WOMEN AND AMERICAN TRADE UNIONS

WOMEN AND AMERICAN TRADE UNIONS

JAMES J. KENNEALLY

EDEN PRESS
WOMEN'S PUBLICATIONS
Montréal Canada

WOMEN AND AMERICAN TRADE UNIONS
JAMES J. KENNEALLY

Credits:
Cover Design: J.W. Stewart

ISBN: 0-920792-10-3
Library of Congress Catalog Card Number 77-9240
Second Edition

Printed in Canada at John Deyell Company
Dépôt légal — deuxième trimestre 1981
Bibliothèque nationale du Québec

Canadian Cataloguing in Publication Data

Kenneally, James J.
  Women and American trade unions
(Monographs in women's studies)

Includes index.
ISBN 0-920792-10-3

1. Women in trade-unions - United States -
History. 2. Women - Employment - United States -
History. 3. Trade-unions - United States -
History. I. Title. II. Series.

HD6079.2.U5K45 331.4'0973 C78-001356-5

TABLE OF CONTENTS

For Louise

INTRODUCTION

Some years ago I planned to compile a series of biographical sketches of American women whose achievements and contributions had been slighted by historians. The need for a separate study of women in the labor movement became strikingly apparent due to the disproportionate number of female labor leaders who emerged as subjects of the inquiry. Consequently the entire focus changed and an effort was made to update those monographs dealing with the issue in the period before 1920, to examine still another dimension of the Progressive Movement, and to explore the complexities and limitations that the concept "lady" imposed on working women and labor reformers.

Confined by their perception of the female role, male dominated unions frequently were reluctant to espouse the cause of women. As a result, the most effective champion of women workers for nearly half a century was the Women's Trade Union League, an organization of unionists and middle class reformers. Considerable attention is devoted in this account to the League which prodded government and trade unions into action on issues affecting working females, and with the assistance of suffragists, demonstrated that middle class feminists and working women could surmount class differences in the pursuit of justice.

Rebellion against sexual discrimination in the work force is not a new phenomenon but is only the most recent episode in the enduring struggle of women to achieve equality of treatment with men. With the development of the factory system many women were drawn from their homes into the mills of Lawrence and Lowell. Still additional thousands were lured into the factory during the industrial expansion of the Civil War. Victimized, even more than men, by inferior pay, dehumanizing working conditions, and lengthy hours, women fought back. Their search for humane treatment was sometimes thwarted by unions, for like many non-working female reformers, trade unions viewed the employment of women as an anomaly reflecting upon the inadequacy of male providers. Thus working women were forced to struggle on two fronts: first against exploitation by management, and second against a recurring sexism which circumscribed union efforts on their behalf and precluded them from full partnership in these organizations.

Post World War II inflation, feminism of the 60s, and the limitation of family size have dramatically changed the composition of the work force by the permanent employment of millions of women. Strengthened by their numbers and fortified by their conviction that work is a "right," these women have confidently begun an assault on trade unions, described by many of them as one of the few remaining "bastions of male supremacy." Groups such as the recently established Coalition of Labor Union Women have begun a new chapter in the relationship between working women and trade unions by confronting union misogyny and demanding a modern emphasis on ideals as old as the Knights of Labor, that unions provide protection regardless of sex or color.

In addition to revealing the "roots" of this struggle for equality in the work force, a history of women in the labor movement should be of service in that very quest. For women workers it can provide a sense of historical identity and traditions as well as models and heroines; for males it should correct erroneous stereotypes of working females by demonstrating their determination, courage, and loyalty under adverse circumstances. Finally, a history of women and unions is still another response to the challenge of Arthur M. Schlesinger to break "the silence of historians" that makes it "appear one half of our population have been negligible factors in our country's history."

I would like to acknowledge the assistance I received in the preparation of this study. Special gratitude is due Eleanor Flexner, whose *Century of Struggle*

(Cambridge, 1959, revised edition 1975) first roused my interest in women labor leaders, my students in "Progressivism" for generously encouraging my enthusiasm, and, for their helpfulness, the nameless staffs at many libraries but especially the cooperative and courteous personnel at the Schlesinger Library on the History of Women in America, Radcliffe College. My wife's insights, criticism and understanding have added still another facet to our "partnership."

North Easton, Massachusetts, April 1978.

In addition to updating statistical data the only significant revision of the 1978 edition pertains to changes in the Equal Employment Opportunity Commission and the Office of Federal Contract Compliance during the Carter administration and the heightened concern of the AFL-CIO in dealing with women's issues. Finally, it appears that the trade union movement has come to accept women's changing status, and as Secretary-Treasurer Ray Schoessling of the Teamsters recently stated, "A woman's place is no longer in the home. A woman's place today is anywhere she chooses to make it."

North Easton, Massachusetts, February 1981.

MAJOR ABBREVIATIONS USED IN THE TEXT

ACWU	Amalgamated Clothing Workers Union
AFL	American Federation of Labor
AFT	American Federation of Teachers
bfoq	Bona Fide Occupational Qualification
CIO	Congress of Industrial Organizations
CLUW	Coalition of Labor Union Women
CWA	Communications Workers of America
EEOC	Equal Employment Opportunity Commission
FERA	Federal Emergency Relief Administration
GAO	Government Accounting Office
ILGWU	International Ladies' Garment Workers Union
ILO	International Labor Organization
ITU	International Typographical Union
IUE	International Union of Electrical, Radio and Machine Workers
IWW	Industrial Workers of the World
K of L	Knights of Labor
NAWSA	National American Woman Suffrage Association
NFTW	National Federation of Telephone Workers
NIRA	National Industrial Recovery Act
NLU	National Labor Union
NRA	National Recovery Administration
OFCC	Office of Federal Contract Compliance
TWUA	Textile Workers Union of America
UAW	United Automobile Workers
UEW	United Electrical Workers
UGW	United Garment Workers
UMW	United Mine Workers
UTW	United Textile Workers
WEAL	Women's Equity Action League
WEIU	Women's Educational and Industrial Union
WFM	Western Federation of Miners
WPA	Works Progress Administration
WTUL	Women's Trade Union League
YWCA	Young Women's Christian Association

Chapter 1

POSTBELLUM (1865-1875) [1]

"The physical organization, the natural responsibilities, and the moral sensibility of woman prove conclusively that her labors should be only of a domestic nature." This dictum appeared in an 1836 report to the National Trades' Union from its Committee on Female Labor. The report went on to state that the employment of women was a disgrace to "freemen" that could lead only to "degeneration." Thirty years later the judgment of organized Labor had hardly changed at all even though Civil War demands greatly increased the number of women in the labor market.

Due to the shortage of male workers and wartime industrial expansion over 100,000 new jobs were available for women in factories, sewing rooms and arsenals. By 1870 one out of every four non-farm wage-earners was female as were ten per cent of all industrial workers. Labor unions, practically destroyed by the panic of 1857, were revived by the same boom that created positions for women. By the war's conclusion, 61 different trades had been organized into 300 unions, 13 of which were newly established national organizations. Three years later membership was estimated at 600,000 by William Sylvis of the Molders International.

Growth of male membership far exceeded female membership, for society held that woman's normal occupation was in the home and that employment, especially of wives, violated natural law and endangered the nation. To stimulate the ambitions of women Mrs. M.L. Rayne, a novelist, compiled a list of female occupations, yet contended that "it is in the natural order of things that all women should be housekeepers." That female work led to functional disturbances, contributed to "lasciviousness," endangered child-bearing, and undermined "the perpetuation and ennobling of the race," was the charge of Azel Ames, a medical specialist employed as an investigator by the Massachusetts Bureau of Labor Statistics. She recommended that women be excluded from unsuitable occupations and when employed safeguarded by legislation.

Working women themselves shared the societal norms that perceived employment in factories merely as a temporary and often necessary interlude between school and marriage. Reluctant to be considered permanent members of the work force they were little interested in unionization and often hostile toward striking. Their attitude contributed to such degrading working conditions and low pay that many were tempted to abandon the hardships of industrial life for the relative luxury of prostitution.

Middle class women usually ignored the hardships of female workers, whose lifestyle they considered unladylike. Their efforts were focused on more traditional causes such as temperance and world peace. Even Congressman Benjamin Butler (Republican, Massachusetts), an important advocate of the rights of labor and later a vigorous defender of factory girls, argued in 1869 against equal pay for male and female clerks of the House of Representatives. Since these women were already being paid more than seamstresses, he claimed they did not need higher wages. Besides, he felt equal pay would increase competition for jobs.

Those who urged work reform tended to be unrealistic advocates of long range solutions rather than supporters of practical proposals with immediate benefits. A former school teacher, Virginia Penny, who ran a "ladies" employment agency in New York City, naively believed that the worker could improve her status by preserving her "purity" and making the most of opportunities to become better educated. Through hard work she could win her employer's appreciation and higher wages. To rectify working conditions others championed ballot extension to women even though some suffragettes harbored strong anti-union feelings. Lucy Stone, founder of the American Woman Suffrage Association, opposed unions; in her opinion the Knights of Labor was an "unreasonable and destructive element." On the other hand, Susan B. Anthony, a more radical feminist, urged the merger of suffrage and labor interests through workingwomen's associations but her ideas alienated trade unionists who felt that employed women needed "not the ballot, but bread."

2

WORKINGWOMEN'S PROTECTIVE UNION

Although frequently visionary and impractical, reform advocates helped bring about increased protection for female workers. In November 1863 representatives of New York seamstresses, probably the nations's most exploited manufacturing employees, met with Judge Charles P. Daly, and assisted by Moses Beach, editor of the *New York Sun*, established the Workingwomen's Protective Union. This organization provided legal aid against unscrupulous employers. Financed by Mr. and Mrs. William E. Dodge, Mrs. Russell Sage, and other philanthropists, the union was surprisingly successful. It found jobs for several thousand women and initiated action against firms that tried to defraud employees of their wages.

By 1878 the Workingwomen's Protective Union had taken 6,192 cases to court and had reportedly settled 12,000 out of court. Moreover, it secured the passage of legislation against businesses that advertised for "girls to learn the trade" as a ruse to obtain help they would not be obliged to pay. The union also provided occupational training, kept records of employers' practices, listed acceptable places for employment and encouraged women to organize. Its generally conservative approach won the editorial support of the *New York Times*, which feared the ascendancy of professional "labor agitators" and the eruption of strikes. Accomplishments of the Workingwomen's Protective Union encouraged emulation in other cities such as Chicago, Detroit, and St. Louis and inspired the Young Women's Christian Association and the Women's Educational and Industrial Union to undertake similar programs.

NATIONAL LABOR UNION

Most reformers who believed in advancing the rights and dignity of labor remained convinced that women should not work outside the home. This dichotomy was a serious problem for the National Labor Union established in 1866 by delegates of ten national unions. This first "permanent" national union adopted a vague resolution pledging "individual and undivided support to sewing women and daughters of toil," and a year later recommended that working men endorse equal pay and aid women in forming labor organizations.

These sentiments were put to the test by suffragettes who attended the third NLU convention in 1868 as labor delegates, hoping to use this meeting not only to further the cause of working women but to champion the extension of the ballot to females. Several days before the convention, Susan B. Anthony, aided by Elizabeth Cady Stanton and Mary MacDonald, established Working-women's Association No. 1 of New York "to elevate women and raise the value of labor." Its membership, consisting primarily of women typesetters and clerks employed by Anthony's suffrage paper *The Revolution*, chose Ms. Anthony as a delegate to the NLU. Mary Kellogg Putnam was the representa-tive of Workingwomen's Association No. 2, comprised of women in the sewing trades and organized with the help of male NLU members. MacDonald was a delegate of the Women's Protective Labor Union of Mt. Vernon, a group she founded under the aegis of local women property owners.

These organizations were oriented more toward suffrage than trade unionism. Almost immediately there was a sharp division of objectives between Stanton and Association No. 1's cofounder, vice president Augusta Lewis, who would later become president of the New York Women's Typographical Union. Although Stanton's proposal to name the Workingwomen's Association the Workingwomen's Suffrage Association had been defeated, the organization's platform did not reflect the ideals of aggressive unionism. It gave no indication of conflict of interest between employer and employee, but urged women instead to "perfect themselves," cooperate, obtain skills, and treat their em-ployers justly.

The audacity of Anthony, Putnam, and MacDonald was surpassed only by that of Stanton, who appeared at the NLU convention as a delegate from the Woman's Suffrage Association with credentials certified by Anthony. Stanton's presence led to heated debate during which building trades delegates threatened to walk out. She was finally seated by a vote of 45 to 18, with the stipulation that this did not mean the National Labor Union endorsed "her peculiar ideas," only that it recognized her as the representative of an organization whose main objective was the "amelioration of the conditions of those who labor for a living." Even so, delegates from the Newark House Painters Union withdrew in protest.

Instrumental in persuading the assembly to seat Stanton was President William H. Sylvis of the Molders International Union who was a founder of the National Labor Union. Although Sylvis addressed women's rights meetings and aided female labor organizations, he reflected the confusion of many trade unionists in that he believed it the function of women "to be man's companion . . . [the] presiding deity of the home circle, the instructor of our children . . ."

who should "not labor outside the domestic circle." Since women had been dragged from their exalted position and forced into the factories men should, he contended, support equal suffrage so that women could emancipate themselves from the thralldom to which they had been subjected. Furthermore, the ballot would prevent their moral debasement by protecting their rights as workers.

Thanks to Sylvis' support, the women delegates were able to play a fairly significant role at the 1868 NLU convention. Through their efforts Kate Mullaney, a Troy collar laundry worker, was elected the union's second vice president. After relinquishing this office because the first vice president was from the same state, she was appointed assistant secretary and assigned the special task of promoting the formation of workingwomen's associations. A committee on female labor, whose membership included Anthony and Putnam, presented a resolution endorsing female unions, equal pay and equal suffrage. The delegates discounted Anthony's claim "that it was the power of the ballot that makes men successful in their strikes" and deleted the suffrage clause before approving the resolution. More in accord with their convictions, and passed unanimously, was MacDonald's resolution recognizing the right of working men and women to strike.

For the next few months Anthony, aided by Sylvis, organized women into unions and amalgamated the various Workingwomen's Associations in New York. But other interests soon began to compete with her zeal for the problems of female workers; by the end of 1868, investigations into industries employing women, temperance lectures, marriage issues, and feminism dominated her activity. As a result workingwomen drifted from the association, leaving only middle-class intellectuals whose primary interest was equal suffrage.

During a printing strike in 1869 Anthony found that her commitments to equality for women and to trade union principles were incompatible. She urged women to take the jobs of the strikers and implored employers to finance a school to teach girls the printing trade. "Give us the means," she declared, "and we will soon give you competent women compositors." She defended this policy to the NLU with the assertion that it would enable hundreds of poor girls to earn wages equal to those of men, but this explanation was not satisfactory to unionized printing workers.

At the 1869 NLU convention delegates of Typographical Union No. 6 of New York challenged Anthony's credentials and attacked her as an enemy of labor. Union organizer Augusta Lewis charged that the Workingwomen's Association was in reality a suffrage group and demanded that Anthony be denied a seat. Anthony, who had previously described strikers as "political tricksters," acknowledged encouraging girls to serve as strike breakers in order to learn the printing trade: "Shall I say to the girls, 'Do not go in, but starve' or shall I say, 'Go in and get a little skill into your hands and fit yourself to work side by side with men?' " Despite this admission, she was initially seated by a 55 to 52 vote with the support of labor reform delegates, suffragists, and the Knights of St. Crispin.

The Typographical Union immediately introduced a new resolution demanding her removal since President Lewis of Women's Typographical Union No. 1 had been fired by *The Revolution*'s printer for engaging in union activities. Furthermore it maintained that the paper paid nonunion wages. Despite Anthony's denial that she knew of Lewis' firing or of the anti-union proclivities of her printer, her career as a trade unionist came to an abrupt end when she was unseated by a vote of 63 to 28.[2] During the debate some speakers reflected the prevailing view of women's role, advocating that they not work at all. "The lady goes in for taking women away from the wash tub," protested one delegate, who demanded to know "in the name of heaven who is going there if they don't?"

The convention had accurately assessed her faltering commitment to unions. Anthony reported to the remnants of the Workingwomen's Association that she would never allow it to fall to the level of "mere trade unionism" and she asserted that the votes to seat her should really be interpreted as support for woman suffrage. Her paper, *The Revolution*, flatly stated "that the worst enemies of Woman's Suffrage will ever be the laboring classes of men. Their late action toward Miss Anthony is but the expression of the hostility they feel to the idea she represents."

Although the National Labor Union ended its flirtation with equal suffrage it still upheld the cause of women workers. Its conventions of 1869 and 1870 were attended by delegates from the Daughters of St. Crispin and the Sewing Girls Union, and in 1871 Mrs. E.O.G. Willard of Chicago Working Women's Union was elected as vice president. The NLU continued to endorse equal pay and to encourage activities that "welcome [women] entering into just competition with men in the industrial race of life."

6

Implementation of these principles was a difficult task. During the post-Civil War period apparently only two state-wide organizations for female workers were established - the Massachusetts Working Women's League in 1869 and the Working Women's Labor Union for the State of New York in 1870; neither was very successful. Unskilled and easily replaceable women were fearful that union activities would result in dismissal by their employers. Furthermore, the effectiveness of trade unions was often diminished by women members, who believed that their presence in industry was unnatural, an attitude that hampered the only national woman's trade union (that of shoe workers) in its pursuit of legitimate labor goals.

DAUGHTERS OF ST CRISPIN

The introduction of machinery to the shoe industry in the middle of the eighteenth-century created a division of labor whereby stitching and binding became primarily women's work. Division of labor by sex did not create a barrier to working class consciousness as women and men united to resist the industry's oppressive conditions. In 1860 both sexes protested a loss of jobs and wage reductions in Lynn, Massachusetts and adjacent cities. The shoe workers undertook the biggest strike to date, one so bitter that outside police and militia were brought into the area.

This demonstration contributed further to the tradition of rebellion and fostered, a few years later, the establishment of a shoe workers union. The Knights of St. Crispin, as it was called, excluded females and opposed their employment if it jeopardized jobs for men. But a history of cooperation between workers in Lynn partially overcame these reservations as the Knights expressed sympathy with the women's plight and at their request aided in the formation of separate female "lodges" in 1868. Rapid unionization of women shoe workers followed, and in less than a year the first national convention of the Daughters of St. Crispin, held in Lynn, was attended by delegates from as far as California. Other conventions were held until the Daughters floundered in the depression of 1873.

This organization was never very effective because many of its members were reluctant to participate fully in union activities traditionally viewed as a male domain. In their convention of 1870 the Daughters passed a resolution demanding equal pay but demurely reassured their "fellow citizens that we only desire to so elevate and improve our conditions as to better fit us for the discharge of those high social and moral duties which devolve upon every true woman." Even Jennie Collins, a former textile worker, who dedicated her life to improving the conditions of working women evaluated the Daughters from the perspective of male pre-eminence. To her, theirs was an altruistic, selfless organization of women whose origin and purpose was to help male shoe workers. Generous females, she alleged, rejected the opportunities for increased wages and responsible positions that accompanied strikes. Moved by the justice of male demands they magnanimously organized the Daughters to support their brother workers.

WOMEN IN MALE UNIONS

Although confusion over their role was common, women found that employment in certain trades forced men to admit them into union ranks on equal terms. The first union to do so was the International Typographical Union. In 1867 it created a committee to report on a plan "to regulate and control female compositors, so that ladies in the business may benefit themselves and inflict as little injury as possible upon printers." The committee recommended that locals admit women or organize them into separate units, for exclusion created strikebreakers, a greater menace to male craftsmen than competition within the union. As the result of persistent agitation by women, the ITU implemented the recommendation in 1869 by amending its constitution so affiliates could not discriminate "against women compositors where they conform to the laws and requirements of the International." During the next few years the Typographical Union vacillated on the desirability of separate or integrated locals, probably because obtaining equal pay for women members was difficult. For a while it was suggested that women who received the same pay should join regular locals, while those paid less belonged in female locals.

Female organizing by the ITU first began in New York City in 1868, when Typographical Union No. 6 was threatened by female scabs. During a compositors' strike some women were taught typesetting and hired by the *New York World*. When the strike was settled the women charged that they were dismissed to appease the union. But Augusta Lewis, assisted by New York Typographical Union No. 6, Susan B. Anthony, and the Workingwomen's Association, decided to organize the women to protect the printers of both sexes. Within three months Women's Typographical Union No. 1 enlisted 30 of the best women compositors in New York and had a treasury of more than $400. The new local's president, Lewis, who had been educated at Brooklyn Heights

Seminary and Manhattanville's Convent of the Sacred Heart, requested a charter before the ITU convention in 1869. Her persuasive appeal, backed by the men's local, resulted in an amendment to the International's constitution sanctioning women's unions. A year later President Lewis efficiently served the International as corresponding secretary and encouraged further unionization of women.[3]

Women's Typographical Union No. 1 collapsed in 1878, the victim both of employers who drove a wedge between men and women by refusing equal pay and of male unionists who persistantly resented the presence of women. Lewis had revealed the dilemma of the female unionist to the 1871 convention when she reported: "We refuse to take the men's situations when they are on'strike,' and when there is no strike, if we ask for work in union offices we are told that there are no conveniences for us. We are ostracized in many offices because we are members of the union, and although the *principle* is right, the *disadvantages* are so many that we cannot much longer hold together, and I trust our want of success will be attributed to the true cause." Although Women's Typographical Union No. 1 could not withstand the pressures mounted against it, it provided valuable experience and precedent to many women.

The second international union to admit women also did so reluctantly, wrung by the same fears as those of the compositors. The introduction of the cigar mold, which did away with the need for skill and strength, coupled with the federal revenue tax in 1861, consolidated cigar production - once a household industry - into concentrated manufacturing. The number of women in the trade rose dramatically from 731 in 1860 to 2,615 in 1870, and to 9,108 in 1880. This increase forced the Cigar Makers International Union to amend its constitution in 1875 to permit female members.[4]

Many cigar makers still resented the female invasion and, overlooking women's participation in the Great Strikes of 1877, emphasized instead the hundreds of girls who accepted jobs as strikebreakers. Yet the International continued its policy of enlightened self-interest. Intensifying its recruitment of women workers, it denied the Cincinnati Cigar Mutual Protective Union affiliation because it excluded women. Furthermore, the International lobbied for the regulation of female labor to protect the rights of men. President Adolph Strasser stated: "We cannot drive the females out of the trade but we can restrict their daily quota of labor through factory laws. No girl under eighteen should be employed more than eight hours per day; all overwork should be prohibited; while married women should be kept out of factories at least six weeks before and six weeks after confinement."

COLLAR LAUNDRY AND TEXTILE WORKERS

As male union officers seldom concerned themselves with women's issues, female members of necessity developed the qualities of leadership and loyalty necessary for trade union success. The Collar Laundry Workers of Troy, New York, an organization regarded by many men as the only bona fide women's union in the country, displayed outstanding resolution and solidarity. This laundresses' union successfully raised wages from $2 and $3 weekly to $8 and $14, and prospered to the point that it could contribute $1000 to the Troy Iron Molders strike fund in 1866. Two years later it donated $500 to striking bricklayers in New York City. The National Labor Union Convention of 1868 passed a resolution thanking the laundry workers' president, Kate Mullaney, for her work in support of other unions and appointed her the first national woman labor organizer in American history. Mullaney apparently met with little success in this capacity but she remained determined to advance organized labor's cause. Despite financial backing from the molders, her union was smashed in a bitter strike in 1869 and her experiment of a worker-owned factory manufacturing collars and cuffs was crushed.

Women textile workers also showed aggressiveness and initiative when they struck in New Bedford, Massachusetts in 1867 and patrolled the highways to repel strikebreakers. A few years later in neighboring Fall River they refused to follow the example of male weavers and accept a 10 percent reduction in pay. Instead, they met on their own, decided to strike, inspired men to do the same, and were able to maintain the wage level.

The depression of the mid-1870s destroyed most women's trade unions and brought organizational efforts to a halt, but the decade's activities contributed substantially to a new female role in emerging urban industrialization. Women had helped increase industrial production, had proved that an unorganized work force could be a greater threat to male workers than their entry into male dominated unions, and had demonstrated to society that they could remain as faithful to trade union principles as men. Furthermore, these years provided organizational experience, educated many women in trade unionism, and provided a reservoir of experience and leadership for the future.

Chapter 2

KNIGHTS AND LADIES [1]

The Noble and Holy Order of the Knights of Labor served as a transition from the idealistic, reform-oriented National Labor Union to the pragmatic American Federation of Labor. First organized in 1869 as a secret society among garment workers in Philadelphia, its growth, though steady, was so slow that it was not until 1878 that it held its first national convention. Fearing the effects of new machinery on craftsmen and the increasing use of lower paid unskilled females as machine operators, delegates sought to protect themselves by including in the Knights' constitution the goal of securing "for both sexes equal pay for equal work."

To help achieve this aim Grand Master Workman Terence V. Powderly drafted a resolution sanctioning the admission of women. Before he could offer it to the 1879 convention, however, Philip Van Patten, a Socialist, introduced a resolution approving the admission of women as members and allowing them to form local unions under the same conditions as men. A favorable committee report on Van Patten's proposal was challenged on a point of order: since the resolution would amend the constitution it needed the approval of two-thirds of the voting delegates. Powderly ruled that the point of order was valid. Although it finally received the necessary two-thirds approval, 14 to 6, it was tabled to the next assembly.

In the following year the Knights authorized a select committee to meet at the call of the Grand Master Workman to prepare regulations and a ritual for the induction of women. Powderly never convened the committee, for, as he later explained, "a separate ritual will bespeak inequality, lead to confusion and is

11

unnecessary." To the delegates of 1881 he maintained that it was ridiculous to admit women on an equal basis, demand equal pay for equal work, and then insist on special initiation rituals.

Actually the issue of a distinct ritual was fatuous, not only had an assembly of women been organized but a female had been elected a delegate to the 1881 convention. Early in that year male shoeworkers of Local Assembly 64, Philadelphia, refused to accept a reduction in pay; management responded by slashing female wages thirty to sixty percent. Under the leadership of Mary Stirling the women struck. Local Knights organizer Harry Skeffington promptly inducted the strikers into the Order. When Powderly criticized the aggressive Skeffington, the latter had progressed too far to be stopped. Garfield Assembly 1684, the first local composed entirely of women, was chartered in September 1881. Its members elected Stirling to the District Assembly, which in turn sent her as a delegate to the General Assembly that year. She became quite prominent when chosen Grand Venerable Sage for the 1883 and 1885 conventions.

ELIZABETH RODGERS: MASTER WORKMAN

Elizabeth Rodgers of Chicago was among the first to capitalize on the new membership opportunities for women in the Knights of Labor. Encouraged by her iron molder husband, in 1879 she organized and led the first women's union in Chicago, a small group that had difficulty overcoming the prevailing attitude that "nice girls" did not join unions. But in 1881, a Women's Assembly of the Knights of Labor was established, with Rodgers presiding as Master Workman. This local, composed primarily of housekeepers, met with considerable success in exposing shameful working conditions and promoting labor's cause.

An eloquent speaker Rodgers advanced swiftly, serving as a delegate to the State Trades Assembly for seven years and as an elected member of District Assembly 24 of Chicago for four years. For this assembly of 50,000 men and women she ably executed the office of both Master Workman and "Supreme Judge." In 1886 this indefatigable mother of twelve attended the national convention with her two-week-old daughter. Evidence of the respect in which she was held was reflected by delegates who collected $49.45 to present a gold watch to the child, and nominated Rodgers to the post of General Treasurer, an honor she declined. She continued to serve the Knights, however, in a variety of assignments - for example addressing conventions of the Women's

Christian Temperance Union as a fraternal delegate from the labor organization. Basically this Irish-Catholic leader pursued a course designed to undercut socialism and convince reformers to support labor.

LEONORA BARRY: GENERAL INVESTIGATOR

At the 1885 Knights of Labor convention a motion was made by Miss Mary Hanafin, a Philadelphia saleswoman, to establish a committee to gather statistics on women's work. The following year a committee comprised of Hanafin, Stirling, and Mrs. Lizzie H. Shute, a Massachusetts shoe stitcher, reported that the average female work day was ten hours, the average factory weekly wage was $6.00 and that laws regulating child labor were not enforced.[2] The committee recommended further investigation and agitation for reform. Also proposed was a meeting with all female delegates.

Sixteen women delegates were collectively appointed a committee to review the report. They recommended that the General Assembly establish a permanent committee of women to investigate working conditions, campaign for equal pay, organize women's assemblies, and seek the eradication of child labor. The assembly approved both the proposal and the delegates' recommendation of Hanafin as president of a new Committee on Women's Work, with Mary O'Reilly as vice-president, and Leonora Barry as salaried full-time General Investigator.

A year later the committee was given additional prestige and authority when its responsibilities were assigned to a newly created Department of Women's Work whose investigator was appointed a general officer of the Knights with an office in the organization's Philadelphia headquarters. This agency's mission was "to free from the remorseless grasp of tyranny and greed the 1,000's of underpaid women and girls in our large cities, who, suffering the pangs of hunger, cold and privation, oft times yield and fall into the yawning chasm of immorality." But the department found its efforts circumscribed when its investigator was instructed to organize female locals only "when it will not conflict with more important work."

Investigator Leonora Barry, another unsung hero of the labor movement, was born in Ireland in 1849 and brought to the United States as an infant. In 1879, after eight years of marriage, she was widowed and left with two small children to support. Because of failing eyesight she abandoned her dressmaker's job and went to work in a hosiery mill in Amsterdam, New York. A delegate to the General Assembly, only two years after she joined the Knights, she was appointed General Investigator in 1886, a position she held until her second marriage. Completely dedicated to the Knights and to laboring women, she worked to the point of exhaustion so often that Powderly cautioned her to slow down; nevertheless, only six weeks before her wedding in 1890 she accepted organizing assignments in New York and Vermont. Her zeal flowed not only from her faith in the Knights, but also from a deep religious conviction that she was God's instrument.

Traveling throughout the United States and Canada, Mrs. Barry lectured, distributed literature, and checked on local assemblies at Powderly's request. To make female membership in the Knights more attractive she instituted a sick and death benefits fund. During the late 1880s her success in securing passage of a child labor statute in Pennsylvania won her the title "Mother of the State Factory Law." In advocating that legislation Barry was handicapped by societal restraints; she feared for her reputation if she lobbied at a state capitol or went "button holing legislators."

Barry's efforts were welcomed by many; she received more than 500 requests in 1888 to appear before various locals scattered around the country, and, surprisingly was able to fill 213 of them. Because of these heavy demands, Powderly finally ordered her to ignore requests from men's assemblies: "Devote every moment to the service of women for their affairs have been kept too long in the background and no one ever had the opportunity you have at hand to make the indignities heaped on defenseless women a burning question in the near future. To do so you must waste no time on men, except it be to secure their intercession in behalf of struggling women."[3]

Despite her efforts and popularity, Barry was unsuccessful in winning wide public support. It must have been disheartening for this religious woman when a Roman Catholic priest denounced her as a "lady tramp" and labeled the Knights "a vulgar immoral society" for encouraging women to organize. Male Knights, many of whom were Catholics, shared nineteenth-century Catholic antifeminism and thus contributed to the membership's unsympathetic attitude toward female organization. Barry found the men ignorant of the Knights' egalitarian principles and frequently uncooperative. It became necessary for Powderly to remind them that her work was as important to men as it was to women.

Women's response to Barry's efforts must have been even more discouraging than male reaction. Many females were penalized by their employers for talking to her, but a great many more were simply indifferent. She attributed this apathy to misplaced pride, to religious scruples, and to the conviction that the debilitating hardships of women's employment were apparently best escaped by marriage. She was so discouraged over the failure of women to respond to her efforts that in 1889 she recommended the abolition of the woman's department and the redirection of efforts toward the general good of all members rather than toward any concentration along sexual lines. The committee on legislation, however, ignored the recommendation.

Her discouragement over female inertia was ironic, for Barry became a labor leader only reluctantly; she never was a genuine feminist. She cautioned her "sisters" in the Knights to appeal to the noble qualities of men rather than to antagonize them. Barry believed that nature intended men to be the bread-winners so that women could raise a family in "the old fashioned home," which should be the basis of all reform. If women were forced to work, they should organize, for unions protected their "honor" and "purity" and thereby the national good. This could be achieved, she wrote, as the labor movement created favorable conditions for "the mothers to whom a nation must look for her strength of manhood and womanhood in future generations." Unions nevertheless were still to be run by men. Female members would assist the male leader "as God intended them to do," and the local would protect the ladies from men who swore, smoked cigars, chewed, or drank.

In 1890 she married Obadiah R. Lake, a St. Louis printer and brother Knight, and resigned as organizer. Powderly's light-hearted account of her forthcoming marriage predicted her separation from the Order: "Soon the name of Sister Barry will exist only in fond rememberance of the members of our Order and her many friends outside it. She has not yet been called across the dark river but she will soon be buried in the bosom of a Lake that shall wash away all claim that we may have to her."

Leonora Lake was never again active in the Knights of Labor concentrating instead on causes considered more typically female. Introduced to the temperance movement through the Order, she became a co-worker of the doughty president of the WCTU, Frances Willard, who described Lake as "that noble Irish woman." An officer for fifteen years in the National Catholic Total Abstinence Society, she lectured tirelessly on behalf of that organization, frequently addressing Chautauqua and Lyceum groups as well as suffrage

15

conventions on temperance and the woman's ballot. Lake had earlier manifested interest in the vote when she represented the Knights before the International Conference of Women in 1888 and the Women's Suffrage Association of Detroit.

Powderly had supplemented Barry's endeavors by reserving a portion of the Knights' official newspaper, *The Journal of United Labor*, for news of the activities of the "sisters." Directed to both sexes, its columns exposed degrading work conditions, publicized the achievements of women, called for the support of suffrage and female unionization, and provided a vehicle for Barry's reports.

TERENCE POWDERLY: OLD-FASHIONED FEMINIST

Believing that the Knights should be "a power for good" in the struggle for "humanity regardless of . . . sex or color," Powderly advocated equal suffrage and temperance. At conventions he repeatedly championed prohibition, distributed WCTU resolutions to local assemblies, and exchanged fraternal delegates with the Temperance Union. Under his persuasion the officers of the Knights pledged abstinence; in reciprocation President Frances Willard addressed the 1886 convention and joined the Knights. Miss Willard was so impressed with the dapper labor leader that she kept a picture of him on her desk and rhapsodized uncharacteristically, that he was able "to convince millions of doubtful Protestants that a thoroughgoing Catholic can be a thoroughgoing Christian." Despite the opposition of Willard's anti-labor friend Lucy Stone, the Temperance Convention of 1886 proclaimed that the Knights' "triumph is our own," created a department of labor, and advocated an eight-hour day and social legislation. Willard offered her services to Powderly by telling him that "if there is anything you would like me to say on the labor question let me know."

Powderly pressured his conservative workmen toward an acceptance of woman suffrage. Although lack of time prevented him from speaking at suffrage conventions, he initiated Susan B. Anthony into the Knights of Labor, welcomed suffrage delegates to its assemblies, and led the fight for prosuffrage resolutions. In 1892 he championed an equal suffrage plank at the Populist party national convention and in a futile effort to get it adopted cast 82 labor votes for it.

16

Powderly, however, was always far more sympathetic to the cause of women's rights than were the members of his organization, either male or female. When the Washington, D.C. District Assembly introduced a resolution for equal suffrage in the convention of 1886, the women's committee reported that "there is more important work for women to do before they are prepared to vote." Some locals openly rejected women workers solely on the basis of sex; other Knights were apparently unaware of their plight. George McNeill, one of the most prominent labor leaders in Massachusetts, wrote a lengthy book in 1887 entitled *The Labor Movement: The Problem of Today*, in which, although very sympathetic to women, he displayed little concern for them as workers. He expressed a typical male attitude when he encouraged Cyrus Field Willard, a master workman, to recruit young women into mixed assemblies to attract new young male members.

Male apathy was to a certain extent attributable to female Knights themselves. Women frequently requested separate assemblies, consequently the Order publicized the possibility of this type of local and charged only $11 for women's charters rather than the usual $16. Powderly received so many requests from women's assemblies to induct men as officers that the appeals were treated routinely and a special form was designed for granting the required dispensation. The women cited several justifications for such policies: the smallness of their assembly, their lack of experience, and the leadership qualities of a male master workman. After 1886, despite the appointment of additional women organizers, female membership began to decline along with that of males. When Barry resigned as General Director of Women's Work in 1890 the women's department collapsed. The only female delegate at the convention, Alzina P. Stevens, refused to take the department's leadership, probably because she was already overcommitted to other areas of women's rights.[4]

Powderly and his sympathizers, far ahead of their time, left a legacy for American women. Much pioneer work had been done, and many Americans, both male and female, had been exposed to the working girls' plight. More important, the Knights of Labor had demonstrated that women could organize themselves and take effective collective action to protect their interests. On one occasion a woman was fired for joining the Order; the strike that followed led to the arrest of women pickets. When these determined females finally had their job and wage cuts restored to them, Powderly was prompted to declare that "women are the best men in the order." In so doing he exposed his own limitations and typified nineteenth-century reformers, male and female. Courageous and dynamic women were perceived as "men" for society still thought these qualities unladylike and unnatural in women.

17

Chapter 3

THE QUANDARY OF THE AFL [1]

The "Gay Nineties" was an arduous decade for American labor. Increased immigration, the demoralizing depression of 1893 to 1896, violent conflicts with management, and struggles between the Knights and skilled trade unions counteracted the benefits usually accompanying industrial growth. Conditions, hours, and wages of working women were especially oppressive, for to improve standards they frequently had to contend with the enmity of male workers.

Women's unions were ineffective or subordinate to those of men. In many trades such as the tobacco industry females were kept unskilled and allowed to learn only a portion of the craft as the union recorded its opposition to their employment. Separate locals and discriminatory wage scales for each sex existed in bookbinding. The International Shirt Waist and Laundry Workers Union and the textile unions stood powerless, their fields remaining difficult to organize both because of the seasonal nature of the work and the employment of children; a union label campaign had failed to provide protection. Little influence was exercised by women in those unions where they held policy making positions, the International Glove Workers and the United Garment Workers of America. The only powerful affiliate of the latter, the predominately female Overalls Union, owed its success to an effective use of the union label.

Women contributed to their own degradation for despite the organizational successes of the Knights of Labor most continued to resist unionization. In 1888 less than 2 percent of the female work force was organized. The typical woman worker in 1890 was young, single, and usually the daughter of ambitious immigrants or native farmers. Only slightly educated or trained, she continued to view her unskilled city job as an interlude between school and marriage, an attitude that hindered working-class consciousness and encouraged passive submission to employer exploitation. Frequently she was rather naive in defending her own interests. In Boston, for example, the female employees of department stores, restaurants, and factories disregarded the advice of the state factory inspector, Mrs. E.J. Ames; instead of unionizing to protect themselves in a glutted labor market, they criticized the employment of married women.

AFL: THE FIRST DECADE

The newly formed American Federation of Labor, organized in 1886, asserted the practical necessity of protecting male wage scales and working conditions from the competition of women. Due to the disaffection of skilled workers within the Knights of Labor, the Federation of Organized Trades and Labor Unions of the United States and Canada, a direct forerunner of the AFL, had been established in 1881 in Pittsburgh. The next year it approved a resolution by Samuel Gompers to extend representation to all women's labor organizations. Consequently in 1883, Mrs. Charlotte Smith, president of the Women's National Industrial League, was admitted as a delegate and addressed the convention. She appealed to that body to advise, cooperate, and assist in the formation of women's unions, and promised that females would stand by male unionists, thus making concerted action feasible and effective. After her impassioned speech the convention drafted "An Address to Working Girls and Women," urging organization and cooperation with men and, in return, committing the new union to the principle of equal pay. Succeeding conventions reiterated this appeal to women to organize, and endorsed maximum hour legislation for females.

AFL president Gompers emphasized that unionization had become increasingly important because women were being brought into factories deliberately to reduce wages. He recommended educational endeavors in 1889 "so that they [women and girls] may learn the stern fact, that if they desire to achieve any improvement in their condition, it must be through their own self assertion in the trade union."

Not until 1891 was Gompers' suggestion carried to its logical conclusion with the appointment of a woman organizer; nevertheless the Federation appeared sensitive to working women's needs. It launched a permanent commitment to universal suffrage in 1890, endorsing an equal voting rights constitutional amendment. It also supported a suffrage petition to Congress signed by 270,000 organized workers. Twenty-three year old Ida M. Van Etten, secretary of the Working Women's Society of New York addressed the AFL's national convention in the same year on the subject of working women. Interrupted repeatedly by applause and cheers, she warned that women were now permanently in industry and that men, if only to protect themselves, had to unionize these newcomers, preferably in separate organizations with female officers but affiliated to local and national bodies. The following year Van Etten reemphasized that theme, as did another speaker, a former factory worker and Knights of Labor organizer, Mrs. Eva MacDonald Valesh, who graphically depicted the hardships of working women. After a decade of rhetoric, Gompers was authorized to appoint a national women's organizer for five months.

MARY E. KENNEY: ORGANIZER

Selected for this precedent setting post was Mary E. Kenney, president of Bookbinders Union No. 1, whom Gompers had met in Chicago the year before. Kenney, a deeply religious Roman Catholic, was born in 1864 in Missouri to Irish immigrant parents. After completing the fourth grade she began work, and at fourteen years became the sole support of her widowed mother. Trained as a bookbinder, Kenney established a women's bindery union in Chicago.

While living in a working women's residence she came to the attention of Jane Addams, who invited her to dinner at Hull House. Kenney had heard neither of Addams nor the settlement, but at the urging of her mother she reluctantly accepted the invitation. As Addams related: "She came in a rather recalcitrant mood, expecting to be patronized and so suspicious of our motives, that it was only after she had been persuaded to become a guest of the house for several weeks in order to find out about us for herself, that she was convinced of our sincerity and of the ability of 'outsiders' to be of any service to working women." Addams offered to assist Kenney's union, which soon met regularly at Hull House, and Addams distributed union materials at factories. Finally at Addams' invitation Kenney and her mother moved to the settlement, where she organized the Jane Club, a residence for working women.

At Hull House Kenney met Henry Demarest Lloyd and Clarence Darrow, both of whom supported her efforts to start a cooperative garment factory. She also organized shirtwaist workers and Chicago cab drivers, and lobbied for labor reform legislation, as a result of which Governor John P. Altgeld offered her a position on the State Labor Commission. She refused, however, recommending Florence Kelley instead. Hull House always remained in Kenney's affections. Returning to Chicago in 1898 after a six-year absence, she joined in the settlement's efforts to defeat the local alderman and ward boss, Johnny Powers, and by her participation demonstrated that Addams' opposition to Powers was not rooted in anti-Catholicism.

Kenney began her service as an AFL organizer in New York City in May 1892. She resided in Gompers' home and tried to convince him to dress more attractively. Daily she urged factory employees to unionize, concentrating her efforts on garment and bindery workers, preaching the union gospel in Albany and Troy and, from July to September, in Massachusetts. At the 1892 convention Kenney presided at one session during Gompers' absence. The AFL president lavishly praised her organizational successes, nevertheless, the Executive Council, possibly because of financial constraints, rejected his recommendation that the Federation continue her employment.

At the request of socialite reformer Mary Kehew, Kenney had been sent by Gompers to Boston, where the Federation's organizer handsome Jack O'Sullivan, had been instructed to assist her. O'Sullivan was soon entranced by her lively eyes and friendly smile. Within a few months they were engaged and, shortly afterward, married, with Gompers as a witness.

For ten years they promoted social justice and trade unions. Much of the success of Boston's celebrated Denison Settlement House was due to the O'Sullivans who conducted union meetings there. Their Boston home became a center of reform, including among its famous visitors the settlement house founder Robert Woods, the "People's Attorney" Louis D. Brandeis, and the future British Labour Secretary John Burns. A close friend and guest, Elizabeth Glendower Evans who was instrumental in the passage of the first minimum wage act for women, was inspired by Mary to a lifetime commitment to labor and social reform.

Joint endeavors did not preclude the O'Sullivans from separate achievements. While serving as a troubleshooter for the AFL, Jack lobbied for reform bills, and reported on labor activities for the *Boston Globe*. On one occasion, during a talk on the "World's Workers" he attempted to organize his audience, the Wellesley College Faculty. Mary served on the board of directors of the Women's

Educational and Industrial Union, was president of the Boston Label League, founded a study group called the Union for Industrial Progress, helped unionize women garment workers and was an AFL organizer in Chicago for a short period. Typical of her dedication was an incident that occurred in 1899 when a determined and pregnant Mary, ignoring her husband's advice and defying a blizzard, addressed a mass meeting of striking shoeworkers in Marlboro.

Despite the deaths of a child and of her mother, the O'Sullivan's had a happy marriage but it came to a tragic end in 1902 when Jack was killed alighting from a train on his way to a union meeting. Yet Mary's greatest contributions still lay before her.

In the years immediately following the expiration of Mary Kenney's AFL appointment little progress occurred in female unionization. The federation directed its limited funds elsewhere; the depression of 1893 resulted in a surplus of unskilled workers, thereby making the organization of women virtually impossible. Conventions did little more than record their support of unionization and maximum hour legislation for women, and welcome women guests and fraternal delegates. Among these were Florence Kelley, who addressed the thirteenth convention on the pioneering Illinois hour law for women and children; Charlotte Smith of the Women's National Industrial League who spoke on organizing women; and Susan B. Anthony, now apparently forgiven by organized labor, who vigorously reiterated the necessity for woman suffrage. Frances Willard of the Temperance Union sent a message to the 1894 convention, and in 1895 two fraternal delegates from that organization were speakers. Willard, invited to address that convention by President John McBride (this was the only year from 1886 to 1924 that Gompers did not serve as president), was unable to appear. Her speech elucidating the virtues of temperance and fraternity was read to the delegates.[2]

ELIZABETH MORGAN: NOMINEE FOR VICE-PRESIDENT AFL

In 1894 Elizabeth Morgan, the convention's only woman delegate, was nominated for vice-president. Although overwhelmingly defeated by P.J. McGuire, the incumbent, it was a tribute well deserved.

An English native, former mill hand, and mother of two, Morgan was founder of Ladies Federal Union No. 2703 of Chicago consisting of clerks, book

22

binders, candy makers, dress makers and others. In addition to establishing 23 locals for craftswomen the Federal Union under Morgan's leadership organized the Illinois Women's Alliance to promote the protection of women and child workers. Successful in obtaining legislation for compulsory education and in restricting child labor Morgan directed the Alliance's investigation of the sweated clothing industries of Chicago whose disclosure resulted in new factory inspection laws.

EVA MACDONALD VALESH: EDITOR

A year after Morgan's nomination and again in 1900 Mrs. Eva MacDonald Valesh addressed the convention on trade unions for women. After her appointment as an organizer in 1900 the Federation was seldom without women organizers, but because funds were short, they usually served voluntarily or received only $3.50 a day plus expenses. Consequently it was difficult for the AFL to obtain competent women for extended periods. Valesh was an exception. A member of the Typographical Union, a regular contributor and managing editor for nine years of the AFL official journal, the *American Federationist*, she also spoke at labor and women's gatherings, sometimes as a surrogate for Gompers. She organized women in the Federal Bureau of Engraving and Printing, and served at Gompers' request on the women's section of the National Civic Federation, a private organization whose purpose was to arbitrate and conciliate industrial disputes. She resigned from the *Federationist* in 1909, however, when Gompers refused to put her name on the masthead. Valesh told him indignantly: "I'm tired of your picking my brain and not giving me any credit."

Gompers also employed the vivacious and beautiful Irene Ashby Macfadyen for various duties in the South, primarily the investigation of child labor conditions and agitation for the passage of regulatory legislation in Alabama and Georgia. Macfadyen, who also advocated compulsory education laws and who risked arrest in her factory investigations, addressed women's clubs, church groups, and union locals on working conditions and women. Gompers was so pleased with her efforts that he published her exposés in the *Federationist* and arranged for her to lecture before Northern organizations.[3] At the same time he commissioned Mrs. Alma Lee to unionize cooks, seamstresses, and laundry workers in the South. At his urging Mary K. O'Sullivan and Florence Kelley contributed articles on child labor to the *Federationist*. Economic exploitation of children was of special concern to the AFL for the organization believed that inadequate adult wages were the cause of child labor.

Whenever possible Gompers promoted the activities of women who were proponents of the Federation's goals. When affiliates subsidized a Women's International Union Label League organizer in the field, he personally encouraged her activities and had AFL organizers recommend promising locations for locals. Similarly after the prominent Bostonian Martha Moore Avery resigned from the Socialist party, Gompers praised her decision. He hailed her public attack on Socialism and her endorsement of trade unions, and publicly presented her with a bouquet at the 1903 convention. At his urging she, too, contributed articles to the *Federationist*, and publicly assailed the possibility of obtaining justice for working men and women through political action.[4] Also at Gompers' request, Mary O'Sullivan in the same year inspected factories in New York for the Federation.

CONFLICTING PRIORITIES IN THE AFL

But neither Gompers' support of working women nor AFL resolutions on their behalf were sufficient to achieve much real progress. Like the Knights of Labor, the Federation's affiliates and members were not ready to acknowledge by unionization the permanence of women in the work force. Some AFL affiliates even excluded women; others merely ignored their petitions for locals. When accepted, women's unions often were separated from men's, even in the same shop or factory, and an inferior women's pay scale was negotiated. An AFL organizer in New York refused to help servant girls establish a union. The Cigar Makers International narrowly defined eligibility for strike benefits, if women's locals were established after a strike had begun, its members were not eligible for relief funds.

Articles frequently appeared in the *Federationist* that revealed the trade unionists' myopic concept of women. It was alleged that their employment was contrary to the best interests of the country; women's work was detrimental to the home and to the nation's character because it endangered motherhood and divided the family. One contributor claimed it would so weaken the nation that a foreign power would be able to conquer the United States with ease. Edward O'Donnell, secretary of the Boston Central Labor Union, emotionally described the employment of women as an "evolutionary backslide" undermining the community, an "insidious assault upon the home; it is the knife of the assassin aimed at the family circle - the divine injunction."

Even the leadership of the AFL shared these sexual prejudices. George McNeill, a founder of the Federation, testified before the Congressionally created United States Industrial Commission that women were not qualified as wage earners because their mental and physical make-up rebelled against work outside the home. As Agnes Nestor of the Trade Union League learned, many labor leaders believed work for women was unfeminine, tending "to unsex them and make them masculine." Valesh, who contended that the AFL "realizes that the normal place for women is in the home," justified the organization of women as a device to protect men's wages. Ultimately, she contended male earnings would rise to such a level that women could "emancipate themselves" from the industrial field and return to their homes. Until the Shirtwaist Strike of 1909-1910 convinced him that women could adapt to a limited wage-earning role, Gompers himself shared many of these retrogressive assumptions. Women had a right to work, he claimed; however, they should not exercise it unless necessary, for their greatest contribution to society was as an indispensable homemaker and mother. Gompers also believed that women should be excluded from industrial labor. Consequently he supported the Boston local that forced women out of the coremaking trade, because such employment contributed to the degradation of womanhood.

Victorian views were further reflected in an overweening concern for the morality of female unionists. Gompers desired membership limited to females of the highest character. Prevention of moral degradation was an objective of the most important women's organization affiliated with the AFL, the Ladies Federal Union No. 2703 of Chicago.

Gompers' dedication to skilled crafts, coupled with his misgivings about working women, led to policies that impeded their unionization. He championed initiation fees and dues set sufficiently high to exclude low-paid women and not only ignored an appeal in 1900 that the AFL persuade the Boot and Shoe Workers Union to reduce dues so that women could join, but also actively fought an amendment to the constitution of the Cigar Makers International to reduce dues for that purpose. His trade union philosophy that the economic power of unions was more important than political power in protecting the worker curtailed his support of working women. Strong unions should be built to negotiate directly, he urged, rather than rely on governmental assistance.

Consequently the AFL became trapped by its own philosophy. Although female unionization was necessary to protect men from the competition of women workers, it was undesirable; and protective legislation would establish dangerous precedents.

As a result the Federation made only gestures toward organization of women and only verbal commitments to protective laws. No campaign for legislation was undertaken unless the proposals favored male workers by restricting women's activities. Most members must have approved this policy, for they resented efforts to do legislatively for women what organization had done for men. Only after women seized the initiative, organized themselves, and success-fully undertook a major strike (Shirtwaist Makers in 1909-1910) did Gompers unequivocally advocate the trade union remedy for the injustices that victimized women workers. But his conservatism still prevented him from asserting leader-ship in an organizing campaign or cooperating with those women who were in a position to found and sustain such unions.

Chapter 4

STIRRINGS OF REFORM [1]

Traditional sex prejudice sharply limited reforms for working women, but some advances in their status did occur at the end of the nineteenth century. Humanitarianism, the "social gospel," and the organized charities movement all attempted to ease the nation's adjustment from a rural agricultural society to an urban industrial one. If these activities seldom related directly to unionizing females, attempts to improve the life of a working woman led naturally to efforts to obtain living wages, ameliorate working conditions, and limit hours. This increasing concern coupled with new educational endeavors by public and private organizations made women more aware of their own dignity, worth, and potential for a better life. Such self-confidence did in time aid them in their social and economic development.

A most serious problem faced by young working "girls" was lack of adequate housing at reasonable cost, a situation so critical that it was precarious to settle in an unfamiliar area of a city. In 1877 a group of wealthy Bostonians established the Home for Working Women so that "women desirous of making an honest living, but penniless and friendless, may find shelter and employment until able to secure a permanent position." There, surrounded by the Puritan ethic and a variety of petty rules to promote good habits and "respectability," the girls worked at laundry and sewing without pay to defray the costs of room and board and to learn skills. A decade later the New England Helping Hand Society was founded to provide homes for working girls "and otherwise to extend a helping hand to them whenever it is deemed expedient." The Society investigated complaints of ill treatment and helped "worthy" young women procure employment.

The dedicated example of Jennie Collins provided the inspiration for this organization of 400 women and for similar establishments. Hailed by the journal of the Knights of Labor as one of the most noble women in America, Miss Collins was a former mill worker, a political and social activist, and well-known advocate of women's rights. With the help of leading Boston merchants she established a temporary home for unemployed women in July 1870. Known as Boffins Bower, it was named after the home of the benevolent parental figures in Charles Dickens' *Our Mutual Friend*. Working women met there to talk and share their experiences as well as to use the reading and work rooms. The Bower also provided entertainment, legal services, and special aids for the unemployed - free meals, loans, and an employment bureau. Wendell Phillips, the labor reformer and former abolitionist, and Mary Livermore, the suffrage and temperance leader, aided Collins in administering and financing the Bower; the state Board of Health, Lunacy, and Charity also provided financial support. Collins further attempted to get the state to establish a girls school to specialize in needlework, machine work, and scientific house work. A champion of women's suffrage as a means of remedying women's wrongs, she addressed the National Woman Suffrage Convention in 1870.

Like most feminists of her generation, Collins' naivete limited her efforts. She defended the employment of ten-year-old girls on the grounds that it taught these children "punctuality, economy, and industry." "Shop-work" reflected the American democratic spirit, she believed, as "side by side may be seen the child who formerly begged its bread, but who is now an expert in the business, and the child who was carried to school in the arms of a servant, but who, having escaped the slavery of a fashionable life, is now working out a happy destiny, rendered easier perhaps by her happy childhood."

YOUNG WOMEN'S CHRISTIAN ASSOCIATION

Collins' solution to the problem of living accommodations and education was adopted and implemented by the Young Women's Christian Association, founded in Boston in 1866 for "the temporal, moral and religious welfare of young women who are dependent on their own exertions for support." Despite administrative confusion from two separate national headquarters differing in their emphasis on evangelicalism, the organization spread rapidly throughout the United States. As part of a concerted effort to reach female workers the "Y" frequently conducted meetings in factories and mills. Nearly 15,000 working women were attending its classes by 1909 and over 20,000 were placed by its informal employment bureau that year. Workers were further attracted by its vocational and educational programs for girls, industrial bureau and unemployment relief program.

Its commitment to young women pushed the "Y" toward other working-class reforms. As early as 1874 it conducted a fairly successful campaign in New York to limit Saturdays to a half day for working women. Delegates to a national meeting in 1891 concluded that the "Y" should attempt to raise women's wages, although it was "not necessary to organize trade unions" to do so; within a few years, however, this stance was abandoned. The report of the sociologist, Annie M. MacLean, who was commissioned by the National Board in 1907 to investigate the condition of working women, hailed the achievements of the "Y" and advocated female unions to improve workers' status. To the acclaim of the Reverend Walter Rauschenbush, the leader of Christian Socialism and an advocate of women's unions, the "Y" resolved in 1911 to support legislative efforts for minimum hours. A few years later it endorsed the right of women to organize. To implement this, activities were undertaken jointly with the Women's Trade Union League and "Y" programs were further extended into factories and shops.

Despite these endeavors the "Y" remained for the most part a middle-class organization, since the "ladies" it served lived outside working-class ghettoes and had a modicum of public-school education. Yet its influence transcended its membership rolls, for it investigated working conditions, endorsed reform legislation, and revealed needs, problems, and abuses of female labor.

WOMEN'S EDUCATIONAL AND INDUSTRIAL UNION

The Women's Educational and Industrial Union was founded in Boston in 1877 to reach the very class of women missed by the "Y." The need for such an organization was reflected in its rapid growth in thirteen states. Organized, financed, and directed by well-to-do women, its purpose was to serve the poorer women of the city. The union lobbied for protective legislation for women, investigated and reported on working conditions, researched for the Massachusetts Bureau of Labor, maintained an employment bureau, and offered a variety of vocational courses. Providing reading rooms, parlors, and inexpensive lunches for working girls, it was careful not to patronize them. Its prudent concern, humanistic endeavors, and elite leadership foreshadowed the settlement-house approach and inspired other prominent and wealthy women to take an active role in union activities.

SOCIALITE REFORMERS

Mary Morton Kehew, described by Wellesley professor and settlement worker, Emily Balch, as "the greatest social statesman I have ever known," was active in the Women's Educational and Industrial Union from 1886 to her death in 1918, serving as its president from 1892 to 1913. Convinced of the necessity of organizing women, and armed with Gompers' consent, she persuaded the AFL organizer Mary Kenney to leave Hull House and come to Boston in 1892. Kenney became a member of the board of the WEIU and, with Kehew, established the Union for Industrial Progress to foster trade unionism among women. In time both of them played significant roles in establishing the Women's Trade Union League. Kehew's adeptness at politics and concern for workers was rewarded with membership on the Massachusetts Factory Inspection Commission and the Massachusetts Minimum Wage Commission. One of the founders of Denison Settlement House, she participated in the establishment of the Massachusetts Department of Labor and Industry and in the institution of public trade-school classes for women.

Another prominent socialite who promoted the cause of working women was Grace M. Dodge of New York, who from an early age believed in serving Jesus by serving humanity. Miss Dodge started a program of practical study on the responsibilities of womankind consisting primarily of weekly meetings with her friends. Working women were invited, and the meetings evolved into the Working Girls' Society. This organization provided comfortable rooms for evening relaxation, a lending library, cultural classes and discussions, as well as instruction in vocational subjects like dress-making and machine operations. A woman physician was usually available for consultation, and arrangements were made for summer "farm-house" vacations. Dodge conducted an intensive campaign to obtain members; the society was publicized in newspapers and magazines, on lecture platforms, and in her visits to brothels and factories. In little over a year it attracted 800 members, spread to other states, and soon began to hold national conventions.

The society's philosophy was based on the Puritan work ethic. Cautioning the girls to save and use their earnings effectively, Dodge preached that hard work uplifted and strengthened those who labored with love and pride. Neither Dodge nor any of her colleagues, however, really accepted the notion of woman as worker. With Mayor Abram Hewitt and other prominent citizens, Dodge sponsored a lecture by Ida N. Van Etten, who undoubtedly expressed the opinion of the group when she claimed: "If all women were happily married and no man died and left widows and daughters unprovided for, the question of woman as workers would be forever settled."

Dodge's traditionalism did not prevent her from trying to coordinate the efforts of her organizations. In this "philanthropic era for women," the effectiveness of women's associations was frequently impaired by proliferation. Dodge established the Association of Working Girls' Societies in 1884 with a central policy-making council whose members included workers, officers from locals and wealthy leisured women forewarned to avoid patronizing attitudes. Twenty-five organizations and settlements, including the Alliance Employment Bureau and the Church Association for the Advancement of Labor, joined the association.

Dodge's dedication to social progress was not confined to working women. She helped institute industrial education for children in New York public schools and consequently was appointed to the board of education. After encouraging the establishment of the New York College for Training Teachers (later Teacher's College, Columbia), she was selected as a trustee. She also was one of the founders of the Travelers Aid Society and was active in YWCA affairs. An early member of the Women's Trade Union League, she generously donated money to that group and encouraged it to establish a training school for women labor organizers.

Other reformers of wealth and status, like Dodge, publicized the injustices of American women. They frequently agitated for change and formed specific organizations for female workers. In New Orleans in the 1880s, a Woman's Social and Industrial Association was established to assist them. The New Orleans Woman's Club also helped working "girls" acquire skills and find employment. Under the presidency of Ellen M. Henrotin, the Chicago Woman's Club sponsored a two-day symposium on Women in Modern Industrialism that dealt with wages and trade unions. A conference to discuss increased wages convened by women socialites, including Anne Morgan and Mrs. J. Borden Harriman, established the New York Woman's Committee to Improve Wages and Conditions of Working Women and Men. By 1899 over 400 women's clubs responded to a national survey, stating they were engaged in the study of social and political economy and were doing practical work in those areas. State Federations of Women's Clubs established industrial committees, and the General Federation supported and encouraged the Women's Trade Union League. The Federation became such an outspoken advocate of work reform that the President of the National Association of Manufacturers warned his colleagues of the dangers of meddling women's clubs.

CONSUMERS' LEAGUE

Frequently this alliance between workers and wealth was tenuous; for aims and objectives were not clearly defined. Sometimes the "elite" were condescending, and in their charity were often contemptuous of labor. The strain between genteel Victorian reform and aggressive trade unions was reflected in the Consumers' League. This powerful and prominent association originated in 1886 in a dingy East Side room in New York. Led by Leonora O'Reilly, a garment worker (who in time became one of the most significant women in the labor movement), working women met to exchange ideas on the improvement of dehumanizing work conditions. The philanthropist, Louise S.W. Perkins, attended the meetings and joined in establishing the Working Women's Society. At its first public meeting at Cooper Union she proclaimed "the need of a central society which shall gather together those already devoted to the cause of organization among women, shall collect statistics and publish facts, shall be ready to furnish information and advice, and, above all shall continue and increase agitation on this subject." Her friend, Josephine Shaw Lowell informed the crowd that one of the society's objectives was to establish trade unions, "the natural remedy for low wages." The audience was cautioned, however, to exercise carefully the right to strike and urged in the name of "brotherhood" to ally with nonworking women and to love all, even the rich.

The Working Women's Society effectively carried out its purpose by gathering data, helping working women and encouraging labor legislation; it was credited with the passage of the New York Women's Factory Inspection Law of 1890, but its endeavors were not always supported by trade unions. The New York Central Labor Union in 1896 challenged the society's justification of a bill to allow factory inspectors to investigate department store abuses, then after heated debate at a joint meeting refused to support the measure.

The society publicized violations of a city ordinance requiring seats for saleswomen, exposed unsanitary conditions of lunch and rest rooms, and began to unionize department store employees many of whom were members. These efforts were often fruitless, for saleswomen frequently failed to realise the degree of their exploitation. Furthermore, they were not sufficiently labor oriented, believing unions beneath the dignity of genteel workers.

To improve working conditions the society adopted a new approach by relying on women who patronized department stores. Inspired by Lowell and sponsored by prominent men, women, and clergy an 1899 mass meeting resolved that the Working Women's Society prepare a list of shops that dealt fairly with their employees and encourage the public to patronize these firms. A committee, the Consumers' League, was established to carry out this program and to organize "salesgirls."

The league's first president was Josephine Shaw Lowell, who had resigned as the first woman commissioner of the New York State Board of Charities in order to serve working people more directly. She was the only sister of Robert Gould Shaw killed while leading black troops in the Civil War and widow of Colonel Charles Russell Lowell who was also slain in that conflict. A deeply religious Unitarian involved in many social justice activities, she worked in the postwar South for freedmen's education and as a member of the State Board of Charities persuaded New York to establish a women's reformatory devoted to rehabilitation. Lowell also founded the Charity Organization Society of the City of New York, opened playgrounds for the city's children, was treasurer of the Outdoor Recreation League, and organized the Woman's Municipal League to reform politics and obtain civil service.

Under her leadership the Consumers' League publicized the list of approved stores and urged women not to shop on Saturday afternoons so that merchants would find it unprofitable to remain open. It also investigated workers' complaints, gathered and publicized data on working conditions, and lobbied for labor legislation.

Sensational exposés in the book *Prisoners of Poverty* by the journalist and educator, Helen Campbell, contributed to the rapid expansion of the Consumers' League into sixty-four cities and states. The leadership in these new chapters frequently overlapped with that of other organizations for women workers. Among the founders of the Massachusetts league were Kehew of the Women's Industrial and Educational Union, and Jack O'Sullivan, the AFL organizer and Denison House leader. In Illinois the league was established at the initiative of Hull House residents. Its first president, Mrs. Charles (Ellen M.) Henrotin promoted the organization through her position as national president of the Federation of Women's Clubs. The branches supported wage, hour, and safety legislation, and investigated and publicized the justice of strikes and the injustice of working conditions. One of the investigators for the Massachusetts Consumers' League was W.L. McKenzie King, who was paid seventy-five cents an hour to examine home-work in the women's and children's clothing industry as well as the working conditions of women in Boston stores. This was a valuable experience, although not the usual preparation, for one who was to be Canada's prime minister for twenty-two years.

Increasingly Consumers' League members demanded a label for their guidance. At the suggestion of the Massachusetts branch, the New York City association called a convention to organize a national consumers' federation to foster acceptable working conditions through the issuance of labels to manufacturers. A label committee was instituted to obtain data from trade unions and to investigate "conditions under which goods are made to enable purchasers to distinguish between the product of sweat-shops and that of the well ordered factory."

With the adoption of a label system a national league was established, and Florence Kelley, a founder of the Chicago chapter, was hired as executive secretary. The Socialist daughter of Congressman William D. "Pig-Iron" Kelley (Republican, Pennsylvania) was serving as chief factory inspector of Illinois at the time of her appointment and had recently obtained a law degree to insure the proper prosecution of Factory Law violators. An early member of the American Economic Association, Kelley who lived in Hull House, had spurred its residents "into more intelligent interest in the industrial conditions" and had gained renown as an opponent of child labor.

Despite the practical objectives of the Consumers' League and its efforts to maintain warm relations with organized labor, the trade unions were suspicious of Brahmin women. Organized labor regarded them as too visionary, on the other hand, league members were condescending toward the pragmatic unions. The consequent impasse was best expressed at a Boston meeting by John Graham Brooks, president of the National Consumers' League for sixteen years: "To work with trade unions is to antagonize much of present member-ship, to ignore them is to antagonize working people." As a result the Massachusetts league adopted an "entirely neutral position in regard to Trade Unions." However, an impartial attitude was not sufficient to overcome the antagonism engendered by two labels - that of the league and that of the unions.

Families of union wage earners frequently ignored the union label when making purchases; thus Women's Union Label leagues were established in 1899 to encourage the consumption of only those items with union labels. League membership was confined to wives and daughters of union members and female unionists. With the support of the American Federation of Labor in 1903 the local leagues were formed into the Women's International Union Label League. Allied with Samuel Gompers' Federation this organization grew quite rapidly. Soon there were thousands of members in city and state branches.

One would expect that the Consumers' League, whose literature stressed the obligation to purchase goods with a consumer's label, would complement the activities of the Women's Label League. This was not the case however. Resentful unions believed that the label idea, stolen from them, infringed on their rights and feared that its award to nonunion firms would make organization extremely difficult. At the 1903 AFL convention, Gompers criticized the league as an organization of well-meaning young ladies who issued the label when they found working conditions sanitary but ignored wages and hours. Several times the Ladies' Garment Workers Union complained that the Consumers' League had granted a label to factories with unsatisfactory working conditions.

Part of labor's objection might have stemmed from resentment at the effectiveness of the Consumers' League label. By 1910 the union label, which guaranteed union shops, had little appeal to society at large; however, sixty-nine manufacturers were using the Consumers' League label. By refusing to carry nonlabel products department stores such as Boston's William Filene and Sons forced improvements in the white goods industry (women's and children's white stitched cotton underwear, to which the label experiment was confined). The label was so efficacious that it was imitated. In 1914 the league obtained an injunction and instituted a suit against the Triangle Shirt Waist Company for using a similar label without its permission.

The Consumers' League responded to union charges by claiming that union labels failed to guarantee sanitary working conditions, the prohibition of child labor, compliance with factory inspections, and even were awarded to products manufactured in tenement houses. Furthermore, it charged, responsibility for proper working conditions, wages, and hours could not be relegated to unions; but was the responsibility of the community which should support the Consumers' League label and its work for protective legislation.

A cold war between labor's champions could only serve the cause of labor's foes. In the interest of effective harmony the Consumers' League strove for a rapprochement. After two years of deliberation it abandoned the label program in 1918, an action prompted by difficulty in administering the project, errors in issuing labels, and the possibility of imperiling "our connection with the American Federation of Labor."

Concentrating upon a minimum wage law instead, it established a special national committee to lobby for this legislation. Among its members were the settlement house worker and Wellesley professor Emily Balch, and economist and Catholic University professor Reverend John Ryan.

LABOR STATISTICS

By the time the decision to discontinue the label was made, large numbers of Americans had been made aware of the working women's plight. Although late nineteenth-century society remained faithful to its *laissez-faire* philosophy, in an increasingly technological and statistical society, government of necessity began to collect and disseminate data on American life and thereby served labor's cause. The Massachusetts legislature reluctantly created the Bureau of Statistics of Labor in 1869. This office, nearly abolished in 1872, was ineffectual until the appointment a year later of Carroll D. Wright, a Civil War veteran. Many of his annual reports dealt with working females: they revealed the neglect of protective legislation and emphasized the need either to strengthen labor's bargaining position or to further restrain employers. Pressured by labor and reform groups twenty-seven other states emulated Massachusetts and by 1891 created similar bureaus. All operated on the optimistic theory that when the facts were known the public would insist that the evils be corrected.

On the national level Senator John T. Morgan (Democrat, Alabama) in 1882 proposed an investigation of the causes of recent industrial strikes, a measure believed to be little more than a shrewd stroke to achieve tariff reduction. In order to thwart the stratagem and please labor lobbyists, the United States Senate commissioned its Committee on Education and Labor "to take into consideration the subject of the relation between labor and capital, the wages and hours of labor, the conditions of the laboring class."

Committee hearings presented an opportunity for women to testify to abusive working conditions. Most of the female witnesses, however, were from the upper or middle classes. They ignored the possibilities of women's unions and instead offered woman suffrage and/or temperance as the means to labor reform, higher wages, and an increased standard of living. An exception was Charlotte Smith of New York, president of the Women's National Industrial League, which was established to further employment opportunities for women when Secretary Henry M. Teller in 1882 refused to employ them in the Interior Department. Mrs. Smith capitalized upon her committee appearance to assail the Western Union Company for its inferior female wage scales and to urge women of the nation to donate funds to striking Western Union women. Her union orientation contrasted sharply with the attitude of Adolph Strasser, acting president of the International Cigar Makers Union, who described as "evil" the phenomenal growth of female employment in the trade from 300 in 1863 to 10,000 in 1882. Cleverly claiming that he was not opposed to their employment but interested in their health, Strasser advocated that women's hours should be regular and controlled by means of working certificates issued by physicians.

Testimony at committee hearings, coupled with election year pressure from the Knights of Labor, led to the establishment in 1884 of a Federal Bureau of Labor Statistics, the only legislation resulting from the investigation. First commissioner of the new bureau, Carroll D. Wright of the Massachusetts agency, now had a national forum. His data revealed that women were paid less than men because they were unskilled in a competitive labor market, and employers believed them to be working only until they married. Even when management thought them as efficient as males, wages remained discriminatory. Furthermore, women usually were hired as they worked for less or were deemed less likely to strike. Since his research demonstrated that working women's problems were exacerbated by the community's lack of respect for their status; Wright appealed to the churches of the nation to welcome these women. The Church Association for the Advancement of Labor (Episcopal), founded by the Reverend William D. Bliss and Bishop F.D. Huntington of New York, was in total sympathy with this request. To Protestant, Catholic, and Jewish clergy it issued a circular on the hardships of the working "girl" and urged that congregations be addressed on the subject. As part of its campaign to obtain overtime pay for the "girls" the Church Association also advocated all goods be purchased before six P.M. during the holiday season.

Congress, concerned about the "growing concentration of economic power," provided in 1899 for an Industrial Commission to investigate problems related to business and labor. After lengthy hearings the commission issued a report linking prostitution to low wages and demanding equal pay for equal work. However, it failed to recommend protective legislation for women and even ignored the existence of the eight-year-old International Association of Factory Inspectors, whose purpose was to develop work standards and encourage industrial legislation. The committee placed the difficult burden of implementing its recommendation on trade unions.[2]

EXPOSING EXPLOITATION

The end of the nineteenth century was not a time merely for dispassionate, statistical accounts of the plight of the working girl. Emotionalism was dominant in colorful accounts by reform journalists in the age of the muckrakers. Conditions under which women labored were dramatically portrayed by educated, reform-minded, female writers who temporarily abandoned their professional lives for the crass, hard world of the worker. A pioneering landmark in this type of exposé was a series of articles by two Philadelphia socialites, Marie Van Vorst and her sister-in-law Mrs. John Van Vorst, published in *Everybody's Magazine* in 1902 and as a book in 1903. This controversial series was designed to help the working girl "mentally, morally, and physically." The indignant authors hoped that the articles would persuade readers that unpleasant working conditions were unnatural and could be corrected. Though shocked by their experiences as factory workers the Van Vorst "ladies" never mentioned trade unions as a remedy. Instead they unrealistically advocated that bread winning women be separated from those who worked only for luxuries. The former group should seek employment in lace-making and similar trades, which required special training and paid well. Furthermore, some legislative remedy should be adopted, for "the question should not be left to the decision of the private citizen." Despite their disillusionment the Van Vorsts remained optimistic, believing that the factory girls' dream of "something better" would eventually be realized.

Rheta Childe Dorr was a more thorough investigator, more deeply committed to reform and women's rights than were the Van Vorsts. A journalist whose career began on the *New York Evening Post*, where she was paid half of a man's wage, she became the leading muckraker of American feminism. Dorr criticized the Van Vorsts for their failure to observe the most startling transmutation of all, "the significance of the woman's exodus from home to factory work." Her realization of the importance of this fundamental change alerted her to the evils that accompanied women's employment. Relating her experiences as laundress, seamstress, factory worker, and salesgirl, Dorr exposed oppressive working conditions and management's failure to comply with protective legislation. She repeatedly demanded reform and implored her readers to help the exploited department store clerk by shopping early for Christmas. Her devotion to social justice and journalism even resulted in her arrest for picketing while researching an article.

In 1904 the year that Dorr became chairperson of the Industrial Committee of the General Federation of Women's Clubs, its president declaimed before the national convention: "Dante is dead. He has been dead for several centuries and I think it is time that we dropped the study of the Inferno and turned our attention to our own." Capitalizing upon this opportunity Dorr implored member clubs to aid the cause of women workers and arranged for factory girls to address the Federation thereby providing a national platform for Agnes Nestor, president of the Illinois Women's Trade Union League, Josephine Casey of the Illinois Street Elevated Railway Union, and Mary McDowell of University Settlement in Chicago.

The revelations of the millionaire waitress Maud Younger were not in themselves very surprising, but Samuel Gompers' belligerent observations concerning them were unusual. A socialite whose residence in a New York settlement house inspired her to work for labor reform, Younger covertly assumed employment as a waitress and then published an account of the harsh working conditions and her gradual conversion to union remedies. However, as Gompers condescendingly pointed out, *McClure's Magazine*, the publisher of the piece, was a nonunion shop. Gompers refused to write an introduction to the articles unless Younger would "advocate practical, straight-out organization of the woman workers into trade unions, and to become part of the bona fide movement of trade unions and the American Federation of Labor." Younger returned to her San Francisco home and organized the city's waitresses. Elected president of the union she served as a delegate to the Central Labor Council, AFL conventions, and became a friend of Gompers.

Other significant exposés were Helen Campbell's *Women Wage-Earners*, wherein industrial education and unions were advocated as the remedies for deplorable working conditions, and the famous *How the Other Half Lives* by Jacob Riis, which acclaimed the devotion of working girls to each other and inspired the future Secretary of Labor, Frances Perkins, to a career in labor.

Even more emotional than the professional muckraker's account of women in industry was the heartrending personal story by women workers themselves. Among the earliest and most significant examples of this genre was Dorothy Richardson's *The Long Day*, a tale of a young schoolteacher forced to work in New York City when her parents died. Richardson's experiences in the factories alerted her to the sexual degradation of American working "girls." Young innocents were continually subjected to obscene and lewd stories by their male co-workers, who fondled, squeezed, and pinched them whenever opportune. Increasingly the "girls" became immoral, many were even recruited for prostitution by procurers who worked in factories. For these allegations *The Long Day* was bitterly criticized by the labor leader Leonora O'Reilly, who charged that it was not the story of working "girls," but of a reporter in search of sensational copy. Unlike other reformers, O'Reilly claimed workers' morals were beyond reproach, that many would choose starvation before prostitution, and that they seldom behaved as Richardson described. In fact, O'Reilly claimed, they never fought, spit or pulled hair, and rarely allowed a lewd joke in their presence. Despite her protestations critics raved over the work and many sermons were based on it.

In arousing Americans to working women's plight, exposés were supplemented by more scholarly and detached studies undertaken by private groups. The Women's Welfare Department of the National Civic Federation, under the honorary chairpersonship of Mrs. William Howard Taft, was formally organized in 1908. This committee collected and distributed information, sponsored lectures, and educated many socially prominent women to the aims and aspirations of the labor movement. It also attempted to stimulate the interest of employers in their employees. The Consumers' League publicized its investigations of women's working conditions, as did Jane Addams' magazine, *Survey*. A multitude of studies were subsidized by the Russell Sage Foundation whose trustees in January 1908 granted funds "for investigation into trades for women and women's lodgings." Supervised by Mary Van Kleeck, a fellow of the College Settlement's Association, its research resulted in publications on working girls in evening schools and in the bookbinding and artificial flower trades. In one of its most important studies, *Women and the Trades*, Elizabeth Butler, former secretary of the New Jersey Consumers' League, revealed the means by which men's unions circumscribed women's opportunities.

SETTLEMENT HOUSE MOVEMENT

More effective in generating reform than all of the statistical studies, exposés, and charitable organizations was the burgeoning settlement house movement. Idealistic upper-class women became allied with pragmatic female workers in a joint endeavor to obtain freedom for women through the ballot and humane working conditions.

Inspired by the establishment of Toynbee Hall in England in 1884, settlement houses spread rapidly throughout the United States. The constitution of University Settlement of New York City, pledging "to bring men and women of education into closer relations with the laboring classes for their mutual benefit" reflected the movement's objectives which appealed to the idealism of American youth. An outlet for religious energies was provided by the settlement's buoyant spiritual and service-oriented outlook. In a society in which organized theology was increasingly meaningless, daughters of professional and business men were now able to engage in responsible activities outside the home without sacrificing social standing.

Settlement house residents realizing that the lack of organization contributed to worker's isolation and helplessness and endangered the community, were drawn to the labor movement. Providing it with well-educated, articulate, and socially prominent defenders when it had few other acceptable spokesmen, settlements strove for a higher standard of living and an orderly life for the workers. As the residents emphasized the ethical aims of labor and attempted to develop its historical consciousness they tended to oppose radical elements such as the Industrial Workers of the World and allied themselves with more conservative movements.

In Chicago the most prominent settlement was Jane Addams' Hull House, where concerted efforts to organize women evolved so naturally that Alice Hamilton explained: "One got into the labor movement as a matter of course, without realizing how or when." Hull House residents assumed the initiative in organizing two women's unions, establishing a Council of Women's Trade Unions, and supporting strikers and protective legislation. During the depression of the 1890s Addams even succeeded in cajoling the city to undertake make-work projects for the unemployed.

Hull House further served as a liaison between the workers and socialite reformers of Chicago as Addams and her friends defended labor's right to organize, strike, and bargain collectively. Important labor speakers were brought to the settlement, and many individuals, later prominent in the union movement, were first introduced to labor issues there. Among others who enjoyed the congenial atmosphere of Hull House were Dr. Alice Hamilton, the Christian Socialist pioneer of industrial disease research; Florence Kelley of the Consumers' League; Mrs. George (Elizabeth) Rodgers, Knights of Labor Master Workman; Mary Kenney, the first woman organizer for the AFL; Margaret Dreier Robins and her husband Raymond, mainstays of the Women's Trade Union League; Gertrude Barnum, secretary of the Illinois Women's Trade Union League, and Alzina Parsons Stevens of the Knights of Labor and AFL, who in her function as deputy inspector of the Illinois Factory Law was accused of being "unsexed," "no lady," and a "termagant" by Marshall Field.

Lectures, unionization, or propaganda meant little if women did not have adequate means to continue a strike once it had begun. In a Hull House meeting factory girls pointed out that female strikers capitulated quite rapidly when faced with eviction from boarding houses because of non payment of rent. Thus to promote the independence of women workers, a home for working girls was established with the assistance of Mary Kenney. Two nearby apartments were rented, furnished, and turned into a cooperative self-governing boarding club. Within three years the Jane Club, as it was known, grew from a membership of seven trade-union women to fifty, and with the receipt of a $15,000 donation became a significant part of Hull House services for over a decade.[3]

Mary McDowell, who was one of the first residents in Hull House, helped to organize a women's club in 1893. That same year Addams recommended her to a faculty committee to become director of the University of Chicago Settlement House in the "Packingtown" area of Chicago. McDowell's religious views made her an ideal choice, for she sought the humanization of religion through service and brotherhood. She believed that "democracy and Christianity must be blended. Are not both loving God with all your heart and your neighbor as if he were yourself?" This concept of hers meshed well with that of the Christian Union, a faculty organization that as an example of religious and educational principles in social service had founded the stockyards' settlement to search for the causes of contemporary unrest.

McDowell and the settlement became increasingly involved with labor reform. With the aid of Michael Donnelly, Local 183 of the Amalgamated Meat Cutters and Butcher Workmen of North America was established by her at the settlement where it met regularly. A member and president of this first union of women stockyard workers, McDowell also sustained it during the Stockyard strike of 1904 by raising money for relief, publicizing the injustices of the workers, and helping negotiate the final settlement. At the same time her inspiring leadership helped the Chicago Women's Trade Union League survive its early years. More attached to this organization than any other and its president from 1904 to 1907, she still found time for activities on behalf of protective labor legislation, woman suffrage, and the betterment of interracial relations, an interest that grew out of the shocking race riots of 1919.

Boston settlement houses were as involved in the labor movement as those in Chicago. Denison House (Women's College Settlement), aided by its "devoted and inspiring" friends from organized labor, was founded in 1892. Its Executive Committee was convinced "that the Industrial Problem is the most important one presented to this generation, we feel that a settlement place among the working people must stand not merely for the help of individuals in the neighborhood, but quite as much for education, for the study of conditions affecting the mass of working people, particularly for the study of the labor movement." Consequently members vigorously promoted the cause of labor and unions. Invaluable in this respect was Jack O'Sullivan, labor reporter for the *Boston Globe* and AFL organizer who married one of the settlement's notable residents, Mary Kenney. Zeal and efficiency of the settlement house workers resolved his doubts as to their practicality. O'Sullivan soon described a working women's organizational meeting at Denison as "one of the best labor meetings he ever attended," and his enthusiasm inspired the chronicler to inscribe in the House diary: "Bravo! Mr. O'Sullivan's getting converted."

Many women's locals were founded at Denison House, including tailors, bindery, and dry goods clerks unions. When Local 37 of the Garment Makers Union was established Mary Kenney was elected president and the House head-worker, Helena Dudley, treasurer. This local of over 800 members met regularly at Denison and selected Vida Scudder and Dudley as its delegates to the Central Labor Union, which also met there.

These two women were both important to the success of Denison House and Boston reform movements in general. Wellesley professor Scudder was hostile and bored with the limited objectives of traditional feminism. Asserting that it was not enough for women to be free, she claimed they must also be useful and should study economics as well as support movements for equality and social reform. In her classes and writings she pressed literature into the service of

43

society. A founder and director of Denison House, she enthusiastically supported all of its undertakings, and presided over the Boston branch of the Women's International Union Label League, a House-sponsored organization.

Helena Dudley, a Bryn Mawr graduate and Christian Street Settlement (Philadelphia) head-worker before coming to Denison House, was as enthusiastic a champion of labor as Scudder. After joining the AFL she directed much of the House's labor activities along with her close friend Kenney. Dudley's vigorous support of the Lawrence strike of 1912 so antagonized some of Denison's benefactors that she resigned for the good of the institution.

A Denison House achievement was the establishment of a Federal Labor Union in 1894, primarily a women's organization consisting of manual and nonmanual workers, professional people, and labor leaders who agreed to pool their talents and experience for labor's benefit. This union was in part an attempt to bridge the gap between classes by promoting better understanding of labor's goals. It publicized the intellectual and moral ends to which unions were committed, urging peaceful settlement of labor disputes, and strove "to secure for working women the benefits of organization." Meeting regularly at Denison House the Federal Labor Union organized women, conducted classes for them and thereby brought the settlement into frequent contact with wage-earners and the Central Labor Union. In 1894 Kenney was the union's fraternal delegate at the AFL national convention held in Denver.

Emily Balch of Denison House attended the same AFL convention as a Central Labor Union delegate. A Wellesley College economist, she became interested in social reform after attending the Summer School of Applied Ethics led by Dr. Felix Adler, founder of the Ethical Culture Society. In keeping with her advocacy of a broader role for women in the social order, she helped to establish Denison House and served temporarily as its first head-worker. Balch was one of the handful who planned and started the Women's Trade Union League; she was acting president of its Boston branch and a member of the Massachusetts State Commission on Industrial Education.

Although Denison House favored settling labor disputes peacefully, it nevertheless supported many strikes on Boston's turbulent labor scene. Its residents also alleviated Boston's unemployment. During the depression of the 1890s they established a sewing room that provided work three or four days a week to over 324 women tailors. On a more permanent basis Denison House instituted a training school for dressmakers and seamstresses and, in cooperation with the South End House and with the Women's Educational and Industrial Union, founded an employment bureau for boys and girls.

Like most settlements Denison House also promoted education. Lecturers addressed the residents and the community on social and labor issues. Among these speakers were Mary McDowell, president of the Illinois Women's Trade Union League; Jane Addams of Hull House, and male presidents of local unions, who urged the further organization of female workers.

Other Boston settlement houses also sustained women's needs. Philip Davis, a former Hull House resident and worker at Civic Service House in Boston, organized men while his young wife, Polly Shorner Davis, concentrated on women. Supported by the philanthropist and suffragist Mrs. Quincy Agassiz Shaw, Polly unionized waistmakers, wrapper makers, and white goods workers, and established an evening college. Philip Davis, too, was a part of that small group that created the Women's Trade Union League. Even all male Andover House (later called South End House) cooperated with Denison House in the Federal Labor Union by publicly advocating better working conditions and vocational training for women, and proclaiming that unionization was more necessary for women than for men.

Like those of Boston and Chicago, New York's settlement houses were also inevitably drawn into the labor movement. Greenwich House endorsed unionization, and its founder, Mary K. Simkhovitch, active in the New York Organization of Working Girls' Societies was also associated with the Women's Trade Union League from its early years. Lillian Wald, described by the anarchist, Emma Goldman, as one of the few American women genuinely concerned with the economic conditions of the masses, used her position as director of the Henry Street Settlement (formally the Nurses' Settlement) to improve working conditions. Co-founder of the Child Labor Committee, she also lobbied for investigative and protective legislation for workers. The Henry Street Settlement formed unions and supported strikers even though some contributors withdrew their funds as a result. Of tremendous help in all worker-oriented activities were Leonora O'Reilly and her mother, two shirt-waist workers and Knights of Labor members who resided at Henry Street and inspired Wald. Backed by wealthy reformers they established a shirtwaist factory to train young girls in vocational skills.

Meeting regularly at Henry Street and providing further liaison between the settlement and the unions was the Social Reform Club. The self-styled intellectual, Edward King, a Socialist, who taught classes in Greek and Roman history to lower East Side workers, was on its executive board. A founder of University Settlement, King used the Social Reform Club as a platform to encourage and inspire both Wald and O'Reilly. Originally founded to spread the use of the trade union label, the club, on whose advisory board Gompers served, broadened its objectives to improve the condition of wage earners and to draw workers and their sympathizers together through equally proportionate membership.

The appearance of women of wealth and leisure in the labor movement via the settlement house was in part attributable to American society that had severely limited activities considered appropriate for "ladies." Agitation by these upper class women for legislative remedies publicized and ennobled labor's cause. Nurturing by such organizations as the Social Reform Club and the Federal Labor Union led easily into the establishment of a special organization of well-to-do and working women whose purpose was to unionize women - the Women's Trade Union League.

Chapter 5

THE PROMISING YEARS: EARLY ACTIVITIES
OF THE NATIONAL WOMEN'S TRADE UNION LEAGUE [1]

By the end of the nineteenth century it had become obvious that the American
Federation of Labor was not the vehicle for organizing female workers and
protecting their rights. Handicapped by its conviction that a woman's place was
really in the home and its policy of protecting the skilled worker at the
expense of the unskilled, the AFL virtually ignored the needs of five million
female workers, except for routine convention resolutions sympathetic to
women. Yet settlement houses and charitable organizations had demonstrated
that many female workers were receptive to unionization, and that there were
men and women with sufficient leisure, interest and ability to organize them.
Both the feasibility and the necessity of a new society specifically concerned
with the welfare of the female worker was increasingly apparent.

ESTABLISHING THE WOMEN'S TRADE UNION LEAGUE

The formulator of such an organization was a man, William English Walling, the
grandson of a Kentucky millionaire and a graduate of the University of Chicago.
Inspired by the achievements of Hull House he became a worker and resident
at University Settlement in New York, and with the encouragement of Lillian
Wald and Florence Kelley, spent the summer of 1903 in England investigating
the possibility of an American organization similar to the British Women's
Trade Union League. In Boston, during the AFL convention in the fall of that
year, he explained his ideas to Mary Kenney O'Sullivan, who enthusiastically
agreed to help him.

Philip Davis of Civic Service House in Boston, hearing of their plans, also became an eager participant. Support was then solicited from other settlement houses. A committee including O'Sullivan, Robert Woods, and Vida Scudder, with Walling as chairperson, was appointed to draft a constitution. After a conference with Samuel Gompers, Max Morris of the Executive Council of the AFL was selected to represent that organization at formative meetings. Other key participants in these early sessions were Mary M. Kehew (Women's Educational and Industrial Union), Emily Balch and Helena S. Dudley (Denison House), Harry White (President, United Garment Workers), Michael Donnelly (President, Amalgamated Meat Cutters and Butcher Workmen) and John R. O'Brien (President, Clerks International Protective Union). O'Sullivan announced the formation of a female labor association from the podium of the AFL convention. Probably in deference to the newly formed group, the convention adopted resolutions calling for special efforts to organize women and for the appointment of at least one female organizer.[2]

The new society, known as the National Women's Trade Union League, opened its membership to males and females, union members or not, who would assist unions that allowed women members and would aid in the formation of new women's unions. Ties to the AFL were reflected in the provision that an annual conference would be held jointly with the Federation's convention. Its link to the social workers was manifest in that nonunion members were eligible to hold any office. For the trade unionist, as distinguished from the social reformer, the only protection was the requirement that a majority of the elected members of the Executive Board had to be, or have been, union members. Other officers were to be earnest sympathizers and workers for the cause of trade unionism. Elections were held and Kehew, O'Sullivan's nominee, was chosen as president, O'Sullivan secretary, and Jane Addams vice president. On the Executive Board were two settlement house workers and three trade unionists, Mary Freitas of the Textile Workers Union and Leonora O'Reilly and Ella Lindstrom, both of the United Garment Workers Union.

Although enough women had changed their attitudes toward work and unions to inspire the formation of the NWTUL, serious obstacles to unionization remained, since the majority of women still adhered to traditional values. Most female workers continued to view themselves as temporary members of the labor force soon to assume their natural role as homemakers.[3] As they did not find traditional union advantages sufficient incentive to join, the League contemplated a dowry benefit to make membership more attractive. Nevertheless, many working women remained reluctant to degrade themselves further by joining rough, crude, male-dominated unions, which frequently were immigrant controlled. To obtain immediate gains some women even served as strike breakers. These attitudes reenforced the reluctance of male unionists to spend their scarce funds on females. Yet in a society that still feared so-called class legislation and whose court system checked any tendencies to enact such laws, unionization appeared to be the only solution to the exploitation of working women.

During its first few years the new organization's activities were limited and results were insignificant, for the NWTUL had to clarify its structures, objectives, and means of achieving its goals. In January 1905 Gertrude Barnum, a University of Wisconsin graduate and Hull House resident who would later become an organizer for the International Ladies' Garment Workers Union, was appointed full-time executive secretary and national organizer. Branches were rapidly formed with the help of settlement house workers in New York, Boston and Chicago; twenty cities were represented at the 1908 interstate conference.

The League was given an excellent opportunity in 1906 to publicize its work, champion suffrage, and report on general areas of concern to women and labor. A Women's Department was established in the *Union Labor Advocate*, the official journal of the Chicago Federation of Labor, whose office adjoined that of the Illinois branch headquarters. Anne Nicholes, secretary of the Illinois WTUL, edited these columns until 1908, when Alice Henry succeeded her. Henry was editor until January 1911, when the League began its own journal. The new periodical, named *Life and Labor* by Senator Robert LaFollette (Republican, Wisconsin), was also edited by her for four years. Henry, an Australian reform journalist who had studied worker movements in England, came to Chicago in 1906 to help Jane Addams campaign for municipal suffrage for women. Her meeting with NWTUL President Margaret D. Robins led to her appointment that year as office secretary of the Illinois branch, the beginning of a long career of service to the League. Only her return to Australia in 1933 terminated her endeavors for American women.

Notwithstanding the dedicated efforts of social workers, the WTUL suffered from inadequate financing. Despite a farewell gift of $1,000 from Margaret Dreier Robins the New York branch almost collapsed when she resigned the presidency. A lack of funds seriously impaired the League's programs and attendance at its convention. Ignoring the constitutional provision for annual conventions with the AFL, in 1905 to the embarrassment of Gompers, who had already included them on the printed program, the WTUL decided not to meet with the AFL in Pittsburgh but rather to convene separately at Hull House in order to obtain better attendance. Despite the change in location, only sixty people attended the conference and banquet. Their enthusiasm and optimism could not offset the smallness of their numbers. No national convention was held in 1906, but in 1907 three branches representing thirteen states met simultaneously a few months prior to the League's convention with the AFL at Norfolk, Virginia. However, because of financial exigencies only eight representatives, most of whom were also AFL delegates, attended the League's convention. To maximize publicity and attendance in 1908 three inter-state conferences were again held in Chicago, New York, and Boston. In the latter city one observer attributed poor attendance "to a less forward movement generally among the women of that section."

Not until 1909 did the NWTUL hold its second formal convention, now described as biennial. Seventy-one delegates from four branches and twenty affiliated unions heard an address by Mary MacArthur, secretary of the British Women's Trade Union League, who had been lecturing in the United States at Ellen Henrotin's request. The spirit of the delegates greatly exceeded their numbers. When they received an invitation from Marshall Field to visit his Chicago store, they resolved: "The convention on behalf of the out-of-town delegates unanimously and respectfully declines to accept the invitation because of the known opposition of this firm to the organization of women workers and to efforts to raise the individual status of women."

LEAGUE TENSIONS: WORKERS AND MIDDLE CLASS MEMBERS

Financial difficulties were relatively minor when compared with the problems posed by many trade unionists' distrust of social worker associates. The title "nonunionist" for these members was soon dropped because of its antilabor connotation, and the term "ally" substituted. However, the change of name did little to create understanding and sympathy, for both elements continued to grate on each other. Rose Pastor Stokes' bitter attacks on the condescending attitudes of the rich were substantiated for in 1908 the Boston WTUL still held separate meetings: allies in the afternoon at a home, working "girls" in the evening in a hired hall. Leonora O'Reilly had resigned from the League in 1905 primarily because of the allies' attitudes. She believed that this group frequently confused working women, made trade unionists feel like interlopers, and unnecessarily approved Richardson's *Long Day*, a book that adversely reflected on workers. Even an ally as dedicated as Mary McDowell caused some consternation when she described the organization's fundamental purpose: "I am not certain that the Women's Trade Union League would call it getting a living wage. I would call it guarding the home. After all the biggest thing we can hope to do is to make women - and men - think of the welfare of society."

Eventually this breach was healed. By 1907 a major purpose of the NWTUL was defined as discovering and developing the leadership inherent in working ranks. Furthermore the role of the ally was also clarified as one who "must have great patience, lofty faith and unalterable humility. It is the girls who must ever be the movement but the ally can help immensely. She has often time, money, and the touch with the outside world . . ." Perhaps the greatest reassurance to workers was the arrest of many allies for picketing at a variety of strikes beginning in 1909. The first public display of solidarity occurred when Margaret Dreier Robins headed a League delegation in a labor parade to protest the civil liberties violations of two Industrial Workers of the World, "Big Bill" Haywood and George Pettibone. Many allies were distressed by Robins participation in the demonstration on behalf of these men who had been spirited out of Colorado to stand trial for the murder of the former governor of Idaho, Frank Steunenburg. The Chicago Women's City Club rescinded her membership.

The attitude of Margaret Robins and her equally dedicated sister Mary Dreier reassured working women of the allies' partnership. Not only did the Dreiers empathize with workers, but believed that in helping them develop talents that "industrial feudalism had throttled," they could learn from its victims. Rose Schneiderman was one of those workers whose suspicion the Dreiers overcame. With their help she emerged as one of the most prominent women in the American labor movement. A petite immigrant from Russian Poland she was only thirteen years old when she began working to support her widowed mother. As a direct result of her efforts a women's local of the United Cloth Hat and Cap Makers Union was chartered in January 1903. Schneiderman served as its secretary and representative to the Central Labor Union. The following year, at twenty-two years of age, she was elected to the General Executive Board, the first woman to hold such a position in the Cap Makers. While leading a thirteen-week strike in 1905 against the open shop, she was assisted by the New York WTUL and through this contact met the Dreier sisters, who became her lifelong friends. Her suspicions resolved, Schneiderman joined the League, appealed for union cooperation, and was elected a vice president in 1906.

Two years later one of the allies provided funds to enable her to leave work and return to school on a full-time basis. While a student she spent her evenings recruiting for the WTUL, particularly among the garment workers, and assisted in the famous Shirtwaist strike of 1909-1910. Schneiderman was hired as full-time League organizer, and after the horrible Triangle Shirt Waist Company fire of 1911, served on the New York factory investigating commission with Al Smith, Gompers, and Mary Dreier. She took a leave of absence from the WTUL in 1912 to campaign for woman suffrage, particularly among female workers. After three years she became a national organizer for the International Ladies' Garment Workers Union but resigned in 1917 to succeed Leonora O'Reilly as chairperson of the Industrial Section of the Woman Suffrage Party of New York. That same year New York women were enfranchised, and she returned full-time to the New York WTUL. Schneiderman later became instrumental in preventing wartime repeal of New York State's 54-hour law for women, worked for females in the International Labor Organization, and helped establish Brookwood Labor College. During the 1920s she grew friendly with Eleanor and Franklin Roosevelt, and during Roosevelt's presidency was the only woman on the Labor Advisory Board of the National Recovery Administration. Schneiderman was elected president of the New York WTUL in 1926 serving in that capacity until 1950.

THE WTUL ENDORSES PROTECTIVE LEGISLATION

Confusion between the allies and the unionists was exacerbated as the NWTUL attempted to determine the best way to achieve its objective, protection of the woman worker. As late as 1909 the Executive Board was sharply divided between those who believed it more important to organize and strengthen unions, and those who contended the major purposes of the League were education, investigating industrial conditions, securing legislation, and interpreting trade unionists and allies to each other. These purposes were not mutually exclusive, but lack of resources impaired League attempts to achieve both.

The United States Supreme Court must have encouraged many League members to agitate for protective legislation at the expense of organizational activities. After the Court found unconstitutional a New York statute establishing a maximum ten-hour day for bakers, in *Muller v. Oregon* it upheld a state law limiting women laundry workers to a ten-hour day. The latter decision dwelt upon the inherent differences between the sexes, women's "maternal functions" and the "well-being of the race." Because of earlier state court decisions invalidating protective legislation, Florence Kelley, an advocate of women's unions, urged the WTUL to organize women and to agitate for a congressional investigation of their working conditions. However, Kelley, who had helped prepare the Muller brief, responded to the Court's decision by abandoning her earlier union position and emphasizing protective legislation as the remedy for female exploitation.

League conventions and local meetings passed resolutions urging such laws and persuaded other women's groups to support their program. A legislative package calling for an eight-hour day, the elimination of night work, maternity leave with pay, and a legal minimum wage in the sweatshop trades was drafted by the WTUL. Leaguers also exhorted the AFL to organize an independent labor party in order to achieve such goals and lobbied for the federal government to investigate women's working conditions. After obtaining the backing of Theodore Roosevelt, the General Federation of Women's Clubs, and the AFL, a measure to initiate such a study was enacted in 1907.

Meanwhile branches agitated on the state and local scene. A city history of women and trade unions was completed by the Boston League. In Illinois the WTUL campaigned successfully for a ten-hour law for women. This endeavor first brought Agnes Nestor into prominence and helped make the young attorney Harold Ickes a devoted friend of the organization. Efforts on behalf of Chicago's children drew the wrath of conservatives, particularly when the League urged that working certificates be issued only after children were made aware of the laws that protected them. To reach more workers free concerts were presented in Chicago parks and a Committee on Immigration was instituted. The response to the latter was so enthusiastic that it became a separate undertaking, the Chicago Immigration Society.

STRAINED RELATIONS WITH THE AFL

These programs, advanced primarily by the allies, explain in part why Samuel Gompers did not completely abide by his pledge to the 1905 WTUL conference to cooperate as a matter of "right" and "fraternity." Never very enthusiastic about the organization, as late as 1904 Gompers was unaware of the names and addresses of its officers. In two lengthy papers on the subject of women and trade unions, he avoided the distinct problems of females and completely ignored the existence of the League, for he thought that its main value lay in the area of public relations. Convinced that the average employer did not discriminate against capable women, Gompers opposed the policy of governmental protection of the rights, wages and hours of workers. He believed that, under the inspiration of the allies, the WTUL was frequently working at cross purposes with the AFL. This conviction was reenforced when the League refused to endorse a Federation proposal on the exclusion of Japanese and Korean immigrants. Consequently Gompers publicly condemned the "superficial sympathy doled out by philanthropists for the women and girls" and criticized the organization for directing too much energy in "utilizing possible 'allies.' " He cited lack of funds in refusing to appoint female organizers in 1904, and at the 1907 AFL convention he avoided conferring with a League committee on that very issue. Despite the League's effective action in strikes in Fall River and Chicago its fraternal delegates were denied the vote at AFL conventions, even when the Amalgamated Meat Cutter and Butcher Workmen urged that the policy be changed.

Distrust of the League was not rooted in suspicion of the allies alone, the Federation had been unable to overcome the sentiment that work outside the home was unnatural for women. The Federal Labor Union of Owensboro, Kentucky, resolved at the 1908 convention that the U.S. Congress should exclude women from all government employment. Defeated only after considerable debate, the resolution was intended to "relegate [women] to the home" away from work that might possibly injure them and endanger motherhood. As late as 1914 Andrew Furuseth, of the International Seaman's Union, because he attributed growing unemployment to working women, offered a resolution proposing that social and racial health be restored by returning them to the home. Since Furuseth believed women the cornerstone of the family, his anger was aroused when the Committee on Resolutions recommended that "health" be "restored" by making the employment of women as "congenial" as possible. It was only after Vice President James Duncan warned the convention delegates to deal with conditions as they found them, not as they would like them to be, that the amended resolution was adopted.

In dealing with conditions as they found them the vacillating AFL cooperated with the WTUL in early years, creating a sense of optimism in League members. The WTUL was allowed to use "Indorsed by AF of L"on letterheads, and AFL officials including Gompers, frequently attended League meetings.

President Robins was elected to the Education Board of the Chicago Federation of Labor; in 1909, along with Agnes Nestor, she was appointed to the Industrial Education Committee of the AFL. Gompers finally appointed a female organizer in reponse to NWTUL-sponsored resolutions. But his lack of complete confidence in the League was again revealed when he ignored their objections and selected Annie Fitzgerald, secretary of the Label League, for this position.[4] Fitzgerald's work, confined to Illinois, did much to demonstrate the effectiveness of women organizers. She "stimulated our weak kneed element," stopped hostile demonstrations by management, and worked toward the establishment of a local of the Teamsters Union, the Barbers Union, and a Federal Union.

Women were supported in other ways by the AFL. Conventions continued to endorse woman suffrage and to cooperate with suffrage organizations. In 1907, Gompers promised Anna Howard Shaw, President of the National American Woman Suffrage Association, that he would work for equal suffrage, equal rights, and equal pay "so long as life shall last it will by my pleasure to do everything within my power, both on the platform and by the pen, in behalf of the movement." Consequently he advised suffragists in their Oregon campaign and urged all affiliates to assist them.

The AFL journal, the *American Federationist*, ran a series of articles in 1905 on women and labor that included contributions by Henrotin and Walling. At the convention that year, various locals donated $1,000 to the League. WTUL delegates, although unenfranchised, were still treated courteously. Nestor presided temporarily in 1906, and President Robins addressed the 1908 convention. The Federation endorsed the League's proposal for a government investigation of women in industry and lobbied in Congress for its passage. The League reciprocated by lending its support to a resolution on the alien contract law, apparently at Gompers' request. Its new constitution of 1907 redefined its objectives as assisting in the "organization of women into trade unions to be affiliated with the AF of L."

Mutual opportunities to organize women and support their strikes were never fully exploited, yet the League and the AFL occasionally cooperated in such endeavors. With the assistance of Michael Donnelly of the AFL, Mary McDowell, at one time president of the Illinois WTUL, had established the first women's union in the Chicago stockyards. She also served on the General Packing Trades Council, played a major role in the strike of 1904, and often urged Gompers to encourage efforts in the stockyards. As president of the Cattle Butchers Union, Donnelly obliged new members to swear support of women workers. When the United Textile Workers of America, many of whom were women, struck in 1904 in Fall River, Massachusetts, Gompers raised money for them. The Boston League not only supported the strike but found employment for 130 strikers and underwrote the costs of transportation, food, and lodging to accompany their relocation. The Amalgamated Meat Cutter and Butcher Workmen were so impressed by League efforts in these two strikes that they proposed granting voting privileges to League representatives at AFL conventions. Despite the defeat of this suggestion, the Federation did encourage special efforts to organize women.

The WTUL participated in other strikes throughout the country. Locked-out corset workers of Aurora were assisted by the Illinois branch. Leaguers furnished moral support, money, and publicity for young girl strikers of the Paper Box Makers Union in New York City. Members were also conspicuous in what one observer described as the most fiercely contested women's strike in history, that of the International Shirtwaist and Laundry Workers in Troy, New York. This action, arising from a reduction in piece work rates, became a city wide general strike when goods were sent to other factories. The New York WTUL helped organize the women, raised strike funds, provided educated leadership, and prevailed upon Gompers to issue a public statement urging labor to support and cooperate with the demonstrators. The strike was eventually beaten, but women had proven that they were "not a disturbing, disintegrating factor, but a strong, sane, reasonable force, sensitive to common needs and alert for a common rights and common justice."

Regardless of these achievements membership remained a problem. To increase it the Chicago branch arranged for medical services for those who paid ten cents a year to the Budget Department, and the Boston League hired Josephine Casey as an organizer. Miss Casey had recently unionized female employees of the Chicago Elevated Railway and successfully led them in a fight for a wage increase. Strengthened by her deep faith in people's basic goodness, she enthusiastically advocated women's rights and became an organizer for the International Ladies' Garment Workers and the United Textile Workers. Increasingly she applied her talents to the broader aspect of the women's movement; she founded the Women's Political Equality Union, became a field worker for the National Woman's Party, and campaigned for an Equal Rights Amendment to the United States Constitution.

Further efforts to make trade unionism attractive to women were undertaken by the WTUL. In order to bind the "girls" closely together and to encourage class consciousness, the League publicized its achievements and promoted social as well as recreational activities in local branches. Even more important, it began to clarify its own role, as reflected in the new constitution of 1907. At that time four classes of membership were provided - local and state WTULs, members at large, and affiliated organizations (national unions, state federations of labor, and women's auxiliaries to trade unions). Annual dues were ten cents for each member of a state or local chapter, one dollar for individuals, and from one to five dollars for affiliates. Ties to the AFL were made more explicit by stating that the League's objective was to organize women into AFL unions and by pledging support to the principles embodied in the economic program of the Federation (this plank was dropped in 1911 as too vague). Other major provisions of the new constitution were equal pay, an eight-hour day, minimum wage scales, and full citizenship for women. But the most significant factor in the development of the League was the long-lasting, devoted commitment to that organization of two women, Leonora O'Reilly and Margaret Dreier Robins, whose disparate backgrounds vividly demonstrated the League's ability to unite factory and parlor for the betterment of women.

MARGARET DREIER ROBINS: MIDDLE CLASS IDEALIST

Margaret Dreier, born in Brooklyn, was privately educated. Raised in a deeply religious family, she believed that one served God by serving humankind and applying Christian principles to social problems. Her long career of service to workers probably originated with her membership in the Women's Auxiliary of the Brooklyn Hospital, which treated many young women whose ill health or injuries were caused by unsafe or improper factory conditions. Dreier rapidly became involved in other reform groups where she met and shared efforts with Mary Kehew. As a member of the board of Asacog Settlement House in Brooklyn, she encountered Leonora O'Reilly, who persuaded her to aid in the organization of the New York WTUL as a means of realizing Dreier's "new concept of social service for remedying industrial evils." In 1905 she met Raymond Robins of Chicago, who had come to Brooklyn to preach on the "social gospel" at Plymouth Church. A bachelor dedicated to promoting the causes of labor, religion, and government Robins found a kindred soul in Dreier. In less than three months they were married.

Her sister Mary succeeded Margaret as president of the New York WTUL when the newlyweds moved to Chicago to reside in a cold-water tenement in the "bloody seventeenth ward." A year later Margaret was chosen national president and served the League in that capacity from 1907 to 1922. The energy and talent she brought to that office were matched only by the generosity with which she dispensed a good portion of her fortune. In a moment of discouragement she wrote to her sister: "There are times when it makes me quite heartsick to realize that it is my money alone which enables me to carry out the plans, and that whatever intelligence or character I have would be utterly useless were it not for the fact that I have money."

Mrs. Robins had to defend herself from the charge of Socialism because she viewed the WTUL and unions as more than mere instruments to improve working conditions. To her they were a means of educating women, teaching them to think and grow while developing self-government, self-respect and self-reliance. This concept, her devotion to trade unions, and her social position enabled Robins to be an effective liaison between working "girls" and the rest of the community.

LEONORA O'REILLY: TRADE UNIONIST

Nearly as significant in the early history of the WTUL was Leonora O'Reilly, whose background sharply contrasted with that of Dreier. O'Reilly was born in 1870, the daughter of Irish immigrants. Her mother, widowed in 1871, returned to factory work and took in boarders to keep the small family together. Young Leonora was strongly influenced by the labor views of her mother, who lost one position because of union activity, and who often brought her daughter to radical lectures at Cooper Union.

At eleven years of age Leonora began to work in a collar factory, and at sixteen - the year she joined the Knights of Labor - she participated in her first strike. In 1888 she became one of the founders of the Working Women's Society, and was later elected vice president of the Social Reform Club. Through these organizations she became friendly with wealthy reform women, one of them, Louise Perkins, arranged for a reduction in her hours at the shirtwaist factory where she worked. With Perkins making up the pay differential, O'Reilly was able to attend school. She studied at YWCA classes, served at the Nurses' Settlement (Henry House) with Lillian Wald, and graduated from the Pratt Institute, where she studied liberal arts and sewing-education. At the same time O'Reilly continued her reform activities, organizing for the United Garment Workers of America, working for the Consumers' League, and advocating female unionization as a contributor to the *New York Journal.*

When she graduated from Pratt in 1900 O'Reilly became head-worker at Asacog Settlement House in Brooklyn, where she began her friendship with the Dreier sisters. Her vocational summer school that taught girls sewing developed into the Manhattan Trade School for Girls, where the curriculum consisted of academic subjects, industrial history, and vocational (machine) training. While a member of the Board of Directors, O'Reilly supervised the Electric Machine Operating Department and taught for seven years.

A founder of the New York WTUL in 1904, she persuaded the Dreier sisters to join the League. To give her "freedom to use her gifts for the people in her own way," Mary Dreier made O'Reilly financially independent in 1908. As a result she worked indefatigably for the cause of working women until a heart attack in 1914 limited her activities. After this she increasingly spent her available time and energy in the suffrage movement. An eloquent speaker, she lectured and organized for the WTUL in its early years and won for that organization the cooperation of New York labor leaders. She served as a liaison between the unionists, the Consumers' League, and suffrage organizations, and also participated in the Moyer-Haywood Inquiry Committee of New York.

Unlike her friends the Dreiers, O'Reilly's commitment to the labor cause was not inspired by traditional Christian affiliation. O'Reilly, apparently a Roman Catholic at one time, later advocated the "Religion of Humanity," frequently referring to herself as a "pagan" to the consternation of her friend Mary Dreier. Her dedication to the working class probably stemmed from her mother, the Religion of Humanity, and Socialism. Most likely her study of Giuseppe Mazzini, whom she viewed as the founder of Christian Socialism, converted her to that doctrine. O'Reilly believed that poverty is an anomaly since productive capacity exceeds consumptive capacity. She taught that labor, which is noble and holy, creates all wealth and therefore should own the wealth. For immediate objectives she urged the collective ownership of railroads and large-scale industry and the reorganization of the government, eliminating the Senate, the presidential veto, and the power of the Supreme Court to curb social legislation.

Although O'Reilly had suitors, she never married, for she was apparently reluctant to yield her independence. She despaired when her Socialist friends traded their economic independence for the false security of marriage. Nevertheless she adopted an infant girl, Alice, whom she loved deeply and who lived with her and her mother until the child's tragic death in 1911.

Energy of women such as these and clarification of the NWTUL's purpose contributed to its fairly rapid growth, and by 1909 the organization was able to participate dramatically and effectively in the women's labor movement.

Chapter 6

THE WTUL COMES OF AGE [1]

One of the most significant episodes in the history of working women was the Shirtwaist strike of 1909-1910. With this action female strikers and the NWTUL won the cooperation of the AFL as well as the respect and sympathy of the nation. In addition, WTUL unionists became convinced that their "allies" were not condescending visiting crosstowners, but colleagues in the fight for the rights of working women.

ORIGINS OF THE SHIRTWAIST STRIKE: 1909-1910

Known as the "uprising of 20,000," the strike began in September 1909 and was directed against two of New York City's largest shirtwaist firms, one of which, the Triangle Shirt Waist Company, would become nationally infamous in 1911 because of the tragic fire on its premises. Original grievances included charging employees for electric power, needles, thread, and oil, and subjecting them to a variety of petty harassments through a system of fines. But the prime issue became unionization when employers responded adversely to the formation of new locals of the Ladies Waist Makers Union. The Triangle Shirt Waist Company turned the strike into a lockout, assumed the leadership of an Employers' Association "to prevent this irresponsible union from gaining the upper hand," and then placed its business with nonstruck firms. On November 22 a mass meeting of shirtwaist makers was held at Cooper Union. Among the many speakers was Samuel Gompers, appearing at the request of the NWTUL, who warned, in his typical fashion, against hasty action. The crowd, however, was not in a mood for conciliatory, dispassionate speeches. Its frame of mind

61

was indicated by the enthusiastic reception given to Mary Dreier, president of the New York WTUL, who had been arrested for picketing; and by its response to the emotional address of Clara Lemlich, a young striker. Urging an immediate general strike, Lemlich dramatically raised her hand and swore the old Jewish oath: "If I turn traitor to the cause I now pledge, may this hand wither from the arm I now raise." Thousands in the audience responded fervently. Production came to a virtual standstill the following day as between 20,000 and 30,000 workers, mostly Jewish and Italian females, sixteen to twenty-five years old, walked out.

The odds against the striking "girls" were formidable for the International Ladies' Garment Workers Union, only nine years old, was not yet firmly established, and the waistmakers' local had only one hundred members and $4 in its treasury. The strikers' courage was unshakable, however. A proposal by the National Civic Foundation was publicly burned as it did not include union recognition. Management tried unsuccessfully to exploit Jewish and Italian antagonisms and drive a wedge between the "girls." At Triangle prostitutes were employed to disrupt picket lines. There was collusion between the employers and law enforcement agencies; thousands of pickets were badgered by the police, over 700 were brutally arrested, and many were sentenced to the city work house. When one arrested picket was informed by a magistrate that "she was on strike against God, whose principal law is that man should earn bread," the WTUL eagerly publicized George Bernard Shaw's barb: "Delightful medieval America, always in the intimate personal confidence of the Almighty."

LEAGUE PARTICIPATION IN THE "UPRISING"

The WTUL immediately rallied to the support of the strikers. Even before the walkout became general, it recruited upper and middle-class women to picket and to persuade scabs to join the union. Dubbed the "mink brigade" by Rose Schneiderman, seventy-five volunteers lent their prestige and respectability to the demonstration for seven weeks; these included Anne Morgan, the daughter of J.P. Morgan, Elsie Cole, daughter of Albany's Superintendent of Schools, and Inez Milholland, daughter of millionaire John E. Milholland. The double standard of law enforcement became evident when the president of the New York League, Dreier, was arrested for picketing. As her case was called, the arresting officer apologetically murmured, "Why didn't you tell me you was a rich lady? I'd never have arrested you in the world." This incident contrasted sharply with the experience of a small Jewish girl badly beaten by a factory foreman in the presence of a police officer. The freelance writer and Leaguer Rheta Dorr, who had been picketing arm in arm with the striker, brought the case to court. Despite her testimony and that of the victim, the magistrate dismissed the charges as "incredible."

The WTUL was particularly zealous for the rights of pickets. It volunteered legal services at police courts, provided witnesses for arrested strikers, cross-examined those who testified, raised $29,000 in bail, and acted as a complainant at police headquarters. As a result of League efforts, Mrs. O.H.P. Belmont, who had visited night courts to ensure that those arrested were treated justly, conducted a mass meeting at Carnegie Hall to remonstrate against police brutality. A protest march of 10,000 to City Hall, organized by the League for the same purpose, was led by Mary Dreier, Ida Rauh, and Helen Marot a former investigator for the U.S. Industrial Commission. The press had tended to ignore police excesses and legal injustice, but was now forced to report events more objectively; it thereby aroused a sympathetic public response unattainable through a coverage of only the issues.

The success of the WTUL in publicizing injustice and in fund-raising was due in large part to the support the allies obtained from socially prominent, well-to-do women whom the Employers' Association castigated as the "uptown scum." Anne Morgan joined the League and was immediately courted by Gompers, with Mrs. O.H.P. Belmont, she obtained encouragement and financial contributions from New York's "400." Miss Morgan raised $1,300 at one meeting at which Dreier, John Mitchell, and Rose Schneiderman defended the strikers. Belmont, who related worker exploitation and police brutality to the denial of woman suffrage, conducted a mass meeting at the Hippodrome and participated in a Carnegie Hall rally. Mrs. Henry Morgenthau Sr., who with her attorney husband founded a settlement house, and Helen Taft, daughter of the President, also contributed time, money and publicity to the cause.

Among the most selfless of the allies was Carola Woerishoffer, millionaire daughter of a Wall Street financeer. A 1907 graduate of Bryn Mawr, Woerishoffer became a part-time resident and worker at Greenwich House. She was also employed as a laundress for four months in order to obtain data for the Consumers' League on this degrading industry. In 1908 she joined the New York WTUL and actively supported the Shirtwaist strike, posting $75,000 worth of property as a bond for arrested strikers. Later she contributed $10,000 to the WTUL to inaugurate a permanent strike fund. Her commitment to workers intensified by her participation in the Shirtwaist episode, she became an investigator for the New York Department of Labor. This fervid young woman died at age twenty-six in an automobile accident.

The WTUL did more than merely protect the civil rights of demonstrating workers. Strike headquarters were at the League office, where the WTUL provided an information bureau, coordinated all activities, dispatched lecturers, defended pickets, revitalized the practically defunct Local 25 of the International Ladies' Garment Workers Union, and — most importantly — promoted the morale of the young demonstrators. Close to $20,000 was raised by the League for relief and in so doing the injustices and petty tyrannies of management were well publicized. WTUL members and strikers edited and sold a special issue of the *New York Call* and *New York Journal*, interspersing appeals for contributions with a dramatic history of the dispute. Accompanied by a sixteen-year-old girl who spent thirty days in jail for picketing, Rose Schneiderman raised money lecturing at colleges and at parlor meetings in Massachusetts with the president of the Boston League. Pauline Newman, a young striker who would later organize for the ILGWU, toured upstate New York for funds. Mass meetings and parades were supported by groups that under other conditions would have been anathema to the allies but were welcomed in these circumstances. New York Socialists rallied behind WTUL demonstrations; the League's O'Reilly addressed a Socialist mass meeting on the strike; and the United Mine Workers' colorful labor gadfly, "Mother" Jones, came to New York to assail the abuses of the industrial system.

Inspired by the New York example Philadelphia shirtwaist makers also struck. Sharing similar grievances and suspicious that their employers were filling orders for New York City manufacturers, about two-thirds of the waistmakers walked out in December. As in New York, the strikers were mostly young, mostly female, and overwhelmingly Jewish. Since the International Ladies' Garment Workers Union was small, with neither the staff nor the funds to manage two general strikes, it appealed to President Robins of the WTUL for assistance. Within twenty-four hours she was in Philadelphia with Agnes Nestor. Other League members, including O'Reilly and Schneiderman, soon followed, as did Mother Jones. Here again they organized, raised money, and provided leadership.

After opening headquarters in the waistmaking district the League conducted a publicity campaign on behalf of the strikers. Money was raised for relief, Robins and Nestor investigated factory conditions and encouraged resistance.

One of the most significant contributions of the League, here as in New York, was the defense of pickets who were arrested and jailed. Not only was bail money raised, but Robins convinced Philadelphia socialites and Consumers' League members to join the picket line. The ensuing notoriety further publicized the strike and reduced the instances of police brutality. With the support of Mrs. George Biddle, Robins formed an advisory council of the cities' leading lawyers to protect the pickets' rights.

A SATISFACTORY CONCLUSION

As the stoppage spread to Philadelphia it came to an end in New York, for many smaller firms quit the Employers' Association and settled. Others gradually followed; however, because of dwindling resources and the intransigence of some large firms, the strike was officially called off on February 15, 1910. At this time, thirteen shops with 1,100 workers were still out. Nevertheless, settlements had been made with 339 New York firms, 300 of which called for union shops; most Philadelphia manufacturers had also negotiated settlements favorable to labor.

As a result of its role the WTUL was recognized as an efficient, capable, and powerful organization. The *New York Journal* praised its share in the workers' "great victory," as did the *American Federationist*, the ILGWU, the Workingmen's Federation of the State of New York, and the president of the Boston Central Labor Union. The latter urged that the League become a full-fledged member of the AFL rather than a mere affiliate. Distrust of the allies was resolved when these women marched in picket lines, and when an embittered shirtwaist manufacturer initiated a suit for conspiracy in restraint of trade against wealthy Leaguers. Even Gompers expressed his appreciation for them, the League, and for women workers as he proclaimed that the strike demonstrated the practicality of unionism among females and "the capacity of those misused toilers to suffer, fight, and dare that justice might be done." [2]

In addition to refurbishing its image the League effected other successes. The entire Ladies Waist Makers Union had been revitalized; membership had increased; a permanent chapter was established in Philadelphia; and two new leaders had matured, one an ally, the other from union ranks. Mabel Gillespie attended Radcliffe for two years before entering settlement work at Denison House. She joined the Boston WTUL in 1903 and in the following year participated in the Fall River strike. For the next five years she worked as a Consumers'

League investigator in upstate New York, exposing exploitative conditions in the canning industry and violations of child-labor laws in the city of Buffalo. From her return to Boston in 1909 until her death in 1923 Gillespie served as executive secretary of the Boston League. Assuming the leadership of the Boston Shirtwaist strike she contributed her savings to help finance it. Linking the League with powerful male unions, she doubled its membership, and organized newsstand, necktie, knit-goods, wire, straw-hat, and jewelry workers. In 1910 she was arrested for unionizing in front of the Gillette Safety Razor plant. Several years later she founded and was elected president of the Stenographers, Bookkeepers, Accounts, and Office Employees Union of Boston. As a result of her influence on the passage of the Massachusetts minimum wage law, she was appointed to the state Wage Commission from 1912 to 1919.

The other leader to emerge from the strike was Agnes Nestor, whose Irish immigrant father, a dedicated Knight of Labor, blended a political career with the grocery trade and factory work. At eighteen, a year after she had begun work, Nestor, a member of the cutters' union, led a victorious strike against the glove factory that employed her. Shortly thereafter she established an operators' union chartered directly by the AFL and composed entirely of women. After helping to organize the International Glove Workers Union of America she was elected first vice president in 1903, and continued to hold national office until 1948. Her efforts in behalf of the Glove Workers Union precluded her from active participation in League affairs until the Philadelphia Shirtwaist strike; then she organized, lobbied, and held office as branch president from 1913 until her death in 1948. An effective bridge between the WTUL and the AFL, she frequently represented both the League and the Glove Workers Union at conventions.

The shirtwaist strike increased the AFL's respect for the WTUL, nonetheless, relations between the two remained somewhat strained because of the Federation's aversion to Socialism and the League's willingness to obtain support from any who sympathized with its goal of improved working conditions for women. The League's leadership included Socialists like Helen Marot, Pauline Newman, Rose Schneiderman, and Leonora O'Reilly. A joint legislative committee composed of members of the Socialist Party and the New York WTUL led to frequent criticism from the right.[3] After her resignation from the *American Federationist*, Eva M. Valesh, in New York to publicize the Shirtwaist strike, charged that the WTUL was dominated by Socialists. To a Woman's Forum audience she described its radicalism as "masked by its perfunctory interest for the strikers" and charged that it used labor disputes to further Socialist purposes. Valesh, never completely in sympathy with the League, promised to start a campaign against Socialism by promoting "sensible" labor unions. This pledge was interpreted by the press as the culmination of Anne Morgan's policies. Morgan, Valesh's friend, had earlier attacked O'Reilly's Socialism and issued a clarion call for new trade unions.

However, little of consequence followed from these declamations. Gompers invited Morgan to a labor conference and to a personal meeting. Appealing for her support of legitimate labor goals he implied that she should join the League, whose members needed her clarity of vision. Valesh, after her public attack, informed the New York WTUL's executive board that, as an AFL organizer her principles were not in accord with the League's Socialist leanings. She did not even bother to attend the board meeting that voted to expel her.

Conservative trade unions never reconciled themselves to the League's leftish tendencies, yet they found it impossible to ignore the organization. At the 1909 AFL national convention Gompers praised the NWTUL and appointed Nestor and Robins to the AFL Committee on Industrial Education, Women's Branch. He even requested that Robins undertake on behalf of the Federation a study in Europe of labor issues. Successfully championing the League's proposal for a congressional investigation into the industrial employment of women and children; the AFL used the study to urge "reasonable restrictions of females and minors in dangerous employment."

Little was done by the AFL to offset the special problems faced by males organizing women or to attract female unionists. Support for the League's efforts to organize women came only from those unions that employed large numbers of unskilled females to operate light machinery (as in the garment, textile, and laundry trades). Those that did not have a division of labor and where women competed directly with men for skilled positions frustrated WTUL objectives. As a result of their antipathy AFL organizational efforts were limited to rhetorical appeals to affiliates and a special campaign directed toward stenographers and typists. Although discouraged by labor's attitude, Robins excused Federation leaders and rationalized their neglect of women because of the more pressing needs of male workers. Nevertheless she believed that the AFL could not claim to be a representative body until a proportionate number of women were delegates at its conventions. To accomplish this goal, she urged women to publicize their injustices, obtain civil rights, and change attitudes.

LEONORA O'REILLY: INDEFATIGABLE ORGANIZER

Leonora O'Reilly attempted to develop that very attitude by addressing large women's audiences on feminism, labor, and the WTUL. Throughout the Northeast her persuasive voice and obvious sincerity fascinated crowds as she linked employer exploitation to the need for suffrage and a viable well-financed League.

The WTUL attempted to involve churches in these issues, by urging congregations to support the label campaign and persuading clergy to allow labor representatives to preach on Labor Sunday in 1910. O'Reilly, a significant part of this program, lectured frequently to these groups. If her experience with them was typical, the campaign could not have been very successful. Although warmly received, she was much perturbed by these appearances. She confided to her diary after one such lecture: "The whole thing went poorly. Church people always have the effect of a vise on my head and brain, so of course my work is but indifferently done, my tongue wags the allotted time — I go away feeling there is no use at all in my work. What a contrast between the night spent with the striking hat trimmers and these Christians."

O'Reilly's alleged failure to reach the religious community was offset by her success on other fronts. She played a major role in organizing laundry workers and corset, shirtwaist, and neckwear makers, for whom she negotiated a contract. Hat trimmers elected her honorary vice president of their union in 1909 in recognition of her efforts on their behalf. She also raised relief and bail money for 2,000 striking jute workers in Brooklyn and obtained funds and publicity for a New York cordage strike.

Workers' problems were not the only concern of this dynamic woman. O'Reilly participated in a program for general education and improvement of living conditions among Italians in New York, and championed black rights by participating in a variety of interracial committees, including the organizational meetings of the National Association for the Advancement of Colored People. Furthermore, she appeared at Albany in behalf of reform legislation; campaigned for the Socialist Meyer London in his bid for Congress; and supported woman suffrage by lecturing, testifying before legislative committees, and staging massive parades. Her friend Arthur Brisbane of the *New York Journal* was encouraged and aided by her to write about equal pay for women and their position in industry; and she herself contributed to the *American Federationist, Woman Voter, New York Call, Life and Labor,* and the *American Suffragette.*

O'Reilly represented the WTUL in its investigation of fire hazards and safety practices of New York manufacturers after the Triangle Shirt Waist Company fire in 1911. As a result of a Newark fire a year earlier, the League had issued safety recommendations for New York. These had been ignored, but now conscience-stricken by the death of innocent girls and haunted by WTUL pressure and publicity, state government could no longer disregard League recommendations, many of which originated from O'Reilly's committee. While investigating and providing relief for the victims' families the WTUL seized upon every opportunity to demand reform. Dreier chaired protest gatherings and Anne Morgan led memorial meetings. Many middle-class and upper-class citizens, encouraged by Felix Adler and Mrs. O.H.P. Belmont, agitated for protection of sweatshop workers. In cooperation with ILGWU Local 25 the League arranged a massive funeral parade for the seven unidentified victims. Flags were flown at half staff, bells tolled, and traffic halted as Schneiderman and Dreier led the cortege through the streets of the city before 400,000 people.

Indicative of the increasingly aggressive working-class consciousness as well as of the League's new attitude was Schneiderman's address before a memorial mass meeting at the Metropolitan Opera House. Holding both hands out before her, she avowed: "We cannot talk of forgiveness. The blood of those dead workers calls to us all to prevent these things." She then related the failure of preventative efforts and concluded that only a successful working-class movement could preclude such tragedies and protect laboring interests. Unionization might eventually provide the most effective protection, but League efforts resulted in some immediate gains. Mary Dreier and Samuel Gompers were appointed to a commission to inquire into factory conditions, a bureau of fire prevention was instituted, and existing statutes were enforced since the League reported violators to authorities.

LEAGUE ACTIVITIES NATIONWIDE

Encouraged by its success in the Shirtwaist strike, the WTUL undertook a variety of campaigns throughout the country. To attract immigrants in New York City, Italian and Yiddish were frequently used in street-corner rallies and in flyers, and a lunchroom was opened at headquarters where debating, singing, and gym classes were taught. The New York League supported strikes, lobbied at the capital, and expanded cooperation with suffrage groups. In St. Louis a new branch helped organize the female brewery employees and won wage increases and other benefits for them. By marshaling one thousand women for a house-to-house canvass and having them distribute flyers at polls, the St. Louis League defeated a representative who had opposed legislation limiting working hours for women. The Boston WTUL and its allies supported the Roxbury Carpet Weavers strike by organizing a union with the help of Sarah Conboy of the United Textile Workers of America. They marched on picket lines and converted the League's office into official strike headquarters. However, when the Bostonians attempted to unionize "girls" of the Gillette Safety Razor Company, the League's organizer was arrested along with Back Bay socialite-reformer Mrs. Glendower Evans. In addition to its usual tasks, the Chicago League opened a worker's library, established an immigrant committee, and provided a physician for members. Former League organizer Josephine Casey, employed by the ILGWU, was arrested in Kalamazoo for conducting a pray-in with pickets of the corset workers' union. The supplication probably reflected the sentiments of female strikers everywhere:

> "Oh, God, Our Father, Who art generous . . . Our
> employer who has plenty has denied our request.
> He has misused the law to help him crush us . . .
> Thou Who didst save Noah and his family, may it
> please Thee to save the girls now on strike from
> the wicked city of Sodom. Oh, help us to get a
> living wage . . . Grant that we may win the strike
> . . . so that we may not need to cry often,'Oh
> Lord, deliver us from temptation'."[4]

National officers were as active as the local leaders. Robins travelled to Cleveland in 1911 to assist striking garment workers. She spoke at union meetings and workers' gatherings, organized a mass rally of over 4,000 citizens, and in cooperation with Alice Henry, Emma Steghagen, and Agnes Nestor, unionized the female brewery workers in Milwaukee. Another important labor dispute supported by the national leadership was that of the button workers in Muscatine, Iowa. This walkout began when the piece workers protested the arbitrary method of counting acceptable buttons.

AFL and WTUL organizers were sent to Muscatine at the request of the strikers and when the WTUL representative was arrested, the issue quickly became union recognition. Strike breakers arrived from Chicago precipitating violence and the mobilization of the state militia. Nevertheless due to the unity of the workers the walkout continued. One thousand skilled females selflessly cast their lot with two thousand unskilled and defenseless workers.

Robins and other League members in the embattled area contributed substantially to the workers' victory. The WTUL obtained legal help for the demonstrators, attacked the practice of home-work, aided on the picket line, conducted mass meetings, and helped to persuade ministers and merchants to support the strikers.

Experience gained in this and other disputes, especially that of the shirtwaist makers, contributed to the development of a specific policy by the WTUL. When asked, the League would cooperate in strikes involving women on the condition that it be represented on the strike committee. Its tasks would be to unionize workers, organize and direct public opinion, patrol the streets, ensure fair play in the courts, and raise funds. Furthermore, on the advice of its counsel, Louis D. Brandeis, the League incorporated to protect its wealthy members against suits for restraining trade because of their participation in strikes.

CHICAGO CLOTHING STRIKE: 1910

These policies were first implemented during a dispute in the Chicago clothing industry in 1910. A strike began when a handful of girls walked out because of a reduction in piece work wages. Protesting a large number of accumulated grievances, 40,000 workers - 10,000 women - joined the movement and appealed to the United Garment Workers Union for assistance. At the request of the UGW, the Chicago Federation of Labor and the WTUL also participated and together formed a joint strike committee.

By obtaining favorable publicity, patrolling the streets, protecting workers' rights, and picketing, the League kept strikers' morale high. Anna Ickes, wife of the League's legal counsel (Harold Ickes), was among those who joined the demonstration. To provide for the workers Robins raised close to $70,000 and distributed $68,000 in cash and goods through a League commissary.

Despite these achievements, relations deteriorated between the League and the United Garment Workers. Thomas Rickert, president of the UGW, was a conservative old-line labor leader interested in developing the union along craft lines. Skeptical of the attachment of unskilled immigrants to unions, he was very eager to come to terms with employers. In November he announced an agreement with Hart, Schaffner, and Marx; however, it was rejected by the strikers because it did little more than provide for a return to work. In January a new two-year contract was signed by the same firm with the UGW, Chicago Federation, and Chicago WTUL. This agreement established an arbitration committee for grievances and implicitly recognized the right to strike by providing for reemployment without discrimination. A number of other manufacturers signed similar settlements, nevertheless, the cautious Rickert, without informing either the Chicago Federation of Labor or the WTUL, suddenly called off the strike. This precipitate action further worsened relations between Robins and Rickert, already acrimonious because Rickert had publicly accused the League of mismanaging the strike fund. Although his charges were proved groundless, the WTUL never again closely cooperated with the UGW. Instead it collaborated with the rival Amalgamated Clothing Workers, formed as a result of Rickert's indecisive and conservative leadership. Collaboration was eased by the League's personal ties with this new organization, whose founder and president, Sidney Hillman, was a friend of Jane Addams and Margaret Robins.

Among the most efficient WTUL representatives during the strike was Mary Anderson, whom Robins appointed to represent the League in implementing the Hart, Schaffner, and Marx contract. Anderson came to the United States from Sweden at sixteen years of age and soon began work in a shoe factory. At twenty-three she was elected president of Stitchers Local 94 (all women) of the International Boot and Shoe Union. A few years later she was elected to the executive board of the union, the only woman so honored; and for fifteen years she was a member of the Chicago Federation of Labor. Through her association with Hull House she became friends with Addams and Emma Steghagen, joined the WTUL, and participated in the garment strike. Employed as an organizer by the Chicago branch and by the National Board, Anderson unionized in Philadelphia and Chicago, investigated mine strikes, represented the League at trade and labor union congresses in the United States and Canada, lobbied for reform legislation, and, like many leaguers, was arrested for picketing. Believing security was to be found outside marriage, Anderson remained single, better able to devote herself completely to the labor movement. In 1917 she went to Washington a member of the Advisory Council to the Secretary of Labor. After participating actively in the International Congress of Working Women, in 1921 she was appointed the first director of the United States Labor Department's Women's Bureau.

LAWRENCE TEXTILE STRIKE: 1912

In clarifying the relationship between the WTUL and the AFL no strike was more important than that of the Lawrence, Massachusetts textile mills of 1912. In January of that year, when the mill owners reduced the work week from fifty-six to fifty-four hours in compliance with a new state law they slashed the already low wages of their employees most of whom were unorganized immigrants. Local 20 of the Industrial Workers of the World, whose entire Lawrence membership was only 287, called a mass meeting, proclaimed a strike, and appealed to headquarters for assistance. National organizers arrived the next day and were followed by Joe Ettor, Arturo Giovannitti, Elizabeth Gurley Flynn and "Big Bill" Haywood. Welding together disparate immigrant groups, these officials inducted new members and established strike and relief committees.

Only after the arrival of IWW leaders did John Golden, president of the United Textile Workers (AFL), journey to the divided city. Despite organizational efforts by his union and the League in 1910 and 1911, only about 208 workers, most of whom were skilled, belonged to the UTW. Golden's "elitist" union was now challenged by the IWW. Wobbly rhetoric and direct action tactics were as repugnant to Golden as they were to city officials, management, old-stock immigrants, and the militia that had been called in to preserve order and property. Fighting back, Golden condemned the strike and requested AFL members to remain at work. He urged the League to stay out of Lawrence, but by the end of January WTUL concern for strikers' welfare was paramount, it established relief headquarters in conjunction with the Lawrence Central Labor Union.

From striker ranks Golden formed three new UTW locals, accepted management's terms, and ordered his members back to the mills. As part of his war against the IWW he attempted to coerce the relief committee into providing only for those who returned to work. Disconsolate and confused, some League members abandoned Lawrence. Golden took over relief headquarters on March 15 and denied aid to 15,000 needy individuals still on strike. Demoralized, embittered, and believing its association with the AFL precluded further activity, the League officially withdrew from Lawrence. Confusion might have been avoided if the Boston chapter had complied with national policy and received headquarters permission to participate and obtain a seat on the strike committee.

Shortly thereafter the strike was favorably settled and the WTUL, especially the Boston branch, reevaluated its affiliation with the AFL. An angry Mary O'Sullivan, who along with a handful of Boston settlement workers had remained in Lawrence, publicly criticized the unimaginative Federation and subservient League. She offered the hope that the threat of syndicalism would make management more receptive to old-time unionism and force dynamism from traditional labor leadership. Other leaguers thought the whole episode a disgrace and questioned the value of an alliance that bound the WTUL to a reactionary AFL and thereby prevented effective cooperation with all facets of labor. At a national Executive Board meeting Gompers and Golden seemed eager to propitiate the humiliated League. (Two years later Golden would charge that organization with IWW sympathies and with supporting the enemies of the textile workers during the Lawrence strike.) With some trepidation, believing there was no alternative, the Executive Board reaffirmed its ties to the Federation as being in the best interests of female workers, and in return was promised $150 monthly to help finance its organizational work among women.

Although the promise of financial assistance had been made by Gompers, Robins was still required to submit a request to the Executive Council for final approval. Her petition was enthusiastically supported by John Mitchell, former president of the United Mine Workers, a gentleman whom Robins described as "unequalled" in "fully and rightly" understanding "the position of the under-paid woman and girl workers." As early as 1903 in his book *Organized Labor*, Mitchell had urged unions to take the initiative in organizing women. Setting an example by his own efforts he provided the League with "constant help and cooperation;" addressed its conventions, furnished encouragement and sage advice when few labor leaders acknowledged its existence and chaired the Industrial Education Committee of the AFL, of which Agnes Nestor was a member.

The AFL subsidy was sorely needed by the WTUL. Despite reorganization and the introduction of more efficient business methods, including a per capita tax, it still teetered on the brink of financial disaster. Even *Life and Labor* usually ran an annual deficit. To curtail expenditures it was required that Executive Board meetings in 1912 be conducted by mail. Only through the contributions of wealthy allies such as Mrs. Walter Weyl, who donated $1,000 annually and the generous sacrifices of Margaret Robins, was the League able to survive. Robins, who cancelled loans and paid her own expenses, subsidized young trade unionists for League work and underwrote the cost of *Life and Labor* for three years. She finally lamented that "I feel as if I were nothing but a money machine."

MARY HEATON VORSE: LABOR'S JOURNALIST

Lawrence was a traumatic experience for many. It resulted in Elizabeth Gurley Flynn's intensified commitment to workers and Mary Heaton Vorse's decision to direct her talents to labor. Born to an old New York family and privately educated, she married Albert Vorse in 1898, an editor, author, and friend of Lincoln Steffens. The newlyweds attended Mary's first labor meeting while honeymooning in Italy. After establishing a cooperative housekeeping venture in 1906, she became friends with the William Wallings, "Mother" Jones, Theodore Dreiser, and other progressives. Four years later, following the death of her husband, she met Joe O'Brien, a reporter for Hearst, whom she married in the spring of 1912. Shocked by the poverty and brutality of Lawrence, these two writers resolved to dedicate their talents to labor's struggle with industrial excesses. In Mary's words: "I could write, I could try to make other people see what I have seen, feel what I have felt. I wanted to make others as angry as I was . . . I believed then that if enough saw what I have seen they would get so angry that conditions such as those as Lawrence could not exist for the very force of public opinion."

In addition to portraying working-class issues sympathetically in books and magazine articles, Vorse (who retained her first married name) was active in the Labor Defense Conference, of which her husband was secretary. This organization was established to secure justice for workers in court cases and to insure objective press coverage for labor. On her return from Europe as a delegate to the 1915 Woman's Peace Conference at the Hague, Vorse encouraged the founding of Montessori schools, helped organize the Province-town Players, and became friends with IWW leaders Elizabeth Gurley Flynn and Bill Haywood. Protected by her status as a reporter, she represented the Workers at the metal strike in the Mesaba Range, Minnesota, after Wobbly (IWW) leaders had been expelled from the area. A few years later while reporting on the steel strike of 1919-1920 she worked at headquarters, aided the organizers, and helped her friend Mother Jones. Her efforts on behalf of the steel workers and her organizing in Pennsylvania in 1920 for Sidney Hillman's "radical" Amalgamated Clothing Workers, resulted in more conservative labor leaders attacking her as "red."

Unlike others attached to the Wobbly cause, Vorse did not oppose American entry into World War I. Four months as a European war correspondent ended her pacifism and persuaded her that the United States would have to enter the conflict. During the war she served overseas as a member of the International Red Cross, and wrote for Herbert Hoover's Food Administration, for the Committee on Public Information on the rights of small nations, and for various journals on wartime labor. In Europe after the war she studied conditions in industrial districts, reporting on Russia in 1921-1922 for the Hearst, International, and Universal news services. Following her return she not only wrote about her participation in strikes at Passaic, New Jersey in 1926, and Gastonia, North Carolina in 1929, but in 1937 was wounded by gunshot while reporting on the Republic Steel strike in Youngstown. A "militant liberal" principally as a result of the Lawrence strike, she championed labor until her death in 1966.

ELIZABETH GURLEY FLYNN: THE REBEL GIRL

The "Rebel Girl," Elizabeth Gurley Flynn, an active Wobbly even before Lawrence, was born in 1890 in New Hampshire. Her father, an Irish-American radical, established an Irish Socialist club and founded its monthly magazine, *The Harp*, a reaction to the remarks of New York Mayor George B. McClellan, who, after criticizing Russian, Jewish, and German Socialists, had proudly proclaimed: "But thank God! There are no Irish Socialists." Convinced by 1906 that capitalism precluded women from becoming free and equal citizens, Flynn joined the IWW and before her father's Harlem Socialist Club made her first public speech, "What Socialism Will Do for Women." This address was followed by another urging government support of children so that women could bear them without depending on men for maintenance. That same year Flynn was arrested with her father for speaking without a permit at one of the many street-corner Socialist rallies they conducted.

Radical women were naturally attracted to the IWW, one of whose founders (Mother Jones) was a woman. Challenging sex discrimination the Wobblies offered special inducements to women members by remitting part of their dues. Charming, eloquent, and beautiful, Flynn left high school to promote the Workers, and for the next decade was one of its leading organizers and lecturers. After 1906 she was a delegate to many IWW conventions, the spokesperson of a militant minority who urged decentralization. At one of these conventions she met John A. Jones, an IWW Minnesota organizer, whom she married in 1908 and left shortly after the birth of their son two years later. She joined in the Bridgeport, Connecticut Tube Mill Workers strike in 1907, and was arrested in free speech demonstrations in Missoula, Montana in 1908 and Spokane, Washington in 1909, where, although pregnant, she chained herself to a lamp post to delay incarceration. Once again she was arrested in 1911 for disturbing the peace during the Baldwin Locomotive Workers strike in Philadelphia.

After organizing New York hotel employees and leading a strike of cooks and waiters, for two months in 1912 she lived in Lawrence directing women pickets and bringing in Socialist women speakers. While there she participated with Margaret Sanger in the Wobblies' most successful propaganda coup, the dispatching of strikers' hungry children to New York for food and shelter. Her Lawrence collaboration with Carlo Tresca, the editor of an anarcho-syndicalist paper, resulted in a thirteen-year love affair.

Inspired by the Lawrence struggle, Flynn organized textile mill workers in Lowell and New Bedford, Massachusetts, and in Paterson, New Jersey, where once again the IWW had to contest with the United Textile Workers for labor supremacy. Golden and Sarah Conboy were invited into the strike-ridden city by the town fathers to organize for the UTW and thereby undercut the Wobblies. Twice in that polarized city Flynn was arrested for inciting to riot and finally was brought to trial and then acquitted. Among the prominent women who joined her defense committee were Mrs. O.H.P. Belmont, Mrs. J. Borden Harriman, Lillian Wald, and Mrs. Walter Lippman.

Travelling through the West she organized for the Workers in California, Oregon, and Minnesota. During this time she met and became friends with Vorse and Kate Richards O'Hare. In 1916 she quarreled with Haywood and temporarily left the IWW. However, she rendered that organization assistance during World War I by helping to launch the Workers Liberty Defense Committee to aid radicals imprisoned under the repressive sedition legislation. Serving on this committee with distinction until 1924, Flynn then helped to establish the American Civil Liberties Union. During much of the 1920s she was involved with the Sacco-Vanzetti defense committee. However, she still found time to participate in several strikes during that decade, including the famous one at Passaic, New Jersey. As the IWW slowly collapsed, Flynn gravitated back to Socialism, but then shocked her colleagues in 1937 by joining the Communist party. Ironically she was expelled from the Civil Liberties Union in

1940 for this membership. Convicted as a Communist under the Smith Act in 1955, she spent twenty-eight months in prison. She became chairperson of the American Communist Party in 1961, a position she held until her death in 1966 at a party congress in Moscow, where she was still actively pursuing her dream of a worker's America.

WTUL achievements in the pre World War I period superficially resulted in better relations with the AFL. Gompers abandoned his parochial view of women's role and now preached that it was a "fantastic fiction to tell girls and women that their place is in the home . . . they are now permanently integral parts of the great industrial and social organization of our country" and should therefore be unionized. Accordingly the AFL conventions of 1913 and 1914 assessed members to organize females in what Gompers characterized as a "movement for justice and human welfare." Sixteen women, including Mary Anderson, were appointed by the Federation for this purpose. In order to avoid another Lawrence, emphasis was placed on cooperating with the League in textile drives. Meanwhile the Dreier sisters were enthusiastically welcomed at AFL conventions, where Robins urged the establishment of a school for female organizers, the education of children for "a knowledge of conditions of industry under which they are to work," and a crusade against poverty. Her sister, Mary, explained the purposes and functions of the League and appealed for subscriptions to *Life and Labor*.

This new cooperation, however, was only a calm in the tempestuous relations between the two organizations. Not only was the WTUL far more liberal than the staid Federation, but the AFL still had reservations about women leaving the home and entering the male trade union world.

Chapter 7

THE FIGHT FOR REFORM: THE BATTLE FOR PEACE[1]

Yielding to AFL conservatism did not initiate an era of trust and cooperation with the League. Political issues complicated any move toward rapprochement. In 1912 the Federation's Executive Board warmly supported Woodrow Wilson, who received a public endorsement for President of the United States from Samuel Gompers. On the other hand some outstanding Leaguers refused membership in the Women's National Wilson and Marshall Association, and instead supported Theodore Roosevelt, the embodiment of their crusade for social justice.

Four years of the New Freedom attracted most of the 1912 Progressives into the Democratic fold; yet two mainstays of the WTUL, the Dreier sisters, fought Wilson's bid for reelection. To Mary Dreier, his advocacy of labor reform was less significant than his indecision on woman suffrage: "The attitude of the labor men to the working women has changed me from being an ardent supporter of labor to a somewhat rabid supporter of women - to feel that the enfranchisement of women and especially working sisters is the supreme issue." Her sister, League President Robins, uncomfortable over Wilson's compromises on the Clayton Act, admired Charles Evans Hughes' labor record. Ignoring Gompers' eager endorsement of Wilson she enthusiastically championed Hughes and attempted to get the National American Woman Suffrage Association to endorse the former Supreme Court Justice. Robins' national tour on the Hughes Women's Special Train was frequently assailed by labor. Refused permission to speak at the Labor Temple in Los Angeles, she was censured by Frances Noel, a League member and one of the most renowned women in the California labor movement.

79

Further exacerbating the division between the Federation and the League was the Clayton Antitrust Act of 1914. Gompers had hailed this law as labor's "Magna Carta," but the NWTUL convention and Robins herself publicly criticized the legislation as meaningless. To them the insertion of the word "lawful" before clauses concerning labor's rights (strike, boycott, and freedom from arbitrary injunctions), emasculated the protective features of the measure. They felt that conservative courts could easily interpret away labor's so-called guarantees. Censuring Robins, Gompers implied that her ignorant objections would discredit the AFL, divide the labor movement, and play into the hands of labor's enemies.

PROTECTIVE LEGISLATION: A DIVISIVE ISSUE

Divergence over presidential candidates and legislative assessments were but a manifestation of a deep dichotomy between the League and the Federation. Gompers still distrusted the allies, and the two organizations were diametrically opposed on the desirability of social legislation for workers.

As early as 1909 the League had begun to agitate for a legal minimum wage and an eight-hour day for women. Supported by other women's organizations, such as the National Consumers' League, Robins urged both state and national legislation to protect the rights of unenfranchised women workers. The campaign met with considerable success, for from 1913 to 1923 fourteen states, fearful of women's political retaliation, adopted minimum wage measures.

Legislative gains were made despite unproductive appeals to unions for support. The only prominent labor leader to rally behind the women was John Golden of the United Textile Workers, who believed that protective legislation would reduce the possibility of strikes in his weakened union. Advocating collective bargaining to achieve workers' benefits, Gompers claimed that legislation was a curb on labor's opportunities, and that the state should do only what "we cannot do for ourselves." Furthermore, he cautioned that political action was a long and dangerous process that could be used adversely to labor's interests. As an alternative to protective statutes he encouraged the formation of women's unions to "protect individual freedom and promote the general well-being." Gompers personally delivered this message to a League convention by proclaiming that working conditions were not sex problems but human ones, and therefore "Industrial freedom must be fought out on the industrial field." However, Gompers was not ready to lead any such fight himself, since he was still unwilling to admit that work was a normal pursuit for women. As late as 1915 he even advocated that they be taken out of factories, where their long hours and low pay endangered the "perpetuity of the country."

Gompers' objections to legislation were shared by the labor reformer Helen Marot. After serving seven years as New York WTUL executive secretary, she resigned in 1913 to protest both union failure to support the League and allied dominance of it. Attacking the programs of social reformers as needless, she feared that circumventing collective bargaining by minimum wage laws would destroy unions. Furthermore, the minimum wage would soon become a maximum wage.[2]

Despite its conviction that the exploitation of women was a greater societal danger than management's maltreatment of male workers, the AFL's Executive Committee opposed female wage and hour legislation. Appealing to "Americanism" as well as chauvinism it condemned legislative remedies as a menace to the liberty of "male" wage earners and as subversive of democratic ideals. The Federation readily followed these leaders, rendering meaningless at the 1915 national convention a female-sponsored resolution calling for cooperation with the League's eight-hour campaign and in the following year refusing to endorse a proposal for a women's division in the Department of Labor. The type of women's legal protection believed necessary by the AFL was revealed in its 1913 national convention. Delegates proposed a law prohibiting the employment of white females in establishments owned or controlled by Japanese or Chinese, since the "moral and economic evils" arising therefrom were a "serious menace to society."

AFL reservations about the League's legislative program were reenforced by lingering suspicion of the nonunionist allies. Paul Kellogg, editor of *Survey* magazine, editorially criticized President Taft's appointments to the congressionally authorized Commission on Industrial Relations avowing there were no "real representatives of the 6,000,000 women workers whose labor problems lie not merely in their relations with employers, but in their relations with men's unions." Bitterly denying the accusation, Gompers stated that women could be represented by men on the board and asserted heatedly that "workers are not bugs to be examined under the lenses of a microscope by the 'intellectuals' on a sociological slumming tour."[3]

Misgivings about the allies led to denigration of League reform efforts by Gompers and unnecessary admonitions that unionization was its rightful purpose. In corresponding with Hull House's Ellen Gates Starr about the Chicago garment strike, he pointedly reminded her that the praise or blame of "outsiders" mattered little, for the "well being" and "future opportunities" of workers "depend entirely upon the organized labor movement." Greedily seizing the opportunity to thank the NWTUL secretary for the League's newsletter he reminded her that activities promoting unions must be strengthened. Gompers even suggested to a secretary of a local of the Ladies' Straw and Felt Hat Operators Union that an amalgamation was desirable between the NWTUL and the Women's Union Label League. Praising the dedication of the latter group he implied that this loyal organization would be dominant in such a merger.

By 1914 Robins was infuriated at the Federation's opposition to labor legislation, charging that its policies toward women were contemptuous and arrogant, and frequently frustrated League efforts to ameliorate female working conditions. No longer willing to rationalize these shortcomings, Robins undertook to embarrass the Federation by promoting closer ties with Canadian unions. She even instructed the editor of the League's periodical, *Life and Labor*, to "pile on the Canadian business," for "I'll lick my chops to see Sammy reading it. Great." Robins also initiated a $25,000 drive to free the League from its financial dependence on the AFL, especially in regard to female organizers.

Relations further deteriorated as the two associations disagreed over the selection of organizers, duration of their commissions, and use of the Federation's $150 monthly appropriation for organizational activities. When the League's secretary-treasurer in 1915 requested an increase in the allotment, Gompers objected that much of the money had been used to establish a school for organizers. In supporting him the Executive Committee asserted that *women* were not qualified to organize *women* and therefore it directed that allocations cease unless the expenditures be supervised by Gompers. Furthermore the AFL president was to approve the selection of organizers and directly receive their activity reports. This new policy apparently was retroactive. The Brotherhood of Carpenters and Joiners had appropriated $500 at their December convention for League organizational activities. However, the secretary of that union, a member of the AFL Executive Committee, sent the $500 to the Federation with the notation that organizational work should "be done by and through the American Federation of Labor."

Robins and other bitter Leaguers held emotionally exhausting conferences with the Executive Council and heads of various internationals. At these meetings, WTUL leaders were accused of being irreligious and under IWW influence. So disparaged were the allies that Robins threatened to have them withdraw from the League if that were the price for AFL cooperation. Although her suggestion of a female on the Federation's Executive Board was rejected and her demands for a restoration of mutual confidence were ignored, AFL officers apparently were intimidated by the specter of allied resignation. Acknowledging their necessity and contributions, the Executive Board agreed that Robins and Gompers would jointly select organizers paid by the AFL. Frustrations over organizing were particularly galling to Robins for despite her advocacy of protective legislation she believed the first purpose of the League was unionization. She thwarted a move of its headquarters to Washington for fear location in the capital would divert it from this task.

WORKERS' SCHOOLS

Precipitating the controversy was the organizer's school, begun in 1914 under inauspicious circumstances. Securing a promise of $50,000 for the institute, from a philanthropic friend of her father, Robins antagonized the donor when she refused to approach another businessman because of his anti-labor policies. Angrily withdrawing his offer the original benefactor retorted: "If his money is tainted, so is mine and I won't help." Consequently the inadequately financed school was forced to begin with just a single student. Without Robins' determination it probably would not have survived.

Located in Chicago, the institution was designed to educate women for duty as labor leaders. Its curriculum consisted of four months of academics, including courses in English, public speaking, economic history, modern radicalism, and judicial decisions on labor. This was followed by eight months of field work under Agnes Nestor or Mary Anderson. Some of the courses were taught at Northwestern and at the University of Chicago, where Paul Douglas was one of the instructors most respected by the "girls." Forty-four women, including Robins' successor Maude O'Farrell Swartz, completed the program on scholarship.

The school was well received. Responding to workers' demands an extensive correspondence program was begun and similar training was sponsored by Leagues in Philadelphia and Boston, where Roscoe Pound was an instructor.

When the school was discontinued in 1926 many of its functions had been incorporated by President M. Carey Thomas into the Bryn Mawr summer school for female workers. As early as 1916 the League had proposed that women's colleges initiate summer institutes for women in industry. Finally in 1921 at Bryn Mawr working "girls" (including a minimum of two blacks each year) attended leadership training courses for two months to "widen their influence in the industrial world" and "help in the coming social reconstruction." After seventeen years at the Pennsylvania institution the school was moved to New York and continued as the Hudson Shore Labor School.

In addition to establishing an educational program for organizers, the League encouraged industrial education for women since one out of seven "girls" left school to enter industry. Believing that it would make women better citizens, ease the task of organizing them, and improve working conditions, proposals for industrial training gained the support of other reformers. However, union labor was reluctant to devote itself to female equality when it endangered male supremacy, many trades demanded that women students be excluded from public industrial education. Consequently, the League diverted its energies from a campaign to include liberal arts and industrial law courses in such programs, to a fight for the equal inclusion of women.

The struggle for equality was carried to legislative chambers. In 1914, in accordance with a bill sponsored by the AFL, President Wilson appointed a commission to make recommendations on federal aid for vocational education. Refusing an appointment to the study group, Dreier successfully urged the selection of Agnes Nestor. A trade union member, she was the only representative of organized labor on the committee. Testifying before the commission Leonora O'Reilly joined Nestor in fighting attempts to bar "girls" from trade courses and relegate them to domestic science. Consequently the Smith-Hughes Act of 1917, providing for federal assistance for agricultural and vocational instruction in the public schools, remained silent on the specific issue of programs for "girls."

Passage of protective legislation and implementation of educational programs did not mitigate the need for organizational drives. The congressional Commission on Industrial Relations reported in 1916 that working women were exploited and were thus a menace to wage standards. Increases in women's employment, it declaimed, were attributable to their low salaries and to the further introduction of machinery that made skill, technical knowledge, and strength unnecessary. To remedy this situation the report urged unionization,

84

protective legislation, and woman suffrage. Observing, rather typically, that women's working conditions endangered men, it described them as a menace to American health and well-being, "and to the ideals of family life upon which civilization has been established."

ORGANIZATIONAL DRIVES

With twenty organizers in the field between 1915 and 1917, the WTUL did not need the commission to encourage its unionization efforts. Rallying to the support of straw and panama hat workers when a manufacturer's association attempted to break the union, New York Leaguers joined picket lines and monitored court sessions regarding strikers. Leonora O'Reilly inspired workers at rallies, Helen Marot was in charge of strike halls, and the president of the Hat Trimmer's Union, Melinda Scott, who would later serve as a League organizer, was on the settlement committee. Under Scott, the League also unionized pottery workers in New Jersey and negotiated favorable settlements in the silk and woolen mills of Trenton. Furthermore, it conducted drives to organize retail clerks and waitresses, undertook a relief and employment program for the jobless, and after supporting the striking bag makers of Brooklyn negotiated a favorable settlement for them. By threatening strikes at potential fire-traps the WTUL compelled factories to remove fire hazards and provide safe egress.

In Massachusetts, too, the League was active. A strike in Holyoke's paper factories was supported by the WTUL and an Office Building Cleaners Union and a female Candy Workers Union were established. Fear of this new union led to improvements in working conditions and wages even in nonorganized factories. But the social distance between the allies and the workers was vividly illustrated when Mabel Gillespie, president of the Boston WTUL, signed the candy workers' contract two hours before her departure for Europe.

Of more importance was the League's endeavors on behalf of Boston telephone operators. Little had been done to organize these workers for the International Brotherhood of Electrical Workers, primarily a union of linemen and cable splicers, considered them flighty and likely dropouts. The first feeble operators' union was affiliated directly with the AFL. However, when twenty toll exchange operators protested lengthy hours by walking out of their jobs in 1912 Gillespie and IBEW representatives established a sublocal for females, the first permanent organization of these women. Under the leadership of Julia

O'Connor, a graduate of the WTUL organizer's school, the strike was successfully concluded and the union prospered. After another victorious strike of 22,000 operators in 1919, separate operator locals replaced the sublocals, and a Telephone Operators Department was established by the Brotherhood.

The Illinois branch was as active as the Massachusetts League. Investigating and publicizing deplorable working conditions of striking spar miners in Rosiclare, the WTUL raised relief funds by sponsoring "self-denying week" - seven days in which working "girls" went without desserts, movies, and street car rides. Leaguers also organized workers, marched on picket lines, raised bail money, and drew public attention to the strikes of broom factory workers and waitresses in Chicago. Ellen Gates Starr, the middle-aged co-founder of Hull House, was arrested for picketing with the waitresses and charged with "disorderly conduct." During the strike of 25,000 men and women in the Chicago clothing trade, she was arrested once again. This strike was defeated, partially because of competition between the Amalgamated Clothing Workers and the United Garment Workers. However, the demonstrators were rendered outstanding support by many League members, including Mary McDowell, Agnes Nestor, Grace Abbott, Sophonisba Breckenridge, Margaret Robins, and Jane Addams, who raised $22,000 for relief. Also sharing fully in the effort was Dorothy Jacobs (Bellanca), who in 1914 led her local, No. 170 Button Sewers, from the conservative United Garment Workers into the newly formed Amalgamated Clothing Workers Association. Her election at twenty-one years of age to the ACWA General Executive Board in 1916 resulted from her endeavors in Chicago. A year later she was appointed first full-time woman organizer and in 1924 head of a special Women's Bureau.[4]

The national office of the League organized "girls" working in the Milwaukee breweries and thereby won for them an increase in wages as well as a decrease in hours. It also raised money to support the Western Federation of Miners in Arizona in 1916. But the era's most significant strike in which the League participated prominently was that of the white goods (underwear) workers in New York City. In 1910 cloakmakers, after a two-month general strike, signed a Protocol of Peace improving pay and working conditions and establishing arbitration machinery. Emboldened by their success and fearful of the dangerous working conditions exposed in the Triangle fire, large numbers of workers, with the encouragement of the League, began to flock to the women's clothing trade unions. So great was this influx that the Waist and Dress Makers Union, Kimono Makers, and Children's Dress and White Goods Workers contemplated a general strike. Deferring action because of a commitment to

86

Cleveland members, the ILGWU anxious to extend the protocol system, endorsed a general strike for 1912.

For several months the League prepared for the walkout; one of its members, under the pretext of writing a college thesis, ascertained the number and location of workers, and their attitude toward unions. In January 1913 wrapper, kimono, and house dress employees stopped work, one day later 7,000 white goods workers, mostly women, followed their example. They in turn were joined in a few days by the dress and waist makers. Closely affiliated with the white goods workers since 1909, when it organized them, the League supported strikers in all the trades. It furnished speakers, provided publicity, operated six of the seven strike halls, and its members marched on picket lines, where Fola LaFollette, the actress daughter of the Senator, was joined by co-eds from Barnard and Wellesley. Thousands of dollars were raised and dispensed by the WTUL for relief. To protect the legal rights of workers the League guarded against false arrest and police brutality, defended the women in court, and provided bail when necessary. By the middle of February the exhausted employers signed protocol agreements with the trades. However, a similar strike had spread to Boston. Encouraged by the experience and leadership of Rose Schneiderman and Gertrude Barnum of New York, the Massachusetts League, led the Boston workers to victory.

The only major AFL women's organizational effort in the pre-war period was led by a former League member, Mary Scully. Hired as a general organizer for the Federation, Scully worked under the direction of James E. Roche, general AFL organizer in Connecticut, recruiting female members in Bridgeport and obtaining eight-hour agreements from every major firm in that city. She was so successful that one observer described her efforts as changing a city of non-union women into one of the most solid strongholds of women's unions in the country.

Organizational success by the League failed to dispel the mistrust of the male-dominated Federation and its member unions. The League and the ILGWU divided over the wisdom of the 1912 white goods strike. Furthermore, the ILGWU resented League demands for a place on the strike committee. Additional difficulties arose between the League and the fledging union of retail clerks when the WTUL insisted on a policy-making role in organizing the workers. Ellen Gates Starr and Samuel Gompers even argued publicly over AFL policies and Helen Marot cited union failure to render the League adequate financial support in her resignation as executive secretary. Embittered over the animus of the New York labor movement toward the WTUL, Leonora O'Reilly seriously considered resigning from the League. Shrewdly persuading her to remain, Mary Dreier reminded O'Reilly that men had never really done anything on their own for women and that, if females had surrendered in the past as she proposed to do now, they would be illiterate still. However, a year later, Dreier herself became so discouraged with misogynistic unions that she decided to devote most of her energy and time to equal suffrage as the best means of improving the conditions of working women.

Recurring difficulties with organized labor were only part of the League's problems. The organization still suffered from inadequate financing, and in 1914 all branches except New York and Kansas City were "bankrupt." Furthermore, zealous but condescending social workers sometimes antagonized working classes, thus creating a resentment easily transferred to the allies. Even some of the League's supporters impaired its effectiveness by justifying trade unions for women on the basis of character formation. On the other hand, some female workers still found unions unnatural, and others, especially those who were skilled, viewed membership as beneath their dignity. If the League overcame this aversion to unions it usually encountered additional resistance, for many trades still resented females and management viewed women's union-ization as a threat to its independence and profit.

To strengthen itself the League sought to increase its membership and change its image. In addition to unionizing workers in new industries and spearheading strikes, it accepted students from the New York School of Social Work for investigative activities. It also developed a Women in Industry Program to pro-vide speakers and pamphlets on the subject of working women. Newspaper advertisements, street-corner meetings, and Saturday night dances were used to attract new members and *Life and Labor* was revamped with short stories, book reviews, and essays. (Among the contributors was Charlotte Perkins Gilman.) Furthermore, the WTUL recommended a percentage of salary rather than a fixed amount for female union dues, and advocated reforms such as government health insurance, old age pensions, nationalization of telephone and telegraph, and governmental operation of railroads.

Leonora O'Reilly contributed immeasurably to the growth of the League in this period. In Pittsburgh, Philadelphia, St. Louis, Youngstown, Bridgeport, and upstate New York she captivated large audiences with her Irish charm and eloquence as she explained the purposes of the League, revived stagnant chapters, organized new ones, and established auxiliaries to trade unions. Two weeks were spent revitalizing the Kansas City branch with the aid of Dante Barton, editor of the *Kansas City Star*, and Frank P. Walsh of the congressional Commission on Industrial Relations. As a result of her endeavors the chapter became financially sound, successfully lobbied for a nine-hour law in Kansas City, and was readily accepted by men's unions in cooperative ventures. When O'Reilly returned to Kansas City a year later, she was greeted by an audience of 7,000 enthusiastic working "girls," who bestowed the accolade "Mother O'Reilly" upon her. In addition to chapters founded by O'Reilly, new branches were established in Los Angeles, Springfield (Illinois), Denver, and Worcester. An optimistic Robins now believed that it would not be too long before a trade unionist became president.

WOMEN'S PEACE MOVEMENT

Before Robins' hopes could be realized, the League became involved in the political and social turmoil that preceded and accompanied World War I. Many League members were idealistically committed to pacifism. As early as 1909 a WTUL convention urged a Court of Arbitral Justice as provided by the Second Hague Conference and objected to further naval expansion as aggravating the armaments race. With the outbreak of the European War, the League, along with other women's groups, assailed the male-dominated society that plunged the world into fratricide. Many Leaguers helped initiate the women's peace movement as early as August 1914 by sponsoring a women's peace parade in New York. A few months later representatives of several female groups, including the WTUL, launched a Women's Peace Party in Washington many of whose members and five of whose vice chairpersons and sponsors, including Elizabeth Glendower Evans, the National Organizer, were intimately associated with the League. Choosing Jane Addams as chairperson, the Party urged an immediate conference of neutral nations to stop the war, and it developed a program for peaceful adjudication of disputes, arms limitation, and neutralization of international waterways. Supported strongly by President Wilson in the early months of 1915, it vigorously opposed preparedness until the United States entered the war.

Almost simultaneously with the formation of the Women's Peace Party, a group of European women, disappointed in the cancellation of the 1915 Berlin meeting of the International Suffrage Alliance, convened a conference at the Hague to stop the war and prevent future conflicts. Forty-seven American delegates sailed on the *Noordon* April 13 and on their arrival in

89

Holland were joined by women representatives from eleven other countries. Many members of the American Delegation had been instrumental in the success of the League. Its leading union organizer, Leonora O'Reilly, attended at Jane Adams' request as a representative of American working women. Delegates established the International Congress of Women, selected Addams as chairperson, and broadened their objectives to include woman suffrage, international cooperation, and the education of children. Shortly after the preliminary activities, O'Reilly addressed the gathering. She asserted that the labor movement was the true peace movement for workers and had done more for international peace than all of the capitalistic peace movements put together. Furthermore, the United States, she charged, killed as many in industrial war as in battle; therefore permanent peace must be in keeping with the rights of labor.

Before adjourning, the Congress organized the Women's International Committee for Permanent Peace to provide a means of continuous mediation. Its task was to invite suggestions from the belligerents, and to consider and submit to the warring powers all reasonable propositions for peace. Selected women presented this plan to the heads of various governments but met with little success. The main results of the Congress were the frequently ridiculed Henry Ford peace mission, and a determination to meet again at the same time and place as the official conference concluding hostilities.

In addition to endorsing the Hague endeavors, the League attempted to resist the drift toward war. Its 1915 convention urged a military embargo and further resolved: "We place ourselves on the roll call of those who are prepared to serve our country by a refusal to engage in or endorse the wholesale murder called war."

This resolution, presented by Agnes Nestor, was graciously received by President Wilson and Secretary of State Bryan. Nevertheless, peace activities probably exacerbated the rift with the traditional unions. Early in the European war the AFL rejected pacifism and supported a preparedness policy. Refusing to speak at a peace meeting sponsored by the Central Federation Union in New York, Gompers advocated that unions oppose peace at any price. Increasingly belligerent, by January 1917 he urged American involvement. A hostile press and sardonic cartoons also reproved the women's peace movement.

Criticism of their efforts was so severe that addresses by O'Reilly, one of the WTUL's most outspoken pacifists, were curtailed by President Robins. Some union leaders actually believed that the peace movement was financed by labor's enemies and was designed "to hurt" working men and women. Ironically the war that women trade unionists tried to prevent accelerated the reforms to which they were committed.

Chapter 8

MOTHER JONES [1]

One of the most fascinating individuals in American labor history is also one of the most frequently overlooked - Mary Harris "Mother" Jones. A paradoxical character, Jones believed that women performed their major service in the home shaping the destiny of the nation by raising their children; however, she herself was one of the most effective labor organizers in the early twentieth century. She excelled in rallying wives and daughters of strikers to parade, protest, and picket on behalf of their men. An exponent of personal nonresistance and civil disobedience to unjust policies, and an advocate of nonviolent demonstrations, she urged workers to arm themselves. Her very presence and inflammatory rhetoric seemed to incite the violence she abhorred. Optimistically drawing sustenance from the gains she had seen labor win, Jones believed in a future of industrial peace, supported by the rationality of intelligent employers and employees. She was, however, incarcerated innumerable times in her efforts to achieve such a utopia. A rather humble woman, her fearlessness, zeal, and personal example helped to better working conditions and inspire male workers as well as female reformers whom she so frequently scorned.

EARLY CAREER: 1830-1901

Born in Ireland in 1830 Jones was brought to the United States at the age of five years. Her father, a naturalized American, worked on a railroad crew and resided in Toronto, Canada, where she attended parochial and public schools. After leaving her position in a Michigan parochial school in 1861 to teach in Tennessee, she married an ironmolder, a staunch unionist. Following the deaths of her husband and four children in an 1867 yellow fever epidemic she began a dress-making business in Chicago. There she met Terence Powderly at a Knights of Labor rally, the start of a life-long friendship. Jones was convinced that all labor reforms achieved during her lifetime, even those obtained after the demise of the Knights, were attributable to Powderly and the issues raised by his union.

There is not much detailed information available on the next two decades of her life; however, during that period she became a familiar and memorable figure on the national labor scene. Many workers encountered this unusual agitator, with her grey hair neatly combed straight back, attired in black bonnet, full skirt, and immaculate shirtwaist trimmed with ruffles at neck and wrists. Her keen flashing eyes, lilting brogue, caustic wit, in addition to her laughter and profanity added to the persuasiveness of her conversation and speeches.

Jones participated in the Baltimore and Ohio strike in Pittsburgh in 1873, in Dennis Kearney's anti-Chinese agitation on the West Coast in the 1870s, and apparently in her first coal strike in 1882 in Hocking Valley, Ohio. As frequently happened in mining strikes, the militia was called in, violence erupted, and miners were charged with murder. Here the men were acquitted because of the efforts of a young lawyer who voluntarily defended them free of charge. Years later, when this attorney was President, Jones came to the White House and successfully implored William McKinley to pardon strikers sentenced to life imprisonment for blowing up a railroad bridge.

From the time of her appointment as a United Mine Workers' organizer in 1891 Jones was in the forefront of the battle for unionization. Her rhetoric had the power to move masses and her personal safety was so unimportant to her that Clarence Darrow compared her fearlessness with that of Wendell Phillips. Consequently she was ideal for this hazardous employment. The suffering she bore from the hands of employers, armed guards, and militia was less disheartening to Jones than indifference, ignorance, and fear encountered frequently from miners. As a former school teacher she often lectured them, criticizing their ignorance, urging them to educate themselves through unions, and imploring them to use their free time during strikes to read. Jones' devotion to the miners was manifested by contributions from her meager salary to the defense of men unjustly accused of breaking the law in labor disputes.

During her first efforts for the UMW in 1891, a mine superintendent in the Dietz fields of Virginia threatened to kill her. As with many similar threats in the years to come, Jones remained undaunted and continued to organize. A few years later in Arnot she demonstrated the unique values of a woman representative. Defying company harassment, including her expulsion from the local hotel and the houses of miners who sheltered her, Jones organized an army of "housekeepers." Armed with mops and brooms, they yelled and hammered on dishpans as they charged the scabs, chasing them away from the mines which the women then patrolled around-the-clock. Furthermore, she convinced the wives of area farmers to support the strike and persuaded a local Swedish colony not to scab. By the end of the nineteenth century her work in West Virginia had earned her plaudits from UMW officials, and she was given the honor of addressing a convention.

Assigned to the anthracite fields of Pennsylvania during the strike of 1900 she stormed through the area haranguing large crowds and organizing mass meetings and marches on various collieries to intimidate those who had remained or returned to work. When UMW President John Mitchell heard of these "raids" (of which he was "officially" ignorant), he fruitlessly advised Jones to stop and then finally ordered her to do so after being informed that force would be used against her. This may have been the beginning of the break between them, for she continued to incite the miners until the strike was settled and was held responsible by the owners for the disorder and riot in the Oneida area that resulted in several injuries and the death of a policeman.

The settlement of 1900 was only an interlude for the operators resented the political pressure that forced them to compromise, and miners were discontent with terms that did not provide for union recognition. Another confrontation was inevitable; but first West Virginia would have to be organized for the union was jeopardized by its weakness there, a condition stemming in part from an 1897 injunction restraining organizational activity in that state.

ORGANIZING IN WEST VIRGINIA: 1902

Mitchell sent Jones to West Virginia in 1902 instructing her to rent property for her activity. Encountering considerable support, she conducted numerous mass meetings, advocated unionization and, if necessary, repeated strikes and intimidation of scabs. Apparently her efforts and reputation, coupled with a renewed strike, frightened the operators. Once again those who provided her with food and shelter were evicted from company housing and a new injunction was obtained in June to prevent assemblies near collieries and interference with employees. Continuing her endeavors, Jones stated that enough injunctions had been issued against her "to form a shroud for me when I am cold in death." At a rented lot in Clarksburg, where she had been attempting to persuade those still working to join the strike she was arrested for violating the court order. Urging her mining audience not to abandon their objective the doughty woman declared: "Goodbye, boys, I'm under arrest. I may have to go to jail. I may not see you for a long time. Keep up the fight! Don't surrender."

Legal officials were reluctant to make her a union martyr. Courageously rejecting the offer of quarters in a local hotel rather than incarceration in jail, she refused to leave the state in exchange for a recommendation of mercy by the prosecution. Judge John Jackson probably searching for such a compromise asked Jones why she did not stay where she belonged rather than enter West Virginia to incite trouble. Restrictions on her freedom of movement were completely odious to this social activist, who replied that as an American citizen she had the right to go wherever duty called her. Years later she would express even more forcefully the relationship between her civil freedom and workers' oppression. To the questions of Chairman Frank Walsh of the Commission on Industrial Relations, concerning her residence she responded: "Well, I reside wherever there is a good fight against the wrong - all over the country . . . Wherever the workers are fighting the robbers I go there."

Charging the judge with being a hireling of the coal companies, Jones infuriated the court. Jackson's decision described union organizers as professional vampires who live and fatten on the honest labor of quiet and well-disposed coal miners. Furthermore he claimed her "utterances" were not those of a citizen who supported American institutions but rather those of a Communist. Her addresses proved the necessity for statutes to curb "seditious comments," for unrestricted license was not to be confused with freedom of speech. To the judge, these offenses were additionally abhorrent because of her sex.

> It seems to me that it would have been far better for her to follow the lines and paths which the Allwise Being intended her sex to pursue. There are many charities in life which are open to her, in which she could contribute largely to mankind in distress, as well as avocations that would be more in keeping with what we have been taught and what experience has shown to be the true sphere of womanhood.

The Victorian pedestal upon which Judge Jackson placed women, coupled with his wish not to make a martyr of Jones, worked to her advantage, as it did on other occasions. Although found guilty of contempt of court for violating the injunction, her sentence was deferred and she was able to persuade the judge to release one of the miners who had been tried with her, a man with a bad heart and very nervous wife. To the end of her life Jones had rather fond memories of this judge, whose views on women's place in society actually approximated her own.

ANTHRACITE COAL STRIKE OF 1902

By 1902 Jones was nationally renowned in the labor movement. That year she campaigned for a Socialist mayoral candidate in Brockton, Massachusetts, and lectured throughout that state. In the West folk songs were composed and sung to welcome her. Although not directly involved in the famous Pennsylvania anthracite strike of that year, Jones did not hestitate to criticize publicly UMW President Mitchell for his role in the settlement. An ambitious man, Mitchell embraced the American business creed of efficiency, stability of contracts, and mangement-labor cooperation to such an extent that he sometimes appeared more a business than a union leader. He seized upon Theodore Roosevelt's plan of a presidentially appointed commission to arbitrate the dispute, at a moment when some observers believed a complete union victory was only a matter of time. To Jones, who had threatened a march of miner's wives on Washington "to shake them up," he was a weak man dazzled by the President, who had abandoned the miners for prestige and glamour. Thus, when the strike commission failed to grant union recognition she bitterly commented that "Labor walked into the house of victory through the back door."

As a result of the strike, relations between Jones and Mitchell steadily deteriorated. An infuriated Jones offended Mitchell a year later by publicly tearing up a petition calling for miners to purchase a $10,000 home for him and his family, criticizing leaders who accepted favors from workers, and advising miners to care for themselves. The breach between the two irreparably widened. In opposition to his policies, Jones resigned as an organizer during the Cripple Creek strike in Colorado in 1903-1904 and did not return until 1911.

CRIPPLE CREEK, COLORADO: 1903-1904

A statutory eight-hour day seemed impossible in Colorado in 1903. Invalidation of an eight-hour law by the state Supreme Court, was followed by an eight-hour state constitutional amendment, ratified in 1902 after an intensive campaign by organized labor, especially the Western Federation of Miners. However, lobbying mine operators, smelter owners, and ranchers prevented the passage of enabling legislation. The WFM, a union of metalliferous miners established by "Big Bill" Haywood, frustrated and angry, struck for an eight-hour day and eagerly awaited support from exploited coal miners with whom it always had close relations. President Charles Moyer of the WFM urged them to join and thereby relieve pressure on the metalliferous strikers and win benefits themselves.

District 15 (Colorado, New Mexico, and Utah) of the UMW responded to the WFM entreaty with an appeal to Governor James H. Peabody. An open letter to the governor condemning the intransigence of the operators attacked major grievances, including the lack of an eight-hour day, payment in script, and company control of miners' lives. A conference between the operators and the union was called by the governor, but this gesture proved futile for representatives of only three small companies appeared. As other attempts at negotiation failed, John Mitchell proposed arbitration in order to avoid a strike. Victor Fuel and Colorado Fuel (the latter controlled by John D. Rockefeller), the largest firms in the area, disdainfully refused, with the ludicrous charge that the union was not representative of the workers. Its options closed, the UMW reluctantly approved District 15's call for a strike to begin November 9. Additional organizers were sent into the field to join Jones, already at work disguised as a peddler.

Challenged by the strike and strong union membership, owners in northern fields changed their minds and finally agreed to an eight-hour day and a fifteen per cent wage increase. When these provisions were submitted to the miners for ratification, Jones, contrary to Mitchell's written request, begged that they be rejected. She warned that if mining were resumed in the northern area, success in the unorganized southern district would be jeopardized. In compliance with Mitchell's policy, a UMW headquarters representative urged ratification to maintain public support. The bewildered miners on a second vote of 483 to 130, finally accepted the terms and returned to work November 30.

As many more workers than anticipated struck, the South was rapidly turned into a battlefield by owners determined to break the union. Management evicted them from company houses and imported strike breakers. Organizers were beaten, and the streets were closed to strikers, who were arrested for vagrancy. Every constitutional right of the strikers was violated, observed the report of the Commission on Industrial Relations. Hurrying to Trinidad, in the center of the strike area, and urging the miners to remain firm, John Mitchell also continued a conciliatory approach by conferring with the governor, a conservative banker, and addressing the Chamber of Commerce. When these efforts failed he travelled to Washington to request presidential intervention.

Despite severe provocation the strikers remained law-abiding and peaceful as they prepared for a special union convention in Trinidad on March 24, 1904. Nevertheless on March 22 the area was proclaimed to be "in a state of insurrection and rebellion" and the militia was sent in. With the proclamation of martial law two days later, homes were searched for weapons and press censorship as well as a nine-o'clock curfew were imposed. National Guardsmen were little more than tools of the owners and a valuable asset in the war to crush both the coal miners and the striking metalliferous miners. Company-employed mine guards enlisted in the occupying militia, guardsmen had their meager state wages supplemented by the operators, and the adjutant general of Colorado boastfully proclaimed: "I came to do up this damned anarchistic federation."

Deported from the area, Jones was also ordered to leave the state of Colorado. Instead she went to Denver and sent a note to Peabody: "I wish to notify you, governor, that you don't own the state . . . The civil courts are open . . . I am right here in the capital . . . four or five blocks from your office. I want to ask you, governor; what the Hell are you going to do about it." As the governor chose to do nothing, Jones ignored the deportation order and, although fearful of her life and "the villains" in Trinidad, resumed organizing for the UMW. Not only did she urge the coal miners to hold out, but advocated cooperation with her radical friend, Haywood, and the striking WFM. As a result Jones was arrested twice, the second time refusing confinement in a hospital she was held in seclusion in a bare room for twenty-six days. Unable to comprehend her defiance of the law "to establish her constitutional right to go where she pleased" Colorado's adjutant general asserted that Jones used her age and sex as a shield for "incendiary utterances" and was responsible for most of the violence in the strike zone.

98

Meanwhile the strike sputtered to an unsuccessful conclusion; in June the UMW withdrew support from an apparently hopeless and financially exhausting cause. Despite District 15's unanimous vote to continue, the spirit of the strikers was broken, for the promise of victory was illusory. On October 12 the strike ended on company terms. Jones, proved correct by the outcome, resigned in protest over Mitchell's policies, resuming organizational duties only after he had been virtually removed from the presidency of the union. Publicly attacking Mitchell and Gompers for their conservatism she sparked bitter assaults on Mitchell's judgment and leadership at the 1905 UMW convention. Jones never quite forgave Mitchell, indicting him in an address at the convention of 1911, criticizing him to various leaders during the rest of that decade, and even assailing him after his death in her autobiography. Yet beneath the rhetoric was a note of sadness, for she believed that despite his sycophantic inclinations Mitchell's intentions had always been good. As she revealed to Mrs. J. Borden Harriman: "Oh, it was a pity, he was a fine fellow, but he had his head turned by feasting with the plutocrats and so he lost influence with the workers."[2]

CHILD LABOR PROTEST

During the years in which the Pennsylvania and Colorado strikes were leading to her break with the UMW, Jones was also an active participant in other labor demonstrations. In walkouts at both Latimer and Hazelton, Pennsylvania, she organized armies of women to close mine entrances to scabs. In Massachusetts and New York, frequently under Socialist auspices, she lectured on the abuses of the working class. Furthermore she was able to focus dramatically the attention of the nation on child labor. About 75,000 textile workers, many of whom were children, struck in Philadelphia in the spring of 1903. Jones' rally there drew a crowd of about 50,000 before whom she exhibited some of the mutilated, hungry, striking children. A member of Coxey's marching army of 1894, Jones then organized a children's march from Philadelphia to New York to raise funds and garner support for child labor legislation. Her contingent starting with a band, flags, placards, eight wagons of food, and 400 children, was reduced to about 50 children and scores of reporters when it reached New York City. Nevertheless, the army attracted massive crowds in Trenton, Princeton, and Coney Island, where Jones assailed the cruelties of the capitalistic system. In New York City she was forced to appeal for a parade permit to Mayor Seth Low, for her request was refused by the police commissioner. After the controversial march she journeyed to Oyster Bay in a fruitless effort to see President Roosevelt. Despite her failure to obtain a personal meeting, she succeeded in publicizing the abuses of child labor and apparently was instrumental in the passage of corrective legislation in the Commonwealth of Pennsylvania.

INDUSTRIAL WORKERS OF THE WORLD

When Jones resigned from the UMW she was unconcerned about supporting herself, for she knew that the "boys of the W.F. of Miners will see that I am not hungry." Believing her new independence freed her to alert the nation to the dangers of industrialism, she was delighted to be one of thirty recipients of a secret letter calling a meeting "to discuss ways and means of uniting the working people of American on correct revolutionary principles."

This 1905 gathering in Chicago had been organized by a small group of six radicals, two of whom, William Haywood and Eugene V. Debs, were Jones' personal friends. Jones and Haywood had come to know and respect each other during the Colorado strike, and her friendship with Debs was one of' many years' standing. In 1897 she joined with him to initiate a political party dedicated to a territorial colonization scheme wherein all industry would take the form of cooperatives, a step toward a National Cooperative Commonwealth. A few years later they organized the new Socialist Democratic Party and together denounced the anthracite strike settlement of 1902. When lecturing on Socialism and the need for unity against "the enemy of mankind, the robbing capitalists," she would sell his book, *Unionism or Socialism*.[3]

After conferring for three days the Chicago group drafted a manifesto assailing the National Civic Federation and attacking craft unions for creating a skilled aristocracy. Instead, they advocated "one big industrial union . . . founded on the class struggle," and then urged workers to convene in Chicago in June to establish this revolutionary industrial union.

At the June convention there were over 200 delegates, ranging from Haywood's Socialist-inclined Western Federation of Miners, the largest union represented, to Jones, who officially represented only herself. This "Continental Congress of the Working Class" (as presiding officer Haywood labeled it) adopted the name Industrial Workers of the World for the new union, and drafted a constitution whose object was to enable workers to control the machinery of production and distribution. Though many delegates feared that an advocacy of political action would impede "direct action" and might result in the IWW's becoming little more than an adjunct of the Socialist Party, the constitution's preamble urged that "toilers come together on the political as well as on the industrial field."

Division over the desirability of political methods rapidly widened and, as control of the IWW passed to the advocates of "direct means," a type of ideological conformity was gradually imposed on the membership. In 1906 the Wobblies - an initially derogatory nickname that stuck - deleted political unity provisions; Debs resigned. Two years later the Marxist Daniel De Leon and his followers were expelled. In 1907 the WFM withdrew and four years later reentered the AFL. Haywood, who retained his IWW membership, was ejected from the Socialist Party along with his fellow Wobblies.

Jones apparently drifted away from the IWW as a result of its repudiation of political remedies. Believing capitalism "soulless" and "loveless," she nevertheless turned to the federal government to mitigate its worst abuses. As she wrote in her memoirs: "Whenever things go wrong, I generally head for the National government with my grievances. I do not find it hard to get redress." Once again she drew close to the UMW and the AFL, yet could not entirely repudiate the Wobblies, for she believed labor solidarity was necessary to ameliorate working conditions. Publicly condemning Wobbly leadership as frequently fanatical she observed: "To bring on a strike and go back licked by hunger is not progress for labor." Thus, she appealed to the IWW and trade unions to stop fighting each other and to join in the cause of the worker. Harmony, cooperation, and unity, primarily through AFL leadership, became her objective. Repeatedly and publicly she deplored internal strife, violence, "dual organization," and anarchism while attacking Socialist sentimentality although remaining a Socialist herself.

As a result of her break with Mitchell, Jones' efforts for the next eight years were directed toward nonminers. By 1910 she had acquired the reputation of a folk hero; it was alleged that children in Omaha had replaced Theodore Roosevelt's picture with hers as a result of the principles learned in Socialist Sunday Schools. She participated in a machinists' strike on the Southern Pacific Railroad in California; was jailed during the American Railway Union strike in Alabama; infiltrated Southern factories to expose the horrors of child labor; joined in the Philadelphia garment strike of 1910; and in street railway and copper strikes in Michigan.

Her endeavors on behalf of labor were not limited by national boundaries for she began to champion the Mexican laboring class. Several Mexicans, who had fled the oppression of the reactionary regime of Porfirio Diaz, were arrested in 1908 on "trumped up charges" in Los Angeles. Jones raised $4,000 for legal expenses and obtained defense witnesses, resulting in an eighteen-day jail sentence for these men rather than extradition and execution. Through her intervention other Mexican emigrés were pardoned by President William Howard Taft and the governor of Arizona. Emerging as president of Mexico in 1911 the revolutionary, Francisco Madero, granted workers the right to organize and consulted Jones on the establishment of mining unions. However, his administration was soon overthrown, and once again to prevent the extradition of Mexican revolutionaries, Jones interceded, this time with President Woodrow Wilson and the federal Department of Justice. In the topsy-turvy world of Mexican politics and revolution, the beneficiaries of these efforts emerged in 1920 as the president of Mexico (Alvaro Obregon) and the minister of agriculture (Antonio Villareal). Consequently on her visit to Mexico in 1921 to attend the Pan-American Federation of Labor Conference, Jones was greeted as a hero by admiring crowds who threw flowers at her feet and shouted, "Madre Yones." Appealing to this conference for unity between Mexican and American miners, the nonagenarian representative of the United Mine Workers urged unification behind Gompers and the AFL, proclaiming that this would do more to advance Christian unity than any church efforts. Recognizing her sacrifices on behalf of Mexican workers, the government offered Jones land, but she refused: "I want no strings tied to me. I want to be free to play my part in the fight for a happier civilization whether that fight is in America, Mexico, Africa or Russia."

ORGANIZING IN WEST VIRGINIA: 1912-1913

When Mitchell resigned the UMW presidency in 1908, Jones resumed efforts on behalf of her beloved American miners by organizing in Greensburg, Pennsylvania. Wives of strikers were arrested when they patrolled collieries and harassed scabs in compliance with her instructions. Unable to pay a $30 fine, they were sentenced to thirty days. Bringing their infants to jail with them, at Jones' urging they sang to the children all night, so disturbing the sheriff and his neighbors that they were released at the end of five days. Jones' Pennsylvania activities, however were rapidly dwarfed by national renown achieved as a result of her fearless endeavors in Colorado and West Virginia.

Organizational campaigns in the latter area ended in 1904 with the ruthless obtrusion of state militia, followed by the hiring of a large company police force to protect nonunion fields. Management so dominated the Kanawha Valley that employees were routinely exploited through payment in script, company stores, and housing. In desperation Paint and Cabin Creek miners struck in April 1912. Union men, fired and evicted from their homes, erected a tent city where they increased their cache of arms to protect themselves from 300 additional Baldwin Felts Agency guards hired by management. The owners erected searchlights, built forts, and tried to reopen the mines with scabs. Inevitably lawlessness began to permeate the fields. Unionization rather than working conditions became the major issue as UMW organizers penetrated the area. Entering the fields as a private individual to protect the union from a damage suit, Jones was as much feared by the operators as she was loved by the miners. The most able and forceful of the organizers, she led the campaign, inciting the waning spirits of miners whenever she spoke. They cheered, hooted or cried in response to her dramatic oratory as she shook her fist at operators or raised trembling hands to heaven to bear witness to injustice. Since gunmen prevented her from using company-owned roads she waded up a creek bed in ankle-deep water to address one meeting. The same guards refused her permission to stop for tea at a miner's "home" after she had sworn men into the union.

These overbearing and provocative mine guards were attacked by infuriated strikers; in July, National Guard troops were ordered into the area. Afraid that unarmed workers would be subjected to the capriciousness of the hired guards Jones appeared before a citizens' meeting designed to persuade miners to lay down their arms and urged instead: "Don't you give up your guns, and if you haven't got good guns buy them."

Constantly reiterating this position and advocating that miners bury their guns if martial law were proclaimed, Jones rapidly became anathema to management and devotees of order. She assailed miners for not having "enough marrow in your backbone to grease two black cats' tails" and urged them to make war until the "Baldwins" were removed. Yet she also cautioned the strikers not to get into conflict with the militia, and reproved them for drinking too much.

Further alienating the forces of conservatism and stability in the area she attacked organized religion for ignoring its duty and not putting the fear of God in capitalists. Her efforts in this direction were probably offset by Bishop P.J. Donahue, who not only accused Jones of sowing the seed of rebellion and discontent, but praised the guards and assailed miners as Socialists. Donahue advocated a restoration of peace and harmony by making "them all go to church twice on Sunday."

Jones abandoned organized religion because of attitudes such as his, and her observation after imprisonment in a religious hospital in Colorado, that the churches were "owned body and soul" by the Rockefeller interests. She testified to the Committee on Industrial Relations: "I don't go to church; I am waiting for the fellows in the church to come out and fight with me, and then I will go in."

In addition to organizing in the fields, Jones endeavored to arouse national sentiment on behalf of the exploited miners by addressing rallies in Cincinatti, Columbus, and Cleveland. Before a protest meeting in Washington, D.C., arranged at her suggestion by Congressman W.B. Wilson (Democrat, Pennsylvania), she castigated mine owners.

Meanwhile, a semblance of order was restored and martial law was lifted. Even though miners were again subject to the "mercy" of mine guards, who made it possible for strike breakers to enter the fields, the strike continued. In August Jones conducted a mammoth meeting on the steps of the capitol in Charleston, demanding that the governor disarm the guards for suppressing civil liberties and precipitating violence. A few weeks later she directed a similar rally in front of the court house, when the militia prevented her from using the capitol grounds for these purposes. In September because of near anarchy in the fields the governor again imposed martial law, leading miners to expect the disarming of guards and the dismantling of forts. However, the opportunity to work peacefully for their demands was thwarted, for the companies, protected by the military, renewed eviction, hired additional strike breakers, and reopened the mines.

With the restoration of order the governor withdrew the troops reestablishing civil authority. Once again the strikers resumed picketing and brought operations to a halt. Tension mounted rapidly, for many of the former militia men were now hired as mine guards. In February 1913, shooting from a passing chartered train into the tent city at Holly Grove, the guards killed one striker and seriously wounded another. To capture their Gatling guns fifty or sixty miners escorted by Mother Jones attacked the Baldwin Felts encampment at Mucklow, where a mining camp bookkeeper was killed. Martial law was imposed for a third time, and many miners were immediately imprisoned.

ARREST AND INCARCERATION

Leading a protest group to the governor, Jones detrained in Charleston and began to walk to the statehouse. Arrested en route with three miners, she was thrown into an automobile, and driven twenty miles into the martial law zone. Here she was handed over to the military, placed under continuous guard, and held incommunicado for twenty-two days. Finally, with forty-eight others, she was tried before a military court on the charges of stealing a machine gun, inciting to riot, and conspiracy to murder. Hoping to bring the case into federal court, the eighty-three-year-old Jones refused to recognize military jurisdiction and neither entered a plea nor made a defense: "I have no plea to offer. Whatever I have done in West Virginia I have done over the entire country and will do again when I get out."

Appeal possibilities were rapidly exhausted. Circuit Judge Samuel Littlepage issued a writ denouncing the military commission as unlawful and unconstitutional, then quickly changed his mind and ruled that a federal judge had no right to interfere with the state-proclaimed martial law. Remaining legal avenues were blocked by the West Virginia Supreme Court's ruling that the governor had the right to arrest and detain suspicious persons during an insurrection.

Rejecting an offer of amnesty that required she leave the state, Jones fully expected to be executed thereby directing public attention to the deplorable and oppressive conditions in West Virginia. Instead she was sentenced to twenty years imprisonment, a punishment so unreasonable when coupled with the bizarre nature of her arrest and trial, that it precipitated the public reaction she desired. Almost as dramatic in alerting the nation to the abuse of civil liberties and exploitation of miners was the revelation that the Associated Press had slanted its news coverage to protect the owners. Fremont Older, the editor of the *San Francisco Bulletin*, dissatisfied with the quality of reports coming out of West Virginia, sent his wife to investigate. Refusing to be intimidated, Cora Older finally interviewed Jones and discovered that the Associated Press correspondent was also the provost marshal. Furthermore, *Collier's, Indepen-*

dent, and the *Masses* denounced AP coverage accusing the press association of suppressing and coloring the news.

Many journals and newspapers, rallying to the defense of civil liberties, attacked military arrest and prosecutions, and in so doing exposed the subjugation of miners. An aroused public inundated United Mine Workers' headquarters with mail protesting Jones' treatment. Appealing to the federal government she urged her friend, Terence V. Powderly to approach Senator Robert LaFollette (Republican, Wisconsin) and implored Congressman Wilson and Senator John W. Kern (Democrat, Indiana) to press for an investigation. Consequently, a Senate Committee after formally inquiring into the strike condemned military rule and the imprisonment of miners. An investigating body appointed by the governor of West Virginia, forced to operate without the cooperation of the owners, concluded that rights of assembly and speech were violated, that management overcharged the miners, and also recommended the abolition of mine guards.

In March Henry D. Hatfield, the newly inaugurated governor, met with Jones and ordered that she and most of the miners imprisoned by military courts be released. Hatfield then pushed through a settlement (hailed by the press as a miner's victory) providing for a nine-hour day and semi-monthly pay. Rights to organize, to buy in other than company stores, and to select weighmen were also recognized.

Believing that the events in West Virginia should serve as an object lesson to the nation, Jones continued to agitate on behalf of the miners and civil liberty. As a result of her efforts it became illegal for deputies to perform duties as guards or watchmen for private firms, or for the latter to be appointed as deputies. Her lobbying and testimony in Washington engendered much support from the UMW and resulted in accolades from union officials. In Carnegie Hall she berated her audience and the working class as "moral cowards" for not stopping military despotism and predicted in Pittsburgh that eventually West Virginia would be unionized if individuals "raised hell" as she did. Although it would be decades before her forecast was fulfilled and West Virginia organized, Jones' role there and in the Colorado strike of 1913-1914 contributed substantially to the winning of 150,000 new UMW members.

COLORADO MINERS' STRIKE: 1913-1914

Evolving into "one of the nearest approaches to civil war and revolution ever known in this country in connection with an industrial dispute," the Colorado strike of 1913-1914 was really a continuation of the labor struggle of 1902-1903. After the militia had ruthlessly crushed that effort, conditions rapidly worsened. Owners were determined to yield none of their prerogatives to unions or even to state law. According to the 1911 report of the commissioner of Colorado's Bureau of Labor every piece of protective legislation enacted by the state was violated in southern fields in order to cheapen the cost of production. If an employee complained, he was fired, or if fortunate, merely beaten by thugs employed as deputy sheriffs by the largest mine in the area, the Colorado Fuel and Iron Company. The commissioner revealed that exploitation of the miners, especially through unfair weighing-paying practices, provided the funds to pay their oppressive guards. As late as 1913 wages averaged less than a $1.84 a day.

In that year the UMW once again began an intensive organizational campaign whose success resulted in demands for union recognition. Refusing to confer with the union, operators also disregarded an invitation to the miner's convention in September 1913 and ignored the U.S. Labor Department's arbitral efforts. They even defied the personal intervention of President Woodrow Wilson. Management controlled churches, schools, and local government, proclaiming that everything had been fine until union agitators appeared, sustained the owners claims there were no issues to arbitrate or any reasons to abandon an open shop policy. Even violence did not shake this contention. Later a refractory John D. Rockefeller testified to the House Committee on Mines and Mining: "We would rather that the unfortunate conditions [strike and violence] should continue, and that we should lose all the millions invested, than that American workmen should be deprived of their right, under the Constitution, to work for whom they please. That is the great principle at stake. It is a national issue."

By September operator intransigence left the miners no choice but to strike. The owners prepared for a long struggle, as workers were evicted from company-owned houses and forced to take up residence in tent colonies and additional guards and strike breakers were hired from West Virginia. "Gunfighters," sixteen of whom were enrolled as deputy sheriffs, were imported from New Mexico, and twelve machine guns were brought into the area. At the end of two years it was estimated that 3,000 weapons had been conveyed into the strike zone.

107

Federal and state mediators fruitlessly attempted to persuade the operators to compromise. The latter's remedy for violence was to join financial and business leaders in inducing Governor Elias M. Ammons to order the Colorado National Guard into the strike zone. Welcoming the arrival of troops in October 1913, miners' attitudes changed rapidly when militiamen were recruited from the company guards and remained on the owner's payrolls. Viewing its duty as breaking the strike, the military protected scabs, forced miners to work, arrested strikers, curtailed freedom of speech, and interfered with the mail. Liberty was so repressed that two representatives from the state's Bureau of Labor were arrested. By April the militia no longer even pretended to be an impartial force.

At the strike vote in September (after typically urging the miners to keep out of saloons and to improve their minds by reading) Mother Jones promised that, unlike 1903, union leaders would unreservedly support the walkout. She herself set the example organizing miners, articulating their demands, and rallying their flagging spirits. Moreover, she railed against workers' exploitation and defied restrictions on civil liberties. By the end of the month the governor blamed the entire trouble in the strike zone on her "incendiary teachings," and the operators unsuccessfully sought to intimidate her: "They are sending me all sorts of threats here. They have my skull drawn on a picture and two cross sticks underneath my jaw to tell me that if I do not quit they are going to get me. Well they have been a long time at it."[2] Undaunted, Jones led a protest march of 4,000 before Ammons' temporary residence in Trinidad. Then journeying to El Paso she persuaded Mexicans not to enter Colorado as strike breakers. Upon her return she defied a militia order by addressing a special convention of the state Federation of Labor in December and leading embittered delegates in a demonstration before the statehouse.

Attempting to return to Trinidad fields in January 1914, she was detained by a detachment of militia for two hours and deported under armed guard to Denver. John Chase, adjutant general of Colorado, supported by the governor, justified this step claiming her presence endangered peace in the area. If she dared to come back, Chase promised she would be arrested and held incommunicado.

Accepting his threat as a challenge, the eighty-three-year-old Jones publicly promised to return. To do so it was necessary for her to avoid detectives at the Denver railroad station and militia at the Trinidad depot. Consequently she boarded a train at a siding outside the capital, alighted on the outskirts of Trinidad, and walked into the city. Shortly after her arrival, she was arrested and incarcerated in the Mt. San Raphael Hospital, a religious institution converted into a makeshift jail. Governor Ammons then announced that she would remain there until she promised to leave the strike zone.

Held under armed guard for nine weeks, Jones' mail was returned to senders with the endorsement "addressee military prisoner." She was denied newspapers and visitors except for her attorney and an army colonel who appeared periodically urging her to leave the strike zone. Introducing a resolution at the 1914 district convention of the Mine Workers, an infuriated Fred Mooney censured the Roman Catholic Church for not protesting her imprisonment and for allowing its hospital to be converted into a "military bastille." Emotionally charged delegates pummelled one another before tabling the resolution. Other objections and demonstrations were triggered by her confinement, the most important labeled "The Mother Jones Riot" by General Chase. On this occasion a protest parade of sign-carrying women, followed by miners, marched toward the hospital shouting for Jones' freedom. Militiamen under the personal command of Chase forcefully blocked their route and finally, at his frenzied command, "Ride down the women," charged the demonstrators. Shocked by the injuries and the incongruousness of American militiamen thumping, slashing, and arresting peaceful females, some military men, normally sympathetic with the owners, joined with the press in castigating the outrage.

The slowness and ineffectiveness of the legal process had contributed to such outbursts. When the UMW requested that Jones be called to testify before the Colorado hearings of the Congressional Subcommittee on Mines and Mining, Chase refused permission fearing her appearance would precipitate a riot. Reconsidering, he agreed to release her, however, the union withdrew its request, since her liberation would nullify proceedings for a writ of habeas corpus. Albeit union efforts to obtain a civil court ruling on her seizure were destined to be frustrated. In February the Supreme Court of Colorado refused a writ of habeas corpus, since the request had not been submitted to a lower court first. Denied a writ in the proper lower court the union was again about to appeal to the Supreme Court, when Jones was suddenly freed under circumstances indicating her release was probably a tactic to preclude a high court decision.

According to Governor Ammons and General Chase, Jones was freed in March consonant with her promise to leave the strike zone after conferring with Ammons. On the other hand, Jones denied that she agreed to leave the area and asserted that the governor had initiated the consultation. At the meeting she informed him that she had the right to go where she pleased including the strike zone. Challenging him further, Jones issued a public statement announcing she would return to encourage resistance to the tyranny and robbery of the operators.

On March 23, one week after her release, a fearful Jones departed for the fields once again. Seized before the train arrived at her destination she had lost none of her bravado, despite her previous incarcerations. When the arresting lieutenant asked, "Will you take my arm, madam?" she retorted, "No I won't. You take my suitcase." Jones was imprisoned in the hospital ward of the county jail condemned as unfit and unsanitary by the state Board of Charities and Corrections. Held in this cold, damp, rat-infested basement for twenty-six days, freedom was dangled before her on the condition that she would promise to leave the strike area.

As Jones resisted the blandishments of surrender, her reputation and character were vilified by the mine owners. A whispering campaign started by operators and repeated by the press accused her of being a worn-out strumpet. Management-sponsored pamphlets in the series entitled "The Struggle for Industrial Freedom" repeated General Chase's canards concerning her revolutionary activities. A slander, charging her with running a brothel, was read into the *Congressional Record* by Representative George J. Kindel (Democrat, Colorado). Terence Powderly, unlike Mitchell a decade before, quickly rallied to her defense. Denying the charge, he pointed out that Jones stayed with him when she was in Washington, and demanded that the libel be deleted from the *Record*. Even if the preposterous accusation were true, Powderly avowed, she still would be welcome in his home.

Jones' arrest and imprisonment engendered stormy criticism of Colorado officials, and the nation's press severely condemned the abuses of civil liberty in the area. Absence of a warrant or suspicion of a crime led University of Colorado legal professor James Brewster (previously a member of the state committee investigating troops in the strike zone) to denounce her arrest as "one of the greatest outrages upon civilized American jurisprudence that has been perpetrated." Nevertheless, once again the UMW was frustrated in its efforts to obtain a writ of habeas corpus. The day before the Colorado Supreme Court was to act on its petition, Ammons withdrew all of the troops, except for one company, and ordered Jones released.

PUBLICIZING THE MINERS' CAUSE

Free once again, she toured the nation for the next few months to raise money for strikers' families, to expose the oppression of management, and to excoriate Rockefeller. In addition to addressing mass meetings from coast to coast, she even journeyed to Canada, rallying strikers in British Columbia. Warmly received at the 1914 AFL convention, Jones called for federal seizure of mines before a responsive New York audience, testified before the House Committee on Mines and Mining, and met with President Wilson.

Before a New York women's group, many of whom were suffragists, Jones utilized a discussion of Colorado conditions to denounce voting equality. Observing that for two generations women had the ballot in that state she affirmed that working men and women were still held in "slavery" there. She asserted that enfranchisement was not necessary for reform: "I have never had a vote and I have raised hell all over this country! You don't need a vote to raise hell! You need conviction and a voice." If females were concerned that agitation was unladylike, they should remember that "God almighty made the woman and the Rockefeller gang of thieves made the ladies." Organization along industrial lines was the remedy for exploitative female working conditions, for "Politics is only the servant of industry. The plutocrats have organized the women. They keep them busy with suffrage and prohibition and charity." On other occasions Jones proclaimed women's unsuitability for politics and unfitness for the ballot, claiming that even if the franchise were extended women would ignore it. Before the 1911 UMW convention she charged that if females remained unorganized they would devote their time to women's clubs, the ballot, and "old meow things" that really did not concern them, resulting in men fighting alone for working rights. Although she continually attacked suffrage as diverting women's energy from realistic reform, like Leonora Barry, she was partially the victim of the American feminine ethic. To her the "most beautiful task" of women and one of "great responsibility" was the training of children, consequently she felt that men should receive enough wages so that women would not be forced to work but could remain at home tending their offspring. As late as 1930 she believed that this function was seriously jeopardized by the Nineteenth Amendment.

While Jones was touring the country in 1914, the "Ludlow Massacre" occurred, one of the most tragic episodes in American labor history. Described in a special city report as "hired assassins" and by the Colorado commissioner of labor as "company hirelings, masquerading as militia," remaining Colorado national guardsmen attacked the tent colony of striking miners at Ludlow on April 20. After firing through the tents from an armored car, they burned and looted the colony and killed twenty refugees. Of the dead, thirteen were women and children, and one striker was severely beaten before he was shot. This barbarism precipitated an armed rebellion in which a total of fifty people were killed.

At the request of the governor and to the joy of the miners, President Wilson sent federal troops into the area and, redoubling his efforts to settle the strike, dispatched a personal representative to negotiate with Rockefeller. When that failed, he had a Labor Department mediator submit an arbitration plan that was accepted by the union but rejected by the owners. At the end of his patience, Wilson appointed an arbitration commission over the mine operators' protests. Ignoring press criticism, he met with Jones, who urged government seizure of the mines. However, federal intervention was too late. Since union resources were depleted, the strike was called off in December 1915, and federal troops were gradually withdrawn from the area.

A bitter legacy remained from the strike. John Lawson, an executive board member of the UMW and *de facto* leader, was indicted along with 162 miners for various offenses. Convicted of murder and sentenced to life imprisonment, the finding was based on a rather bizarre legal ruling. Although Lawson was not present when a mine guard was shot by a unionist, as strike leader he was declared responsible. Repeatedly Jones exposed this travesty in lectures raising money for Lawson's appeals until 1917 when the Supreme Court of Colorado overruled the lower court's interpretation.

Also keeping the strike before the public was the Commission on Industrial Relations, a body instituted by Congress in the dying days of the Taft administration, to investigate cases of industrial unrest. Since representatives of the public, capital, and labor nominated by President Taft were too conservative, Congress refused to confirm them, but the liberally oriented appointments of Wilson were rapidly approved. They not only investigated the Colorado strike but at the insistence of two of its members, George Creel and Jane Adams, held two days of hearings on the Ludlow affair where Jones was a very effective witness on the curtailing of workers' liberty through the use of military men and martial law. This frequently imprisoned woman affirmed that: "No one had dared to file any charge against me in court or make any claim against me that in thought, work or action I have done wrong." To prevent driving labor into the arms of anarchists through the military suppression of workers, she urged the elimination of private detective agencies and recommended government ownership of mines and other vital industries.

Encountering John D. Rockefeller before the commission Jones surprisingly accepted an invitation to a conference in his office. During a meeting lasting for an hour and a half, Rockefeller persuaded her that he was ignorant and therefore inculpable for Colorado Iron and Fuel Company's strike tactics. Finding him personally charming, Jones described Rockefeller to the press as a pleasant young man of good intentions. She rapidly changed her mind, however, when he presented a plan for workers' representation in management without any union. All shadow and no substance, she charged, urging him to go to Colorado and view the situation for himself.

The hearings demonstrated that Rockefeller and other owners were well aware of the policies and political control exercised in the coal fields. Discrediting their veracity, the final report condemned the exploitation and political oppression of the workers, and described the strike as "a struggle against arbitrary power" in behalf of personal liberty. Similar conclusions were reached by the House of Representatives' investigation and in the special report prepared by George P. West for the Commission on Industrial Relations. Although the union lost the strike and the area was not organized until 1934, some observers believed the episode a union victory because of the increase in membership, favorable publicity, and ensuing good will. Furthermore, Rockefeller's reputation and the operators' control of politics had been severely damaged.

The energy and zeal of the octogenarian Jones were in no way diminished by her incarceration and labors in the Colorado strike, for she rapidly resumed her role as labor's gadfly. Not only did she organize Arizona miners in 1915, but in a drizzling rain the following year she harangued a crowd of 3,000 to support an El Paso transit strike, imploring the women to encourage their men. Exhorting New Jersey chemical plant strikers to hold out in 1915, she besought their women to keep men from saloons and prevent them from scabbing. In New York that year she urged 7,000 members of the Ladies Waist and Dress Makers Union to strike if their demands were not granted and to encourage them to do so, related her own experiences as the "old woman with a hatpin" who intimidated armed mercenaries.

A year later in the same city she "incited a riot" that revived a flagging transit strike. According to the *New York Times* the walkout was drawing to a close when Jones arrived on the scene informing strikers that violence frequently resulted in successful agreements. Climaxing a tirade directed at strikers' wives and daughters, she entreated the 200 women to save the carmen by arranging parades and demonstrations: "You ought to be out raising hell this is a fighting age. Put on your fighting clothes. America was not discovered by Columbus for that bunch of bloodsucking leeches who are now living off us. You are too sentimental." As the enraged audience departed from the hall, they attacked a scab-driven surface car. Many of the women, although carrying babies or accompanied by children, flung paving blocks from the newly repaired streets through car windows. While breaking up the melée, police were scratched, kicked, and punched as they arrested six demonstrators. Refusing to apologize for her role in the affair, Jones instead threatened to raise an army of women to prevent further police outrages. As a result of her rhetoric the strike was marked by violent incidents until it finally petered out at the end of the year.

Despite the New York episode, there were indications that Jones was becoming less radical. While still proclaiming her Socialism she nevertheless supported Wilson's bid for reelection in 1916. Stressing that the Socialist triumph would be far in the future, she preached immediate opportunism and the election of Wilson, who had saved the nation from complete demoralization through his labor and farm policy and by maintaining peace with Mexico. Other Socialists also endorsed the President, but Jones' political activities were singled out as a callous betrayal of the party. Both Republicans and Democrats poured money and speakers into Indiana to defeat Eugene Debs, Socialist candidate for Congress. Near the end of the campaign, Jones representing the UMW, toured the mining camps on behalf of the Democratic party. Charged with abandoning her old friend Debs, she claimed her mission really was not to defeat Debs but to reelect Senator Kern, who had helped her in West Virginia and to whom all miners owed a debt. However, she did accuse the Socialist party of treachery and urged it to "clean house." if there were to be "a real revolutionary socialist movement."

Her new-found moderation was also revealed by complying with the President's request and appealing for miners to increase wartime production as well as by her restraint in the Mooney case. During a preparedness parade in San Francisco in July 1916, a bomb exploded killing ten spectators and wounding forty others. Arrested were Thomas Mooney and Warren Billings. An outspoken opponent of utilities companies, Mooney had denounced the parade in his frequent contributions to the anarchist journal, the *Blast*. Billings, a minor union official, occasionally had associated with the former Wobbly, Mooney, and had served a brief prison term for illegally transporting explosives. Both were victims of the hysterical atmosphere surrounding their trial; Mooney was sentenced to death and Billings to life imprisonment. A year later Mooney's sentence was commuted to life and in October 1939 to time served when he was released.

Mooney's relationship with Jones stemmed from his position as secretary of the International Workers' Defense League established in 1912 to help labor radicals with the courts by publicizing cases, raising funds, and providing counsel. Supported by the League in West Virginia and Colorado, Jones became acquainted with Mooney, and later helped raise money for that organization. Publicly defending him, Jones persuaded the AFL to pass pro-Mooney resolutions at its conventions, and intervened with both the President and governor on his behalf. However, her desire to seek justice for a labor agitator did not prevent her from lecturing Mooney of the rights of Americans to have preparedness parades. Indicting him for his association with violence she wrote: "for society after all had made all the progress it has ever made, by anyalizing [sic] the situation carefully and bringing the matter before the public with reason on its side . . . in the great industrial struggles I have been in [I] have prevented more blood shed than any other person in America." Neither her old age nor her new moderation impeded Jones' activities for labor and reform. Once again in 1919 she unionized West Virginia miners. Her exposés of prisoner abuse in the Sissonville camp in that state resulted in improved conditions.

STEEL STRIKE: 1919-1920

But more significant was her activity in the Steel strike of 1919-1920, beginning with her participation in a special year-long organizational drive. Refusing to recognize the union, management rejected negotiations; a bitter strike then began in September 1919. During the ensuing struggle strike breakers were recruited, civil liberties suppressed, and organizers beaten. As a result of violence, federal troops were sent to Gary and state militia to other trouble-some areas. Impressing many observers with her energy, dedication, and courage, Jones was hailed by the AFL strike manager, William Z. Foster, as one who "labored dauntlessly, going to jail and meeting the hardships and damages of the work in a manner that would do credit to one half her age." [4] Holding rallies and revitalizing lagging spirits she reminded the strikers: "There's only one thing you should be afraid of -- not being a man." Urging women to support the men and to fight scabs she reminded them that "the destiny of the workingman is in your hands."

In most areas Jones spoke with only a minimum of legal harassment; however, Pennsylvania was different. In that state she continued one rally in defiance of the police chief's order to stop, and in August was arrested and jailed for conducting a meeting without a permit. With the sheriff's permission and probably at his suggestion, she addressed a mob gathered outside the jail, and rather untypically urged them to go home. In Duquesne, Mayor James Crawford refused a permit for an address by AFL secretary, Frank Morrison, asserting that "Jesus Christ cannot come in and hold a meeting here." But Jones did, and as a result she was arrested.

Proof that her old radicalism still survived was demonstrated in her inflammatory speeches during the Steel strike. She attacked the owners and demanded social and labor reform, even proposing that workers take over the mills in behalf of the government, and hailed Christ as the world's greatest agitator. Her rhetoric, shocking to conservatives, contributed to charges that the strike was Bolshevist inspired for she allowed leaflets demanding an end to the blockade of Russia to be distributed at her rallies, and proudly proclaimed that "If Bolshevist is what I understand it to be, then I'm a Bolshevist from the bottom of my feet to the top of my head." Dedication and efforts of organizers like Jones and the loss of twenty lives proved futile, by January 1920 production was seventy per cent of normal, and union resources were nearly depleted. Consequently the national committee called off the strike.

DECLINING YEARS: 1920-1930

Suffering from rheumatism after 1921, Jones, nevertheless, continued to inspire the labor movement. Once again she organized in West Virginia, and when several thousand armed miners planned to invade Logal County to attack sheriff's deputies and mine guards, she begged them not to do so. Instead she

116

advocated congressional legislation to eliminate private armies and a government investigation; but still she encouraged the miners to continue the strike. In 1922 she begged wives in Kansas (where she was famous because of an organizational drive three years before) "to raise hell" and to assist their miner husbands who had been jailed for refusing to cooperate with a state compulsory arbitration court. When Alexander Howatt, president of District 14, was imprisoned for defying the order, thousands of miners struck in protest. Ordering them back to work, John L. Lewis of the UMW withdrew the district's charter when they refused to comply. To Jones, he had committed the one unforgivable sin, betrayal of his men. Consequently she pushed for his defeat at UMW conventions, and at the age of one hundred expressed the ardent wish to live long enough to see him "licked."

Her antipathy to Lewis was not so great that it prevented her from supporting the same presidential candidate as he in 1924. Appearing before the National Farm Labor party convention in 1923, she urged the delegates to clean out crooked labor leaders among them, to unite politically, and return to the revolutionary spirit of their fathers. Yet, like many unionists, including Lewis, she did not support Senator Robert M. LaFollete, the Progressive candidate, for President. Instead she assured Coolidge of the support of a majority of unionists, insisting that the AFL endorsement of LaFollette was meaningless, for that organization would be unable to deliver its members' votes.

In May 1930, on her one-hundredth birthday, Jones delivered a fiery national radio speech reminding labor that the power to protect its liberty lay in its own hands and should be used intelligently. Urging women to use their talents to reform society, she cautioned them not to allow the capitalists to divert them into clubs or to make ladies of them: "Nobody wants a lady, they want women. Ladies are parlor parasites." Jones also utilized the publicity attendant upon her birthday to renew her decade-old attack upon prohibition "the worst affliction the country has."

A few months later Mother Jones died of old age in Washington, D.C. Since she had returned to the Roman Catholic Church, a funeral high mass was celebrated in that city, and her body was interred at her request in Virden, Illinois, the scene of a bloody battle in 1898 where eight miners were killed by strike breakers and guards. An estate of $2,000 from the proceeds of her book was awarded to the AFL in keeping with her bequest that it be used to help labor.

During her career Jones was constantly castigated by conservative propertied interests; however, during the last decade and a half of her life she antagonized many leftists as well. From their perspective she was confused on the issue of the class struggle, since her heroic efforts were directed at the amelioration of abuses of capitalism rather than its overthrow. Nevertheless some believed that she should be honored as a "period piece," for her activities were undertaken when the struggle was relatively simple. Perhaps it was this growing schism that accounts for her rudeness in later years toward young radical women. Yet her work and zeal inspired Elizabeth Gurley Flynn and "Mother" Ella Bloor, her one time friend and confidante.

There is little doubt that few who knew her remained untouched by her dynamic character and inspirational career. Floyd Dell, the editor of *Masses*, was so thoroughly intimidated by her that when she came to his office he "retreated behind a desk and looked longingly at the fire escape." To most people, however, including thousands of miners, she was a figure to be revered. Mrs. J. Borden Harriman and George P. West, both of the Commission on Industrial Relations, hailed her as one of the greatest American women, a judgment with which Governor George Hunt of Arizona concurred. *Labor Magazine* included her among the six greatest women of the country and even Rockefeller acknowledged her fearlessness, loyalty, and inspirational qualities. Yet her attitude and career were best synthesized by Jones herself when she told a press conference: "I wouldn't trade what I've done for what he's [Rockefeller] done. I've done the best I could to make the world a better place for poor hardworking people."

Chapter 9

WARTIME ASPIRATIONS [1]

American entry into World War I improved the relationship between the National Women's Trade Union League and the American Federation of Labor. Like many progressive organizations, the women's group supported the war's idealistic objectives, even inaugurating a new monthly, called *Women's Work and War*, whose rationale was expressed in its masthead: "The working women are eager to help win the war. To make their help effective is a problem which must be generally discussed. Therefore this bulletin." Many League leaders accepted government appointments, at the 1919 convention it was reported that 38 of these women held defense positions; including Margaret Dreier Robins, Mabel Gillespie, Melinda Scott, Agnes Nestor, Elisabeth Christman, and Mary Anderson.

WARTIME RADICALS

League support of the war convinced radical female laborites that the WTUL was in partnership with the AFL to uphold a tyrannical capitalistic system. Both organizations were condemned with equal dispatch. Charging the Federation with being as ready as employers to oppress women so as to protect skilled crafts and forestall equal pay, these critics further declared that the allies' "economic interest" resulted in their opposing "class-conscious action," ignoring the unskilled and discouraging class-oriented strikes.

Sometimes the women radicals drifted from Socialism into Communism, as did the Russian immigrant Rose Pastor Stokes. A worker in a cigar sweatshop, she became a reporter for the *Jewish Daily News*, and after interviewing J.C. Phelps Stokes, married the aristocratic leftist millionaire. Devoting herself to radical causes, Stokes lectured throughout the country, published poems, plays, and articles on behalf of Socialism and joined with others to protest Haywood's expulsion from the Socialist Party. In April 1917 she abandoned that party to protest its antiwar stand, returning to it after the Russian Revolution in November. During the war she was arrested under the Espionage Act because of her charge that "the Government is for profiteers." Joining left-wing Socialists in forming the Communist Party in 1919, she continued until her death in 1933 to serve that organization and its labor policies despite frequent brushes with the law and an arrest in 1929 for picketing in a needle trades strike.

Participating with Stokes in establishing the American Communist Party was Ella Reeve "Mother" Bloor. Born in 1862, she early aspired to be a foreign missionary and gave her first public speech on the efficacy of prayer. Influenced by her membership in the Knights of Labor and the Women's Christian Temperance Union, as a young woman she began to urge equal suffrage. Married and the mother of four children (one of whom was Harold Ware, named in 1948 by Whittaker Chambers as organizer of a Communist cell in Washington D.C.), she undertook organizational drives among textile workers in Kensington, Pennsylvania in 1894. Becoming friends with Eugene Debs, she joined the Socialist Labor Party in 1898, and organized Socialists in Essex County.

By 1902, Bloor, married for a second time, had gravitated into the left wing of the Socialist Party working chiefly among coal miners as a state organizer in Delaware and Pennsylvania. At the request of Upton Sinclair she investigated packing plants in Chicago for violations of regulatory laws. To obtain data she surreptitiously worked in Armour's and Swift's and then lectured and wrote exposés for the *New York Times, World,* and *Evening Journal.* Sinclair referred to her and Richard Bloor, her co-worker, as Mr. and Mrs. Bloor, a name she retained for the rest of her life. Increasingly viewing suffrage as a weapon against economic inequality she organized Connecticut working women into suffrage clubs with the financial assistance of J.P. Morgan's niece.

Bloor's interest in the ballot did not detract from her primary goals, the improvement of labor and the spread of Socialism. After organizing electrical workers in Schenectady, New York, and establishing a women's auxiliary for the Western Federation of Miners, she formed women's political groups during the Colorado strike of 1914. She served on the relief committee during miners' strikes in Illinois and Ohio, repeatedly entreating miners and their wives to join the Socialist Party. In 1917 she organized in New York and New England for the United Cloth Hat and Cap Makers Union where she was arrested frequently on picket lines.

Giving up full-time union work to become the New York organizer for the Socialist Party, she ran for lieutenant governor in 1918 on that ticket. Nevertheless, Bloor continued to help miners on a part-time basis, agitated for equal pay, and picketed in Utica and Springfield. With Elizabeth Gurley Flynn she established the Workers Liberty Defense Committee during World War I to protect political and labor prisoners and fight deportations of alien radicals. Breaking from the Socialist Party she recruited William Z. Foster as national organizer for the new Communist Party. While serving this group as Eastern organizer, she continued to unionize workers and encourage strikes.

Another Socialist intellectual, Kansas-born Kate Richards O'Hare, suffered war-time imprisonment. In 1894 at the age of seventeen years O'Hare became a journeyman machinist and the first woman member of the International Order of Machinists. After joining the Socialist Party, she met her husband at an orators' training school. Kate O'Hare exhorted substantial change in her role as a newspaper writer, labor organizer, suffragist, and stump speaker. With her husband she edited the *National Rip-Saw*, a sensationally written, powerful Socialist paper that reflected her emotional and radical views and often embarrassed more conservative Socialist leadership. To obtain data on working conditions she toiled in anthracite mines, a New York factory, and a Kansas City department store during the Christmas rush. In the Packinghouse strike of 1904 she spied for the union by working as a strikebreaker in the Armour plant.

A few years later while preaching Socialism with her husband throughout the Great Plains, Kate O'Hare became extremely popular as a speaker; her evangelical approach and revivalist-style camps attracted audiences as large as 5,000 and enabled her to enroll thousands of farmers in the party. As a result of her efforts, there were proportionately more Socialists in Oklahoma than in any other state. Radical rather than politically-reform oriented they provided the nucleus for a secret movement whose purpose was to secede from the Union. Allegedly 34,000 members rounded up arms and dynamite to seize the banks and thereby control the currency and press, halting Oklahoma's contribution

121

to the war. Hoping for IWW support, the participants in the Green Corn Rebellion (a name derived from their diet) burned bridges, blew-up pipelines, and cut telephone communications. The incipient revolution was suppressed by the militia, and 450 rebels and thousands of Socialists were arrested. Thirty prisoners sentenced to Levenworth were released after O'Hare marched their wives and children to Washington to picket the White House.

Shortly thereafter O'Hare's radicalism led to her own imprisonment. The War and Militia Committee of the Socialist Party, chaired by her, denounced the American war effort. Her paper suppressed, she toured the country lecturing on the incompatibility of Socialism and the war, and finally was arrested and sentenced to five years for an antiwar tirade. Devoting much of her life to prison reform after her release from jail, O'Hare conducted a successful campaign to drive prison-labor contract garments off the market.

O'Hare also challenged societal family norms. The mother of four children, she attacked the debasing influence of marriage in a capitalistic society as it led to serfdom and slavery. Proclaiming that the economic power of poverty and the longing to escape oppressive working conditions and substandard wages forced women into miserable, degrading wedlock, she asserted that on the other hand wealthy, ornately dressed upper-class women were nothing more than symbols of their husbands' success in the industrial field. As the "present economic system not only causes mental and spiritual incompatibility, but often forces men and women to sustain the relations of husband and wife long after love has ceased," O'Hare advocated Socialism as a means of humanizing marriage by abolishing the wage system and enabling women to share in the wealth they produced.

O'Hare's analysis of marriage was similar to that of Charlotte Perkins Gilman, who has been described as the major intellectual women's rights leader in the early twentieth century. A divorcee, Gilman supported herself and her child through lectures, club work, writing, and editing her own journal, *The Forerunner*, and yet found time to volunteer for settlement work and suffrage campaigns. A self described "humanitarian kind" of Socialist she was a delegate to the International Socialist and Labor Congress in 1896. Believing her book, *Human Work*, altered the relationship of all sociological knowledge, she thought it her most significant work, but her most famous was *Women and Economics, a Study of the Economic Relation Between Men and Women as a Factor in Social Evolution*. In this study, published in many editions and translated into seven languages, Gilman asserted that marriage had become an economic relationship established by law and sanctioned by religion. Society had so conditioned women that it was to their economic advantage to secure a mate, for "the personal profit of women bears but too close a relation to their power to win and hold the other sex." Sexual functions became economic functions, for women degenerated into house servants, seeking the support of a husband in the inferior relationship of marriage. To achieve equality, women must obtain economic independence, and to maintain it required fundamental change in home and family relationships. Gilman therefore advocated that the duties of housekeeping, cleaning, and maintaining central kitchens and child-care centers be performed by specialists, for only as women think, feel, live, and work outside the home do they become humanly developed and civilized.

Gilman's views were too radical for working women. In 1909 at a WTUL-sponsored debate with Anna Howard Shaw, Gilman justified the ballot as a step toward economic independence and thus freedom from male dominance. In keeping with traditional societal views, Shaw argued that the wife transformed money into food and clothing and that in the home, a product of male and female cooperation, the wife as an equal contributor to the family should be equal politically. The working-class audience overwhelmingly rejected Gilman's unorthodox views and enthusiastically supported Shaw's stand.

There was only one indication of labor support for Gilman's position, an article reprinted in the *Union Labor Advocate*. Contending that housework was a form of economic production contributing much to the financial support of husbands, the author recommended that it be investigated by Congress. She concluded by warning: "Wives today realize that the situation of their work in the home is more intolerable than the possible consequences of their wage-earning."

ORGANIZATIONAL EFFORTS

Radical efforts to disparage capitalism were undermined by the wartime labor shortage. Women flocked into hitherto restricted areas as telegraphers and messengers, elevator operators, streetcar conductors, and armaments workers. As white working women moved into better-paying defense jobs, black women replaced them in traditional women's trades such as the textile industry. The WTUL strove to organize and protect these workers. Articles and editorials in *Life and Labor* demanded equal opportunity and equal treatment of black females. Many local leagues eliminated white only membership qualifications and blacks were appointed to various League positions. A woman who represented the WTUL as a delegate to the National Urban League Convention was appointed organizer in the Chicago stockyards. Emotional appeals were made to locals to unionize blacks who were granted scholarships to the labor school whose curriculum included special lectures on black workers. However, like other League undertakings, recruitment of blacks was hurt by a lack of funds. A black organizer was appointed to direct a national office of Colored Women Workers, but achieved little because the function was inadequately supported due to financial problems.

Wartime employment of Southern women revived WTUL organizational efforts that had begun there in 1916. President Robins addressed meetings throughout the South, and a full-time field representative was assigned shortly after the conclusion of the war. Encouraged by the excellent cooperation of the Central Labor Union in Norfolk the League's drive was centered primarily in Virginia among teachers, telephone, telegraph, and garment workers, white and black.

The only significant wartime strikes with major participation by the League were those in the stockyards and in Chicago garment centers. Despite heroic efforts by Agnes Nestor, the garment strike failed after ten weeks primarily because of injunctions. However, the strike in the stockyards was successful. As meat packers had gradually chipped away at union gains after the 1904 victory, a new campaign became necessary.

Under the leadership of the Chicago Federation of Labor, in 1917 all unions in the industry pooled their resources into a stockyards labor council for a concerted organizational drive. An eager supporter of equal pay demands, Mary Anderson was recalled from Washington to direct WTUL unionization of the women. The successful recruitment was followed by strikes and victories in nine mid-west packing centers.

NWTUL success was not solely contingent on strikes. When a local chapter was established in Grand Rapids, 200 women in a furniture factory were immediately given a raise of $2 weekly to undermine the League's organizational endeavors.

Because of the wartime labor shortage large industrial states attempted to circumvent protective legislation for women, forcing the League and the Women in Industry Division of the federal Department of Labor to devote many scarce resources to this challenge. Nevertheless the WTUL reveled in wartime advances for females, many observers were convinced that new industrial opportunities were permanent and that skilled women were finally an essential factor in American economic life. Believing that a new era, "the Women's Age," was dawning, Robins expected now that females would be able to enter "life and labor" on an equal basis with men.

Preparing for this new age WTUL conventions passed resolutions designed to preserve old values and restructure existing institutions. They urged the protection of civil liberties, a graduated income tax, self-determination for Ireland, withdrawal of troops from and recognition of Russia, public ownership of utilities, and compulsory health insurance. As a "matter of publicity and education" Leaguers sanctioned "the promotion of every movement or device designed to lighten the labor of the woman in the home, particularly the mothers."

Increasingly the League turned to politics as one means of accomplishing these objectives. Combining with the Consumers' League, the YWCA, and the New York State Woman Suffrage Party, the New York WTUL formed a Women's Joint Legislative Conference, chaired by the League's Mary E. Dreier. Asserting that unions had failed to safeguard women, the coalition lobbied for protective legislation. Joining with the Central Labor Unions of Brooklyn and New York City in 1919 the Empire State WTUL established a labor party and nominated Rose Schneiderman for U.S. senator in 1920. Eventually the organization evolved into the Liberal Party of New York. Despite rebuffs from Gompers, a similar party was established in Chicago, where Agnes Nestor of the League and Margaret Haley were on the executive committee. Haley, a Chicago schoolteacher, became a full-time business agent in 1901 for the Teacher's Federation. A long time champion of tenure, pensions, faculty participation in curriculum design, and the WTUL, Haley led the battle for secondary and elementary schoolteachers within the National Educational Association. She also organized for the American Federation of Teachers (AFL), fighting for their right to join unions.

WOMEN'S INTERNATIONALISM

Reform commitments abetted by earlier association with the Women's Peace Party, logically led the League into international peace and social justice movements. As early as 1917 the WTUL urged labor clauses in the peace treaty and resolved that an International Congress of Working Women be convened at the close of the war. Robins, authorized by the Executive Board to contact European women to plan the convention, enthusiastically endorsed a "prepare for peace program" as a substitute for the earlier preparedness for war movement. Consequently, in 1918 the League invited the British Women's Trade Union League and the Federation of Women Workers to join in a working women's conference on social reconstruction. Demanding that working women have a voice in peace terms, the WTUL exhorted the AFL to include Leaguers in its delegation to the International Labor Conference. Leonora O'Reilly, meanwhile, participated in a national meeting of "forward looking Americans" to draft democratic peace terms and to marshal public opinion on significant reform issues.

League cooperation with European workers was encouraged by the AFL. In 1917 Gompers had hoped to have the Lloyd George government send labor leaders to the United States to define postwar labor objectives in conjunction with the WTUL. However, two prominent Leaguers, Melinda Scott of the United Felt, Panama, and Straw Hat Trimmers, and Operators Union, and Agnes Nestor of the International Glove Workers Union, were appointed members of the AFL-sponsored American Labor Mission to Europe, to visit England and France with messages of hope and encouragement for European workers. Investigating working conditions the mission members also discussed with European labor leaders peace terms, efforts for democracy, and an effective International Federation of Labor.

Despite League planning, working women were not represented when labor organizations of the allied countries met in Paris, February 1919, to formulate a program of postwar employment and to advise Paris Peace Conference delegates on labor issues. After pointing out this oversight to Wilson, who agreed that female workers should have a voice, the WTUL, at its own expense, sent Rose Schneiderman and Mary Anderson to the French capital. Arriving too late to present their program, they explored with other women the possibility of an International Working Women's Conference. They met with Professor James Shotwell, a member of the Inquiry, and with President Wilson in an unsuccessful attempt to require women delegates in the League of Nations' International Labor Organization, but the charter of ILO merely provided that at least one female advisor be present for the discussion of issues affecting women.

Undaunted, the League continued to press for women's safeguards in the international labor movement. At its 1919 convention, resolutions were adopted calling for at least one female advisor to each ILO delegation and a women's department in the permanent labor office of the League of Nations. Gompers invited several women, including Mary Anderson, Alice Hamilton, Josephine Goldmark, and Julia Lathrop, to attend the first International Labor Conference in Washington in 1919. Aided by the YWCA, the League, however, convened its own International Congress of Working Women immediately prior to the ILC meeting. With expenses underwritten by Chairperson Robins, it attracted fifty delegates from twelve countries and visitors from seven others. After formulating international standards for the employment of women (including recommendations for an eight-hour day and a forty-hour week, restrictions on night work, and maternity insurance) the Congress forwarded them to the ILO conference.

To encourage further worldwide feminine solidarity a permanent international association of women workers was established in Washington under the aegis of Robins. As president she devoted a great deal of time and money to the organization. At its Vienna meeting in 1923 the International Federation of Working Women, as the group was named, voted to affiliate with the International Federation of Trade Unions. American members withdrew, fearing that affiliation would subordinate women's interests to those of men, however, they publicly justified their action by pointing out that the AFL neither belonged to nor endorsed the International Federation.[2]

WARTIME RELATIONS WITH THE AFL

Except for encouraging WTUL efforts toward international labor solidarity, AFL policy toward women during the war remained unchanged. An astute *New Republic* article, claiming AFL attitudes were inspired by the antifeminism of St. Paul, observed that the Federation never really deemed women permanent members of the work force and had only a tepid interest in organizing them. Apparently more anxious to protect males from competition than to improve the lot of working women, the AFL Executive Council endorsed equal pay and urged special organizational efforts among women, but primarily to protect men. When females were employed in traditionally male jobs the council called for "inquiries" as to the position's suitability and effect on women's health. James Lynch of the New York State Industrial Commission claimed that as women had neither the "nature" nor "training" for war work, their employment would demoralize the social structure. Equally as miso- gynistic was the strike of Cleveland's male streetcar conductors over the emergency employment of women, a violation of the union contract. Despite League protests, the union prevailed, the women were gradually replaced by men.

Gompers himself was so anxious to protect male workers from female competi- tion that eight months after the declaration of war he still denied the need for women in industry. Urging that women be brought into factories slowly, with due regard for their fragile nature, he suggested a committee to determine jobs from which they should be excluded and supported equal pay as a means of reducing their competition with men: "I believe that that proviso estab- lished and maintained would be a sufficient deterrent to any employer to unnecessarily bring women into industry." As late as 1921 still defining certain occupations as exclusively male, he claimed that physical difference accounted for all alleged union prejudice: "There must be some mistake on discriminating against women, it may be that women sought to join unions representing trades to which it is not believed women should work owing to the conditions which would affect their health, or work beyond their strength."

Blinded to women's contributions, Gompers overlooked their industrial record in his wartime speeches and failed to appreciate the League's sacrifices for the war effort. He coldly deferred action on a WTUL request that he appoint two women to the Labor Adjustment Committee of the Council of National Defense, and refused to address the WTUL wartime convention. When a New Haven woman in 1919 volunteered her assistance in securing better working conditions for women, he ignored the existence of the League and suggested that she contact either the Boot and Shoe Workers Union or the United Textile Workers.

AFL provincialism was further revealed when, in an action criticized by the Federal Council of Churches, a national convention rejected as "class-legisla- tion" a proposal from female delegates that two members of the Executive Board be women. Instead of urging full employment for both sexes, one central labor union resolved that women give up their positions to returning veterans and with the armistice the Central Federated Union of New York objected to continuing the training of women workers.

It even appeared that AFL antifeminism might impede federal protection of women in industry. As chairperson of the Committee of Labor of the

Council of National Defense, Gompers ignored women until he was badgered by the League into creating a subcommittee on Women in Industry. Chaired by the wealthy Mrs. Borden Harriman, no trade union women were appointed to this committee until the WTUL protested. Yet even this concession was meaningless for women still had no actual power, the board was kept merely advisory in nature.

FEDERAL PROTECTION OF WOMEN WORKERS

In June 1918, due in part to the efforts of William B. Wilson, Secretary of Labor, and of Felix Frankfurter, Assistant Secretary, a Women in Industry Division of the Department of Labor was instituted to coordinate the efforts of all federal agencies concerning women. As it was planned to draft between two and three million men, the division was tasked to develop policies and procedures to ensure the most effective use of women in war production while retaining favorable working conditions. Advocated by the WTUL since 1909 the division was directed by Mary Van Kleeck who had headed the Women's Branch of the Ordinance Bureau inspecting arsenals and plants employing women. In her new position she maintained close liaison with trade union women through frequent conferences, an advisory board, and her assistant, Mary Anderson, a former League organizer. At Anderson's suggestion she appointed Helen Brooks Irvin, a female black WTUL organizer, to advance equality for black women. Promulgating equitable industrial standards for women, including equal pay, the division agitated to get these protections incorporated into government contracts. As the Women's Bureau, it became a permanent part of the Department of Labor in 1920, and was headed by Mary Anderson, appointed as the result of an intensive lobbying campaign by the League.

SUFFRAGE AND WORKING WOMEN

After fifty-two years of debate the war brought to fruition another reform long championed by labor, male and female, the woman suffrage amendment to the U.S. Constitution. Supported by the AFL since 1890, as a means to improve the bargaining position of female workers, woman suffrage articles were common in the *American Federationist*, conventions habitually passed resolutions in its favor and appealed to state legislatures for support. In 1915 an article urging men to support proposed constitutional amendments in four

Eastern states was written by O'Reilly at the request of Gompers who even outlined the text for her. The Federation was so committed to suffrage that in 1914 Minnie Bronson, secretary of the National Association Opposed to Woman Suffrage, was refused permission to plead her case before the Executive Council, for in Gompers' words " . . . you might as well have a discussion with some person who is opposed to trade unionism as to hear an argument against equal suffrage."

Despite its support, the Federation remained uneasy concerning enfranchisement and warned working women that ballots could never replace the trade union, for votes were unable to solve industrial problems. Achieving protective legislation through suffrage might bring immediate relief to women but the Federation cautioned it could weaken workers in the long run by curbing their freedom. When Gompers' assistant, Eva Valesh, decided to work for suffrage, the labor leader urged her not to do so because women would gravitate toward men's parties and the women's vote "isn't going to help labor any that I can see."

From its inception in 1890 the National American Woman Suffrage Association (a merger of the leading suffrage organizations), made overtures to female workers. Urging the ballot as a means of obtaining equal pay and protective legislation, it invited Carroll D. Wright, U.S. Commissioner of Labor to address its 1893 convention on "Industrial Emancipation of Women." Speakers and delegates from the WTUL were often welcomed to NAWSA conventions, among them were: Florence Kelley, Ellen Henrotin, Alice Henry, Josephine Casey, Mary McDowell, Rose Schneiderman, Margaret Robins, and Leonora O'Reilly. The suffrage association also exchanged convention delegates with the AFL, required union labels on all its printing, and encouraged the unionization of working females. However, only reluctantly, as a result of the urging of its secretary Harriet Laidlaw and WTUL members, did the NAWSA adopt a unionized office.

Although the suffrage association increasingly championed the rights of female workers and the AFL supported the women's ballot, it was the WTUL that provided an effective link between the labor movement and suffrage reform. As early as 1909 the League initiated a special suffrage feature in the Women's Section of the *Union Labor Advocate* and with the establishment in 1911 of its own periodical, *Life and Labor*, regularly supported and publicized equal voting rights. WTUL activities during the 1910 Shirtwaist strike and the revelations stemming from the Triangle fire persuaded both middle-class suffragists and working women that the ballot was needed to protect women of all classes. As a result the suffrage newspaper, the *Woman's Journal*, became more sympathetic to workers and Anna Howard Shaw, president of the NAWSA, publicly supported the waistmakers at a mammoth rally. A year later to promote suffrage among trade union members she hired the League's Rose Schneiderman, who emphasized the ballot as a means of correcting industrial abuses. By 1911 even organized working men demonstrated for the women's vote at a labor-suffrage mass meeting in Carnegie Hall.

A link between middle-class suffragists and female workers was the Wage Earners League for Woman Suffrage, established in 1911 with WTUL encouragement, to persuade working women to agitate for the ballot as an "industrial necessity." Both organizations shared the same headquarters in New York, with the League providing financial support and leadership, as Leonora O'Reilly served on the WTUL's suffrage committee and presided over the Wage Earners League. An eloquent and articulate spokeswoman for the plight and needs of working females, O'Reilly was aided by an effective speakers' bureau and numerous pamphlets in organizing suffrage committees of working women in Baltimore, Albany, Pittsburgh, New Jersey, Pennsylvania, and Delaware. The movement was so successful that League member Harriet B. Laidlaw, national auditor for the NAWSA, in her suffrage handbook, *Organizing to Win*, advocated the further establishment of wage earners' leagues, as well as meetings, parades, and demonstrations held jointly with labor organizations.

By contesting the stance of the National Association Opposed to Woman Suffrage (a women's organization), the WTUL further cemented the relationship between suffragists and women workers. Even before state anti groups had coalesced to form the national association in 1911, the WTUL had censured these leisured, upper-class ladies for their failure to appreciate the difficulties of self-supporting women. Testifying on suffrage before a 1908 Massachusetts legislative committee, Mary K. O'Sullivan, representing trade unions, glared across the hearing table at the female antisuffragists and accused them of insensitivity toward workers and working conditions. Further castigating them as enemies of the people O'Sullivan compared the antis with scabs and strike breakers. A few years later a NWTUL convention, describing the national antisuffragists as "women of leisure who by accident of birth have led sheltered and protected lives," charged them with "selfishly obstructing the efforts of organized working women to obtain full citizenship." Antisuffragists, in turn, attacked League efforts to link the vote and labor reform for women, by asserting that equal suffrage states had less protective legislation than non-suffrage states. Furthermore, these laws, they contended, were in jeopardy, for in demanding the ballot women had to assert an equality with men. On the other hand, social welfare worker and antisuffragist, Emily P. Bissell, writing under her pseudonym, Priscilla Leonard, in *Harper's Bazaar*, claimed that working women neither wanted nor needed the vote to reform labor conditions.

In refuting these charges the WTUL assumed the very stance the AFL had feared, for it justified the vote as a means to reform rather than as a right of women. As early as 1905 Florence Kelley in her book *Some Ethical Gains* observed that women were unable to change dehumanizing industrial conditions and contrasted this failure with the protection working men received through the ballot. Before Congressional committees and state legislatures, reformers such as Mary Kenney O'Sullivan, Leonora O'Reilly, Jane Addams, Margaret Robins, and Mary Simkhovitch testified that suffrage was needed to improve women's working conditions. In New York, Mary Beard, editor of the *Woman Voter*, contended that government regulation of the economy was inevitable, and as the nature of such regulation would be determined by voters, enfranchisement of women was necessary to alleviate working women's injustices. More dramatic was Mrs. Glendower Evans, who led a group of working "girls" to the White House in an attempt to convince President Wilson that a federal suffrage amendment was necessary to protect laboring women.

As Jane Addams later described it, women reformers became convinced of the political connection between equal suffrage and social amelioration, thus supporting enfranchisement to remedy those social conditions responsible for human wretchedness. Capitalizing upon this notion leaguers preached the suffrage gospel to working women, many of whom as lower-class, unskilled slum dwellers had earlier tended to view that reform as irrelevant. Simultaneously the League persuaded many feminists that trade unions were a significant means to improve the status of women. Accordingly the WTUL was described by the Women's Bureau of the Department of Labor as " 'the woman movement' within the labor movement, and labor's spokesman within the woman movement." So intertwined did the two activities become that a mass meeting for suffrage at Cooper Union evolved into a women's rally, and suffragists seized the initiative in organizing a retail clerks union in New York.

Advocacy of the ballot as a means of improving women's working conditions was also attributable to the disillusionment of female leaders with the AFL.

Distrust of organized labor led Mary Dreier and her sister, Margaret Robins, to campaign in 1916 for Charles Evans Hughes after he agreed to support a federal suffrage amendment. Maud Younger also began to concentrate more on suffrage than on unionization. Convinced that enfranchisement was the most efficient way out of our "inhuman industrial condition" Leonora O'Reilly urged women to push for this reform above all others. Accordingly, she devoted the preponderance of her time and talents to that movement, lecturing for the ballot throughout the United States, frequently before Central Labor Unions. Planning and participating in mammoth suffrage rallies, she presided over the Wage Earners' League, and chaired the labor committee of the Woman Suffrage Party of New York. A rather frail woman, who had suffered a heart attack and cared for her elderly, widowed mother, she nevertheless found the energy to organize teachers in New York City.

Despite the reformers' success in associating suffrage with the women's labor movement, arguments for the ballot and for work reform reflected the schizophrenia that long plagued American society. Working women in agitating for the vote contended that it would lead to regulatory legislation and thereby protect "mothers" or "mothers-to-be." Time and time again their case for equal suffrage and improved working conditions was rooted in the assumption that "woman's work" was somehow abnormal, an impediment to her proper role, the raising of children. Florence Kelley reflected a generation of labor women in her testimony on suffrage before the House Judiciary Committee in 1910: "We women are working for the ballot, for the sake of protecting the womanhood and motherhood of over six million working women." Yet, ironically, when appealing for the passage of the suffrage amendment, Woodrow Wilson ignored "motherhood" and emphasized women had *earned* the right to vote through wartime suffering, sacrifice, and labor, an argument readily accepted by men.

As the new decade began, it appeared that a totally fresh chapter in the women's labor movement was about to unfold. Observers were convinced that the war had brought new recognition to women workers and had liberalized societal views on their ability to work outside the home and the propriety of their doing so. As one critic stated, industry had become "sexless in ideology and reality." Not only had the Nineteeth Amendment been ratified and the Women's Bureau instituted, but working women themselves were assuming positions of leadership in union activities. Resigning in 1922 as president of the National Women's Trade Union League, Margaret Robins was succeeded by Maud O'Farrell Swartz of the Typographical Union. Furthermore, 8 percent of trade union membership was now female, and 6.6 percent of working women were organized — a fivefold increase in a decade. At the same time the League was about to launch a campaign to have the AFL issue charters to women's locals in trades in which the internationals prohibited their membership.

Chapter 10

THE NADIR [1]

Expectations that wartime patriotism would lead to a permanent acceptance of working women and an improvement in their conditions of employment were quickly dashed. A resurgence of conservatism followed by the shattering 1929 depression frustrated these dreams.

The Women's Trade Union League was forced to divert its attention from working women's needs to preserving its own image as a feminist and, even more importantly, an American organization. Its revised constitution of 1922, urging that war be banned and that women workers of all countries affiliate closely, aroused the apprehension of conservatives. After initial hesitation for fear of overshadowing its commitment to unionization, the League joined with other liberal groups in establishing a Women's Joint Constitutional Committee to act as a clearinghouse for legislative efforts and to lobby for reformist legislation. These policies in addition to its campaign for the Child Labor amendment to the federal Constitution resulted in the Daughters of the American Revolution and *Woman Patriot* magazine assailing the League as socialistic. (The magazine, successor to *Woman's Protest*, the journal of the National Association Opposed to Suffrage, was dedicated "to the Defense of the Family and the State Against Feminism and Socialism.") The accusations were read into the *Congressional Record* by Representative Thomas F. Bayard (Democrat, Delaware). In New York James P. Holland, president of the state Federation of Labor, denounced the League as "a tail to the Socialist kite." Even more shocking was the canard, first published in Henry Ford's Dearborn *Independent* and widely reprinted throughout the nation, that the League was part of the Communist conspiracy.[2]

135

The director of the Women's Bureau, Mary Anderson, was frequently thwarted in her efforts to promote economic progress by those same forces. In 1938, before the House Committee on Un-American Activities, she was accused of being a Communist tool, a charge originally made in 1924 in the *Independent*. Consequently Anderson was blacklisted by the Daughters of the American Revolution, and the *Woman Patriot* charged the Bureau and its allies with attempting to "Boshevize" the United States by destroying the family.

EQUAL RIGHTS AMENDMENT

League problems were intensified when as a result of pressuring for additional protective legislation it became embroiled with the Woman's Party over the passage of a federal Equal Rights Amendment. A long-time champion of working women, Rheta Childe Dorr, supported the amendment, claiming protective laws were discriminatory as they jeopardized employment opportunities for women. Furthermore, she accused the League of being a tool of male unions, opposing equal rights for selfish reasons. Censuring the League, too, for concentrating on legislation rather than unionization was Josephine Casey, former AFL organizer: "The trouble is, girls, that you are getting old and tired, and want some easier way."

Also contending with the female left over the Equal Rights Amendment was the Women's Bureau. Its National Women's Industrial Conferences of 1923 and 1926 recommending unionization and additional protective legislation to alleviate the hardships of women workers, were disrupted by members of the Woman's Party. Charging that such legislation led to reduced female wages, decreased the opportunities for advancement, and barred the possibility of overtime, these women bolted from the 1926 session and marched on the White House in a futile effort to persuade President Calvin Coolidge to endorse the Equal Rights Amendment. To answer their charges, the conference urged the Women's Bureau to undertake a study of the effects of protective legislation on opportunities for women. Nearly the entire appropriations and staff of the Bureau were engaged in this research for two years. Concluding that although night work restrictions and legislation prohibiting female employment in specific industries were sometimes detrimental to women's opportunities, their report affirmed that the regulation of hours and standards did not adversely affect females. On the contrary, protective legislation generally raised the working standards of both women and men.

Upholding the Bureau's advocacy of protective legislation and opposition to the Equal Rights Amendment to the Constitution were President Coolidge and Secretary of Labor James Davis. Their positions were based not as much on the necessity of protecting working women as on preserving traditional concepts of the female role. Coolidge informed the 1926 conference that "women can never escape the responsibility of home and children, and the working woman as a mother and potential mother challenges universal interest." Proclaiming to the delegates that the physical health of woman workers bore on the future of the race, Davis insisted the question of protective legislation "goes far deeper than the right of the individual woman to work." Uncomfortable with the very concept of female work, the Secretary of Labor had written two years earlier: "All will agree that woman in industry would not exist in an ideal social scheme. Women have a higher duty and higher sphere in life. Eve was the companion and helpmate of Adam and in every way his social equal, but it was for Adam to protect Eve and provide for their posterity . . . I personally prefer to see a woman guiding the destiny of the nation in the home."[3]

WTUL ACTIVITIES

Along with Bureau resources League funds were diverted to fight the amendment and safeguard protective legislation. These unexpected outlays, reductions in contributions from allies, and traditional financial brinkmanship resulted in deficits in 1924, 1925, and 1926. To reduce expenditures, after 1926 conventions met triennially rather than biennially, and the budget for 1927 was chopped 30 percent.

During this trying decade three different women presided over the League. Robins' ambition to have a trade unionist president was realized when Maude O'Farrell Swartz succeeded her. A native of Ireland, Swartz, became a proofreader and member of the Typographical Union shortly after arriving in the United States. Drawn into the League by the suffrage movement, she attended its organizers' school, taught workers' classes, and was branch secretary before her election as president.[4] Overextended by continuing to assist the New York League and campaigning for workmen's compensation Swartz decided in 1926 not to run for reelection. Her successor was Rose Schneiderman, a former needle trade organizer who was national president until the League disbanded in 1950.

Despite trade union leadership for the first time, the WTUL was accused of disregarding organizational activity in the 1920s, for though the female labor force increased 27.4 percent - from 8.3 million to 10.4 million - the number of women union members decreased. However, many had entered unskilled occupations, difficult to organize in any era, but especially in one characterized by an antilabor attitude. Furthermore, the decrease in the percentage of union women in the work force was actually about the same as that of all union members. As a matter of fact the League continued its traditional endeavors among textile workers participating in an eighteen-week general strike of Chicago dress-makers and aiding striking Boston Garment Workers in 1924. Organizing full-time for the Philadelphia Waist and Dress-makers Union in 1927 was the League's national executive secretary, Elisabeth Christman. Mrs. Gifford Pinchot, a national officer, created a Citizens' Committee to rally public support behind these female employees. Their efforts were so successful that a favorable contract was negotiated without a strike. WTUL organizers also helped in the American Thread strike at Willimantic, Connecticut.

Organizational campaigns confined to Northern textile mills, however, were in a sense self-defeating as manufacturers had begun to relocate in the South due to the scarcity of cheap Northern labor, a result of immigration restrictions. As Thomas F. McMahon, president of the United Textile Workers, pointed out, organizational drives in the North were further incentives to such moves and relocation was frequently threatened by management to frustrate unionization. Consequently the League assumed the initiative in unionizing Southern women. Appointing ex-president Robins chairperson of the General Southern Committee, organizational headquarters were established in Richmond under Matilda Lindsay, a WTUL field representative who had recently completed a forty-week unionizational drive for the Wisconsin State Federation of Labor. In addition to educating women workers to the necessity of unions, training leaders, and winning the sympathy of the community, the League organized and directed major textile strikes at the end of the decade.

League drives were not confined to that industry. "Salesgirls" in Boston and glove workers in Indiana were unionized and a plan to recruit women was prepared for the traditionally indifferent International Brotherhood of Bakery and Confectionary Workers. Besides implementing this program with bakery locals, the WTUL also began a very lengthy and frustrating drive to organize laundry workers, resulting in the formation of an unusual New York local with a female president and male secretary.

Women's efforts to protect even the most unskilled and traditionally unorganizable worker coupled with the persistence of female strikers, should have embarrassed male unionists. Urging and publicizing the need to organize black women the WTUL agitated to improve the working conditions of chambermaids. In a General Cigar strike in New Brunswick, women, led by League organizer Sadie Reisch, continued to demonstrate after men had returned to work. Since beauty parlor employees, despite long hours, low pay and inferior working conditions, viewed unions condescendingly, a program of active recruiting was necessary. Unprepared for this task and reluctant to make changes attractive to women the Barber's president requested the assistance of the WTUL and supported its organizational efforts. Close relations developed between the two organizations as the women conducted moderately successful drives in 1931, 1932, and 1934 and helped to formulate the National Recovery Administration codes for beauty parlor operators.

WORKER EDUCATIONAL PROGRAMS

To counter the decade's antipathy toward unions and to ease organizational tasks the League, in consonance with its own traditions, increasingly concentrated on educational endeavors. Every campaign, convention, and meeting was used to instruct the public on working women's needs. Continuing its well-publicized school for workers, WTUL scholarship programs trained women, including blacks and Southerners, in organizational methods and for leadership positions in the labor movement. So successful and so significant was the school that other groups assumed its functions enabling the financially pressed WTUL to discontinue it in 1926.

With League encouragement, a Summer School for Working Women in Industry was established at Bryn Mawr under the direction of Hilda Smith, an alumnus and former social worker. Designed by the League, trade unions, and the students themselves, the curriculum educated one hundred dedicated unionists annually. To meet the demand for increased facilities, the institute, after seventeen years, moved to West Park, New York where it was known as the Hudson Shore Labor School. Smith, continuing as director, also became educational supervisor for the New York WTUL and helped establish a summer school for female workers at Barnard and the women's labor school at Vineyard Shore.

Another workers' school, Brookwood Labor College, was founded in 1921 with the assistance of Rose Schneiderman who served on its board of policy makers. This first resident school for workers in the United States was coeducational with a two-year program and three-week summer institutes. Its ultimate goal was to emancipate the working class and to establish a new social order.

These League inspired institutions encouraged labor to undertake its own programs. An educational clearinghouse and guidance center known as the Workers' Educational Bureau, established in 1921 by unionists and social reformers, soon became an adjunct of the AFL. By 1923 Federation representatives controlled its executive committee, and two years later President William Green hailed the bureau as an "arm of our great movement." Becoming an integral part of the AFL Department of Education in 1950, it had already served generations of unionists by publishing pamphlets and books, teaching workers, and interpreting labor and unions to the public.

One of the national leaders in workers' education was Fannia Cohn who was appointed to the position of organizing secretary when the International Ladies' Garment Workers Union established a General Education Committee in 1916. Emigrating to the United States from Russia in 1904 at nineteen years of age, she joined the ILGWU shortly thereafter. Upon graduation from the first WTUL labor class in 1914, she worked so effectively as an organizer and strike leader in New York and Chicago that in 1918 she was appointed Educational Director of the ILGWU, served on its General Executive Board from 1916 to 1928, and was the first female vice president of a major international.

Under her stimulating leadership, the necessity for workers' education was promulgated throughout the labor and reform movements. In addition to her own writings and speeches, she sponsored panels, forums, and symposia on the subject. Planning educational programs for local union members and their wives, publicizing workers' classes and college institutes, she brought intellectuals and wage-earners together. Her objective was not only to develop well-informed, thinking leadership essential to democratically organized and complex union structures, but to inculcate a sense of idealism in the worker inspiring her "to make the world a better place in which to live" by fighting "inequality and injustices."[5]

Described as "essentially an old-fashioned feminist in the labor movement," Cohn used her ILGWU position and her prestige to promote opportunities, equality, and unionization for women workers. Insisting that worker educational programs give special consideration to the talents and contributions of females she criticized apathetic union attitudes. Modern women, she asserted, refuse to accept the outdated notion that their sphere is the home and if left unorganized will jeopardize work standards. To reach the "new woman," unions must recognize changing values, stress equality, and establish sexually integrated locals. Urging females not to await union initiatives, Cohn implored them to be self assertive and to strive for positions of leadership in the labor movement.

AFL VACILLATIONS

The antifeminism that Cohn assailed was manifested in the early 1920s by the AFL, whose affiliates sometimes banned female members. When women introduced a resolution in the 1921 convention to prohibit any union from denying or abridging "the right of membership . . . on account of sex," the committee on laws rationalized existing discrimination. Claiming that exclusion was not the result of prejudice they attributed it to unladylike work in trades that banned women and offered a substitute resolution that unions excluding females give "early consideration for such admission." A deep-seated distrust of working women was revealed in the ensuing bitter debate. Rejecting a floor amendment for the AFL itself to charter locals if affiliates prohibited female members, the convention accepted the meaningless committee report 164-73. A few months later, warning of the menace of unorganized women, the WTUL directly appealed to the AFL Executive Council to issue charters to women if excluded by affiliates. Again the proposal was rejected, the council claiming it had no authority unless authorized by constituent unions. Defending himself against the accusation of sex prejudice, Gompers explained that the AFL discriminated against "any nonassimilable race."

A change in Gompers' attitude toward working women might have been expected because of his friendship and admiration for the vivacious Lucy Robins Lang. Leaving her position as a tobacco stripper in a cigar factory, Lang became a waitress and joined the AFL. With her husband she crisscrossed the country participating in a wide variety of left-wing causes, demanding a new trial for the imprisoned labor leader, Tom Mooney, and a pardon for Eugene Debs. Originally Lang thought Gompers conservative and spineless, but the very secretiveness of his efforts on behalf of Mooney and Debs convinced her that he was dedicated and pragmatic and thus she came to admire and like him.

According to William Green, Gompers sought her advice and counsel; Lang states that he sought her hand. Describing her service to labor as "remarkable," Gompers hailed her for giving up "everything to establish a better understanding between the 'radicals' and the labor movement." Lang pursued these interests after Gompers' death, assisting his successor, William Green, by investigating working conditions in the South, aiding in the 1927 Mine Workers strike, and studying European labor for the Federation.[6]

Undaunted by AFL rebuffs, in 1922 women again introduced a convention resolution authorizing the Federation to issue charters directly to female workers. Despite a lengthy address in support of this proposal by the WTUL "fraternal" delegate, Mary V. Halas, the issue was again circumvented. A substitution urging all affiliates "to give early consideration" to the admission of women and directing the Executive Council to "take up the subject" with those unions was unanimously approved. Little was done by the AFL for working women during these years other than allowing WTUL delegates to address its conventions and supporting League opposition to the Equal Rights Amendment as harmful to working women who were "potential mothers."

What the WTUL could not induce the AFL to do, the U.S. Supreme Court was able to accomplish. In 1923, in *Adkins v. Children's Hospital*, the Court invalidated a District of Columbia minimum wage law, holding that the "unique" status of women argument used to sustain such legislation in the Muller case was invalidated by the Nineteenth Amendment to the Constitution. Although the immediate effect of the decision was a 50 percent reduction of women's wages in the District of Columbia, the ruling was not entirely unwelcome to the AFL, as it perceived minimum wage legislation as an impediment to unionization.

To protect industrial standards from this new threat, the League called a two-day conference of twenty-seven concerned organizations, including the AFL. Their unanimous recommendation was to unionize women for purposes of collective bargaining and to appoint a committee to recommend ways of implementing this proposal.

In keeping with this suggestion the Executive Council of the AFL requested that the 1923 convention authorize Gompers to prepare a women's organizational drive. Asserting that "If they [women] can not be protected by law we should protect them by organization," Gompers invited forty-five unions to a national conference the following February. There he stated that although the WTUL rendered valuable service during strikes, it was not suitable for an organizational drive, because its mission was primarily educational. Since much fieldwork and extensive action were required, he suggested the establishment, under his direct supervision, of an AFL women's bureau that would include a female executive officer and lead a joint organizational campaign financed by member unions.

Leaguers were convinced that this proposal was little more than a meaningless ruse to undermine the rationale for their existence. Support for the plan by the Barbers and Carpenters, bitter enemies of the League at this time and two of the unions that refused female membership, gave credence to WTUL suspicions as did the first meeting. Of forty-five unions invited, only thirteen sent representatives and they objected to a woman's bureau as an infringement on trade autonomy. After another national conference and several committee meetings, the plan was abruptly terminated by the Executive Committee in August. Convinced that women undermined working standards and really belonged in the home, very few unions were willing to support the drive. At the 1924 convention, the Executive Council announced that it was abandoning the effort; however, it would promote an educational campaign for women and initiate another drive when the time was "propitious."

This time arrived with surprising rapidity. In 1925 the Executive Council, "at the request of a number of international officers," authorized the new president, William Green, "to work out a plan" that avoided the creation of "new agencies or machinery." Believing a woman's campaign necessary, not only to improve economic conditions but also to demonstrate union commitment toward females, Green, nevertheless, feared another failure. Under the direction of AFL troubleshooter, Edward F. McGrady, the drive, centered in Newark, again met with union indifference receiving only nominal support. Backed by just four unions, in 1924 it was again abandoned for an educational effort, with admonishments to the internationals themselves to organize women. An insight into the failure was provided by McGrady's attitude. When Ann Craton, a persistent and experienced organizer, offered her services, he suggested that she go to work for the YWCA instead. When Craton ignored this rebuff, he urged her to get married on the basis that union work was "too rough" for women and that the Federation believed females would not be receptive to an organizational campaign for twenty-five years.[7] At the 1926 convention Green admitted that the campaign had failed, nevertheless, Rose Schneiderman addressed the delegates, pledging League support for their goals.

However, the attitude of most unionists was symbolically revealed as she was followed to the platform by the next speaker, Jeff Davis, "King of the Hoboes."

These abortive drives of the AFL resulted in numerous articles and pronouncements analyzing the difficulties in obtaining women members, assailing unions for their hostile attitudes, and recommending new organizational techniques. Conducting a seminar on the problem, the WTUL published a pamphlet emphasizing that methods must be adapted to the particular trade and size of the community. A member of the Amalgamated Clothing Workers Union research department, Leo Wolman, in a perceptive article in *Survey* and in his book on the growth of trade unions, contended that women were no harder to enlist than men, it only appeared so because female workers were concentrated in industries traditionally difficult to organize. Furthermore, the incentive for women to join was diminished as men kept most of the honors and responsibilities in unions to themselves. A series of articles by the economist, Theresa Wolfson, attributed organizational difficulties to "inability . . . [of unions] to shed [their] heritage of social conception concerning women" and to the lack of group consciousness by women workers, who were women first and trade unionists second. Acknowledging that official AFL policy was more liberal than that of member unions, she still concluded that the WTUL and the organization of women never had whole-hearted labor support. As unions had not developed special procedures to encourage female membership, an organizer, she claimed, must include social and economic inducements to attract them and should form novices into women's branches to be merged later with men's locals.

Of particular concern to Wolfson was union tolerance of wage differentials, prejudicial seniority rules, and even discrimination within the union itself. As progressive an organization as the Amalgamated Clothing Workers, whose constitution proclaimed equal rights with men, eliminated its Women's Bureau after only one year. Despite 50 percent female membership, it had only one woman on its General Executive Board and a mere handful of female local union officers.[8] Charges of sex prejudice against the ACW were made by women members in its own newspaper, *The Advance*. Ann Craton also accused most unions of discriminating against women by protecting male jobs and permitting wage differentials in their contracts. Even those who disagreed over the effects of the Equal Rights amendment on workers were able to agree the unions had failed to organize and protect females.

144

Few criticisms were levied against the AFL's educational campaign which made efficient use of the *American Federationist*. Frequent contributors were Mary Anderson of the Women's Bureau and Fannia Cohn of the ILGWU. Ethel Smith of the League used its pages to urge joint AFL-WTUL efforts and to encourage special approaches to women. Writing editorials to dispel the myth that women worked for "pin money" Green demonstrated that they were an integral part of the labor force and warned that failure to exercise the "patience, intelligence and vision" required to enlist women would result in unions being menaced by female workers. The entire August 1929 issue of the *Federationist* was dedicated to women, the lead editorial stressing the principle that legislation was no substitute for union protection.

TEXTILE WORKERS DRIVE

Events in the predominantly female textile industry should have dispelled the notion that an educational campaign was all that could be done for women, for they proved females could be organized and would remain loyal to unionists even under adverse conditions. As mills moved South to take advantage of cheap labor (by 1925 there were more spindles there than in New England), remaining Northern manufacturers arbitrarily reduced wages, triggering off bitter conflicts and forcing unions to undertake an organizational campaign in the hostile South to protect their Northern base.

Willimantic, Connecticut was the scene of one of the first Northern strikes triggered by these changes. The American Thread Company, the largest thread mill in the world, announced a 10 percent wage cut in January 1925. About 2,600 workers, 80 percent of whom were female responded to the UTW strike call. What followed became in time a familiar pattern throughout the industry. With the aid of state police, French-Canadian strike breakers were recruited and the plant reopened. Strikers, who had been evicted from company housing, survived in a tent colony on minimum relief funds, for despite WTUL contributions, the international was unable to finance the strike adequately. Vanquished workers gradually drifted to other cities seaching for work; a handful even returned to the thread mill. At the end of thirteen months, the only vestiges of the strike were increased poverty in Willimantic and an occasional demonstration at the gates of the plant.

A more direct result of Southern competition was the Botany Worsted strike in Passaic, New Jersey, beginning in January 1926 when the plant slashed wages 10 percent. Spreading rapidly to other mills in the city, there were soon 4,000 mass pickets, many of whom were women whose husbands had been employed on the day shift, on the condition that their wives work at night. These women withstood the ensuing terror and violence as well as their men. Horses were ridden into their lines by police. Fire hoses, clubbings, and tear gas failed to break their spirit. After one vicious police attack on their lines, renewed picketing was led by Miss Elizabeth Kovacs pushing a baby carriage.

To suppress accounts of the violence, freedom of the press was challenged, reporters were assaulted, cameras smashed, and their notes destroyed. Here too, women showed courage and fortitude. Mary Heaton Vorse was in repeated danger during her efforts to cover the strike thoroughly, and Esther Lowell of the Federated Press was one of several reporters arrested. After the imprisonment of Communist strike leaders, the UTW took charge and their moderate leadership, coupled with adverse publicity concerning the violation of civil liberties, resulted in a settlement that compared favorably with those in other textile strikes. Hours and wages remained unchanged and a closed shop was prohibited, but arbitration agreements provided for union recognition and there was no discrimination in the rehiring of workers.

A similar 10 percent wage cut by the New Bedford Cotton Manufacturers' Association was followed by a lengthy and dreadful strike in that city's major mills. Owners justified the reduction by reference to nonunion Southern competition. However, the *Springfield Republican* theorized that it was management's response to the state legislature's refusal to modify laws on night work for women. In any event, on April 16, about 30,000 workers (60 percent of whom were female) walked out. So desperate were they that the strike began with only one third of the workers union members and before the UTW could undertake a membership drive or authorize the employees' action.

Both the Boston and New York branches of the League sent assistance. Performing yeoman service in that troubled city for sixteen weeks was organizer Sadie Reisch who established a New Bedford WTUL branch, scheduled picketing, administered relief programs, and kept the workers' morale high by teaching and leading them in labor songs. Identified by the *New York Times* as one of the three major female strike leaders, she and Elizabeth Glendower Evans were prevented by police from joining the picket lines. Later, along with hundreds of others, Reisch was arrested for picketing and as a result of this "lawlessness" was ordered to move out of her YWCA room.

146

Despite fatigue, hunger and dejection the women remained resolute. In July when the plants attempted to reopen under police and National Guard protection, only about twenty workers returned. However, after twenty-six weeks, an exhausted treasury and the depletion of relief allocations forced the union to accept a 5 percent wage reduction and a promise that any future wage changes would be preceeded by a thirty-day notice.

Dawdling over a Southern organizational campaign because of a shortage of funds the AFL and UTW lost the initiative, as three key strikes broke out in that region before they were ready for a major drive. The first began in the small town of Elizabethton, Tennessee, in March 1929, when women in an inspection plant spontaneously walked out over a wage dispute. Within a few days 5,000 workers (about 75 percent female) had left the mills. Of these, 2,000 under the leadership of UTW and WTUL organizers established a union local. Despite the use of injunctions and National Guardsmen, the strike was settled in less than a month on favorable terms, including wage increases from 5 to 15 percent for men, 11 percent for women, and a commitment to rehire strikers. Matilda Lindsay, the League organizer, envisioned this triumph as the first step in the unionization of the South.

Her enthusiasm was soon shattered as the company reneged on the reemployment terms. In the early morning of April 4 in two separate kidnappings, Edward F. McGrady of the AFL who was sent to save the sagging agreement, and Alfred Hoffman of the UTW, were seized by gangs of armed men, driven out of town and then dumped. Their abductors, probably businessmen, threatened the union officials with death if they returned. The same day, the sister of another AFL organizer prevented a similar incident by brandishing a pistol at her brother's assailants. These events, coupled with company intransigence on the wage increase and dismissal of unionists, led to another strike on April 15. In a determined effort to crush the union, workers were evicted from their homes and National Guardsmen were sent to the town. Over 1,250 strikers were arrested, and machine guns were used to protect scabs in the company union. Morale remained high nevertheless, as many women showed great courage, including Matilda Lindsay, the League's organizer, and the female striker seriously injured when a bus carrying scabs charged into picket lines on the highway.

Its funds depleted, the UTW reluctantly accepted terms negotiated by the twenty-eight-year-old Anna Weinstock of the U.S. Labor Department. These provided for rehiring most workers, establishing a grievance committee, and appointing a new plant manager, whom the workers assumed would be more sympathetic to their needs. However, textile owners, to the delight of Communists who had worked against the agreement, defied the provisions and eventually broke the union.

While the strike at Elizabethton was sputtering toward its demoralizing conclusion, less than one hundred miles away on the other side of the Smokies, mill workers struck at Gastonia, North Carolina. A wage reduction and the introduction of the "stretch out" in 1927 had engendered a spirit of revolt. Capitalizing upon this restlessness was Fred Beal, of the Communist National Textile Workers' Union, a dour Yankee who became a Communist while attempting to turn the New Bedford strike into a class war. Organizing secretly in the South since 1928 and in Gastonia since March, Beal's activities were discovered and the unionists were fired. Although unprepared for a confrontation, Beal was forced to call a strike. Many of the 2,500 workers who immediately responded were women, for as in Passaic, men were hired frequently only on the condition that their wives also work.

Determined to exploit the strike, the Communist party sent in scores of agents who eased Beal out of the leadership and began a massive propaganda campaign. As a result, a management victory was assured for the AFL quickly denounced the walkout and ordered its affiliates to provide no support. Nevertheless, under Communist direction the strike was continued principally for propaganda purposes. Fearful that the dispute was the first step in the overthrow of the government, a near civil war ensued as hysterical mob violence became rather routine despite the presence of National Guard troops. Beatings, including those of female pickets, were commonplace. Mobs destroyed union headquarters and burned relief stores resulting in the need for armed unionists to guard the tent city where evicted workers lived.

During the sixth month of turmoil, a truck load of unionists on the way to a National Textile Workers' rally was forcibly turned around and fired on by a passing automobile of anti-Communist vigilantes. Killed was Ella May Wiggins, a twenty-nine-year-old mother of nine, who had contributed much to the morale of the strike through her frequent presence on the picket line. She sang union ballads so poignantly, she had been sent North to raise relief funds. Wiggins' brief life was a testament to the necessity of protecting workers' rights. When four of her children became ill, the "super" had refused to put her on the day shift so that she could care for them. In desperation Wiggins quit, only to find she could not afford medicine for her ill youngsters: "so they just died. I never could do anything for my children, not even to keep'em alive it seems. That why I'm for the union, so's I can do better for them." No one was ever convicted for the murder of this pathetic woman.

Gastonia had a martyr, but it was too late to save the strike, although it was not formally called off until a few weeks after her death. A melée resulting from the interception of a union parade on June 7 led to a general altercation wounding five policemen, the chief mortally. Seven unionists, all of whom pleaded self-defense and later jumped bail, received lengthy prison sentences for second-degree murder, the last straw in breaking worker resistance.

Adverse publicity at Gastonia and Elizabethton destroyed the Southern drive by Communist unions, but still damaged the AFL. Despite the Federation's hostility to Communism and emphasis that traditional unions provided a viable alternative to it, most textile workers remained ignorant of the differences between the NWTU (Communist) and the UTW (AFL). Southern communities in defending the *status quo* obscured what they considered trivial distinctions between radicals, an important attitude during the labor dispute in Marion, North Carolina. Deplorable working conditions and the new rebellious spirit in Southern textile mills prompted three employees to persuade the UTW Southern organizer to come to Marion. Almost immediately after his appearance twenty-two workers were fired for union activity. Unable to offer relief because of its depleted funds, the UTW advised against a strike; however, desperate employees, including a large proportion of women, walked out on July 11. Lack of effective union support, presence of the militia, and evictions from company housing forced an agreement to return to work two months later.

Reducing hours as they promised, the mills, however, blacklisted over a hundred hands for union activities. Because the company refused to discuss this retaliatory step, the union was left with no alternative, and a second strike began early in October. During a shift change outside one of the mills, deputies fired tear gas at demonstrating strikers. A sixty-year-old lame man, half blinded with tears, struggled with the sheriff. As he was being clubbed and handcuffed, deputies opened fire into the crowd killing six strikers and seriously injuring twenty-five others (one a woman). Most had been shot in the back, yet the plant manager proudly proclaimed: "I understand there were 60 or 75 shots fired in Wednesday's fight. If this is true there are 30 of the bullets accounted for. I think the officers are damn good marksmen. If I ever organize an army they can have jobs with me. I read that the death of each soldier in

149

the World War consumed more than five tons of lead. Here we have less than five pounds and these casualties. A good average I call it."

In the emotionally charged town thirty-six strikers were arrested and four convicted for "insurrection" and "riot," but the sheriffs' deputies were acquitted of second-degree murder. The strike had been broken over the bodies of the workers of Marion.

Emboldened by the textile revolt, encouraged by YWCA resolutions, and inspired by the WTUL example, the AFL launched its own Southern organizing campaign in 1929. Overreacting to the radicalism of the NTWU, the Federation appealed more to employers than to employees, proclaiming that union acceptance, would free management from Communist threats, and AFL efficiency engineers would improve the companies' cost-price position. AFL moderation proved futile, and events inevitably moved toward a dramatic confrontation. Men and women workers in one of the largest cotton factories in the world appealed to William Green of the AFL for help after a 10 percent wage slash in January 1930. A UTW vice president was sent to Danville, Virginia and with the invaluable assistance of Matilda Lindsay, WTUL field representative, established a huge local. After firing union activists management rejected every effort at mediation and negotiation. In September, 4,000 workers struck as other Southern mill owners surveyed this serious challenge.

Under the direction of the League's Lindsay and UTW's Francis Gorman, women played a vital role in the strike. Many of them picketed; others touring the country to raise money, were assisted by WTUL donations of close to $6,000. But, despite their efforts the pattern was the same: injunctions to prevent mass picketing, state police and militia, tear gas, violence, martial law, arrests, eviction from company houses, and a reopening of the factory with scab labor in November. Lindsay's appeals to Green for financial support were no more effective than Green's appeal to affiliates. Unable to fund the strike, after five agonizing months the impoverished UTW called it off without even obtaining guarantees of reemployment. Unionism had been crushed in the Piedmont.

During the strikes Southern women had demonstrated willingness to organize, faithfulness to unions and to fellow workers, and perseverance against adversity, the same qualities being shown by their Northern sisters. By 1924, owing in part to the efforts of female organizers, 40 percent of the

805,000 ILGWU membership was female and over 40 percent of the Amalgamated Clothing Workers Union consisted of women. So successful was the drive that Chicago dress-makers allegedly hired "slick looking fellows," "shieks" "with greased hair, bell-bottomed trousers and patent leather shoes" to mingle with the girls and discourage union membership. Later both unions were wracked by internal disputes and plagued by the Communist-led Needle Trades Union, yet thousands of women remained loyal.

At the end of the decade, these females participated in new campaigns, including the 1930 Needle Workers strike and the 1930-1931 Custom Dressmakers strike where the League's indefatigable Reisch was arrested for picketing. In 1930, 2,500 striking members of the Boston ILGWU were joined on the picket line by their young YWCA teacher in their demands for a five-day, forty-hour week. Participation in the episode generated a life-long commitment to labor by the teacher, the future director of the Women's Bureau and Assistant Secretary of Labor, Esther Peterson, who would never forget those dramatic days.

THE GREAT DEPRESSION

Strikes may have called the attention of the nation to the needs of working women, nonetheless, Americans of the 1920s remained ambivalent toward these issues, an attitude transformed by the Great Depression into outright animosity. As Senator Robert Wagner (Democrat, New York) noted, the female wage earner became the "first orphan in the storm." Unemployment among women was proportionately greater and increased more rapidly than that of men as it became extremely difficult for even trained union women to obtain work. Settling for less skilled jobs, better educated women drove the unskilled into the ranks of the unemployed or into "gypsy" industries that took advantage of the glutted labor market. Work standards were abandoned and sweatshops revived, in one Fall River mill a female employee received only five cents an hour, while the highest paid women earned fifteen cents, a pitiful total of $7.20 for a forty-eight-hour week.

Competition for employment intensified male enmity toward working females. In Woonsocket, Rhode Island men in the spinning mills struck against the employment of women and President A. Lawrence Lowell of Harvard admitted firing scrubwomen and replacing them with men rather than pay women the

151

Massachusetts minimum wage of thirty-five cents an hour. To many, the solution of the unemployment problem was to increase work opportunity for men by curtailing it for women. Urging protective legislation and equal wages at its 1931 convention, the AFL was probably motivated by its conviction that "married women owed primary obligation to the home." Its nine-point unemployment program bemoaning the "unfortunate trend of family life" urged "preference of employment to those upon whom family or dependency rests." Asserting that men had been "crowded" out of their "birthright" because of the increased employment of women, the president of Carnegie Tech proposed that 75 percent of available jobs be reserved for men.

Sharpest attacks were levied against married women who "selfishly" worked for "pin money" or for personal satisfaction rather than consecrate themselves to their designated full-time role as wives. The National Federation of Business and Professional Women's Clubs reported that private employers, with public support, arbitrarily dismissed married women. Legislation to prohibit or limit women's employment in public service was introduced in twenty-four states and employees whose spouses also worked for the federal government were dismissed. A National Education Association study of 1930-1931 revealed that of 1,500 school systems surveyed, 77 percent refused to hire wives and 63 percent dismissed female teachers if they married. All married women workers in 1931 were released by the New England Telephone and Telegraph, and Northern Pacific, while the City Council of Akron, Ohio requested the school board, department stores and rubber companies discharge women workers whose husbands were employed and replace them with men. It was alleged that this policy would not only lower unemployment but it would also decrease the divorce rate. Attitudes were so hostile that the *Woman's Journal* even published a forum article defending the right of women to work.

The economic disaster that created this deplorable situation also curtailed the activities of the WTUL, since it reduced contributions from both labor and allies. To cut expenses, *Life and Labor Bulletin* was temporarily suspended and the Executive Board met only six times between 1929 and 1936 conducting most of its business by mail. After the convention of 1929, another was not held until 1936, for the League's precious funds had to be stretched further to include new commitments: relief and publicity for the plight of unemployed women (frequently overlooked because of a concern for men), an employment agency, and a massive campaign against sweatshops directed toward regulatory legislation, consumer pressure, and union label awareness.

As these objectives could best be realized by legislation, the League's national headquarters was moved to Washington, D.C. in 1930. This was a fortuitous step for one of the WTUL's staunchest supporters was about to enter the White House. In 1919, Eleanor Roosevelt, wife of the Assistant Secretary of the Navy, had attended a tea for delegates to the International Congress of Working Women and in turn hosted a luncheon for some of these representatives, in the process becoming acquainted with Robins, Schneiderman, Swartz, O'Reilly, Anderson, Cohn, and O'Connor. A few years later, after her husband's polio attack, Louis Howe suggested that Ms. Roosevelt become more active. Renewing these contacts by joining the WTUL, she became friends with Schneiderman and Swartz, whom she frequently brought to Hyde Park. These two vivacious women then began to educate Franklin D. Roosevelt in the trade union movement and convert him to their cause.

Eleanor Roosevelt quickly became an enthusiastic supporter of League programs. Lobbying for its proposals at Albany and representing the organization before the 1924 Democratic Platform Committee, she also raised money for its activities, including a working women's clubhouse, taught in its evening classes, and donated to the West Virginia Coal Miners' strike through the League. When her husband's health improved, he participated in the League's Christmas parties for union children at her urging and after his election as governor of New York State was persuaded by Eleanor to attend the twenty-fifth anniversary party of the League and to appoint its former president, Swartz, to the state's Industrial Commission. But her zeal for working women was not confined to those acceptable "lady-like" activities. In 1926 Roosevelt joining in the mass picketing of 300 striking women paper box makers, publicly supported unionization proposals for domestic workers and in 1930 the ILGWU strike of Fifth Avenue dress-makers. There was no doubt but that working women would have sympathetic and articulate representation in the new administration.

Chapter 11

NEW DEAL YEARS - NEW HOPES FOR WOMEN [1]

Under the vigorous leadership of the new President, a wide variety of social and economic reforms became law during the first hundred days of his administration. One of the most important and far reaching measures, according to President Roosevelt himself, was the National Industrial Recovery Act. This measure embodied three programs: the National Recovery Administration, to reduce unemployment and to stimulate business through industrial self-regulation under government-supervised fair trade codes; the National Labor Board, to guarantee the right of labor to bargain collectively; and the Public Works Administration, to provide employment and stimulate business. Section 7 (a) of the act was compared with the Magna Carta by the AFL's Green and with the Emancipation Proclamation by the UMW's Lewis. It required that every code provide for the employees' right to organize and bargain collectively and stated that employers would comply with maximum hours and minimum pay as approved by the President. Furthermore, it prohibited management from forcing workers into company unions. These provisions revived the confidence of American labor. Encouraged by the government, unions broke out of the depression doldrums and began new organizational campaigns - drives that affected tens of thousands of women.

David Dubinsky's ILGWU was demoralized and in debt, its membership plunging from 105,000 in 1920 to 40,000 in 1933. Nevertheless, in May of that year, about 4,500 workers, primarily women, struck nonunion Philadelphia dress plants. With an estimated 95 percent of workers responding management quickly surrendered, settling for a forty-four-hour week, a 10 percent wage increase, and time-and-one-half for overtime. Revitalized and optimistic, the union enthusiastically prepared for an all-out organizational offensive to influence the drafters of NIRA codes. Maneuvering to get the code hearings delayed, Dubinsky, with only 15 percent of New York area dress-makers unionized, audaciously called a general strike in August at the height of the season. About 60,000 dress-makers, most of them women, struck in New York, New Jersey, and Connecticut. Timing and response were so effective that within four days the walkout was mediated and the terms, including a closed shop, prohibition of child labor, and wage increases, were incorporated into the NRA code. A further organizational drive and a series of strikes in other garment centers throughout the nation were rapidly settled on this basis. ILGWU membership and morale soared, and many skeptics became convinced that masses of women could be unionized.

THE GREAT TEXTILE STRIKE OF 1934

Women in the textile industry displayed the same courage and determination as those in the garment trade, but unfortunately with less tangible results. Headed by George Sloan, an industry spokesman, the NRA Cotton Textile Industry Committee drew up a code that failed to offer adequate protection to the workers from the exploitative "stretch out" and set a minimum wage of only $12 weekly in the South and $13 in the North.[2] A processing tax on raw cotton, increased use of the "stretch out," and shorter hours raised production and employment. Over 100,000 new workers were hired in four months, and UTW membership climbed from about 27,000 to 40,000. Fearful of overproduction the NRA then authorized a cutback to a thirty-hour week, thereby reducing wages accordingly.

Economic revival occurred, nevertheless the Cotton Textile Industry Committee disregarded workers' grievances and according to Hugh Johnson, NRA administrator, manufacturers "chiseled" on the codes. Threatening to strike over these issues the United Textile Workers was able to win a position on the Textile Committee. Convinced that this step would do little to alleviate abuses, forty of the forty-two locals in Alabama struck in July. An unsympathetic UTW President, Thomas McMahon, implored unions in other states not to participate, but Alabama workers held solidly, encouraged by the WTUL, which raised relief funds, rallied public opinion, and established a new chapter in Birmingham and a Junior League in Huntsville. A month after the Alabama walkout, infuriated UTW delegates voted at their national convention for a general strike to begin about September 1.

In the largest demonstration in labor history, about 450,000 textile workers throughout the nation struck shortly after Labor Day. Thousands of these were women, sharing threats, hardships, and violence with their male co-workers. In the South the effectiveness of the work stoppage was increased by "flying squads" of travelling strikers, who demonstrated at the gates of mills whose workers had not immediately joined the movement. Surprised by the efficacy of the strike, management fought back tenaciously, using armed guards and spies, evicting workers from their homes, and smearing strikers as Communists. Eventually they prevailed upon governors to call out the militia in North and South Carolina, Alabama, Mississippi, Georgia, Connecticut, Massachusetts, Maine, and Rhode Island, where Governor Theodore Green even considered requesting federal troops. Strike areas became permeated with violence. Organizers were beaten, kidnapped, and jailed causing Mollie Dowd, a WTUL officer and leading Southern liberal to fear for her life. Tear gas was used recklessly, and thousands of pickets were arrested; two were killed in Rhode Island, six in Georgia, and seven in South Carolina. In Atlanta martial law was proclaimed and outdoor internment camps were set up for the incarceration of pickets, including those who were mothers of young children.

At the start of the strike, Roosevelt appointed a board of inquiry for the cotton textile industry. Commission recommendations, issued on September 20, called for a neutral Textile Labor Relations Board and suggested that such negotiations be confined to individual plants. Evading other issues the committee advocated merely that a study be undertaken on wages, workloads, and the "stretch out." Demoralized by the tactics of the troops and the hunger pangs of its members, the UTW ludicrously hailed the board of inquiry's report as a great labor victory and immediately ordered the strikers back to the mills. Disillusioned workers and the liberal press were shocked by this apparently needless capitulation to management and were further alienated when numerous pickets were not rehired. Despite the heroism of innumerable women, textile unionism was temporarily crushed.

ACTIVISTS OF THE MID '30S

In addition to laboring on picket lines during NRA days, many women contributed in a variety of ways to the betterment of working conditions.

Dorothy Bellanca, elected in 1918 to the General Executive Board of Sidney Hillman's Amalgamated Clothing Workers Union, vigorously led drives in western Pennsylvania where garment factories had been established to capitalize upon the cheap labor of miners' wives and their children. As active in NRA inspired campaigns as she was in all ACWU drives, on the occasion of Bellanca's death in 1946, union President Jacob S. Potofsky announced that "she had addressed more meetings, installed more officers, and presented more charters that any other officer."

In Pennsylvania in 1933 Bellanca was assisted by a fellow Leaguer, Mrs. Gifford Pinchot, the wife of the governor, who appeared at factories in Allentown and Northhampton in an official state car. Marching with the demonstrators, Pinchot wore a bright red coat on which was pinned a streamer with but one word, "striker." A month later she picketed in Lebanon with the American Federation of Full Fashioned Hosiery Workers. Massive media coverage of these appearances enabled Pinchot to assail sweatshops and to marshal public support for state wage and hour legislation. Proclaiming "Our ancestors fought for their revolution. We must fight for our economic revolution now," she was instrumental in getting the national Junior League to undertake a public drive to eradicate unjust working conditions.

If any of Rose Pesotta's ancestors rebelled, it was against czardom, but Pesotta was an invaluable fighter in the American economic revolution. Born in 1896 in the Ukraine, she came to the United States in 1913, began work in a shirt-waist factory, and joined the ILGWU. After graduation from the Bryn Mawr Summer School and Brookwood Labor College, she was elected to the local's executive board serving on many strike committees during the 1920s. Appointed a general organizer, Pesotta led drives and strikes on the West coast in 1933, defying injunctions, thugs, and police brutality in order to establish locals and enforce code compliance. Her achievements were such that in 1934 she was elected ILGWU vice president.

As women strove to ensure that employers complied with the codes, others sought guarantees that women would be treated fairly and equally by these codes. Rose Schneiderman, on a leave of absence from WTUL, was the only woman appointed by Roosevelt to the Labor Advisory Board of the NRA. Assisting in code formulation she exerted great pressure along with the WTUL, Mary Anderson, and the Women's Bureau to insure there would be equal pay for men and women. As a result of their "constant nagging" at least sixty codes stipulating sexual wage differentials were revised and 75 percent of the 493 codes provided for equal pay.

Obviously discriminatory were 25 percent of the codes, yet most feminists hailed the NRA as a step toward equality and worker students at the Bryn Mawr summer school praised it for stimulating unionism. Never before had the principle of equal pay been so widely accepted. Claiming that the codes rendered protective legislation for women superfluous, Woman's Party members contended these laws, now obsolete served only to limit opportunities for women and should be invalidated by passage of the Equal Rights Constitutional Amendment. Even after the NRA was ruled unconstitutional, many observers believed that unionization drives and state legislation would achieve equal pay more readily because the codes had familiarized society with this just principle.

There were needs even more pressing than unionization and wages for working-class females. So critical was the condition of unemployed women that there were demonstrations in Washington. Hungry females demanded work and relief equal to males for with public assistance usually not available, women had to rely upon private organizations such as the YWCA and the Salvation Army or the initiative of private citizens such as Mary Ryder of the Typographical Union who established boarding homes for unemployed women in St. Louis.[3]

NEW DEAL PROGRAMS

That policies would change and New Deal relief and reform programs provide for women seemed to be guaranteed by the presence of Eleanor Roosevelt in the White House. In April 1934 she called and keynoted a White House conference where a general program for unemployed women was developed from data compiled at her request by Hilda Smith, an educational specialist in the Federal Emergency Relief Administration. Responsive to Eleanor Roosevelt's ideas and suggestions, Harry Hopkins allowed her to take the lead in all women's programs, resulting in 100,000 women being quickly employed in Civil Works Administration jobs. Other innovative programs followed. A female equivalent to the Civilian Conservation Corps was created with National Youth Administration camps for unemployed girls. By 1937, when the program was abolished, there were twenty-nine such institutions providing vocational training and counseling. With the outbreak of World War II in

Europe, the National Youth Administration also taught women to use drills, lathes, and power saws, and the Works Progress Administration trained them to weld.

Meanwhile, under FERA auspices, residence schools and educational camps were founded for unemployed women, during 1934-1935 seventy such schools employed 750 teachers with 50,000 students. Designed for "physical and mental rehabilitation" the education, length of residence, and number of camps were in no way comparable with the male CCC. Nevertheless, in view of traditional American sexual attitudes, the camps were an interesting social experiment probably contributing to conservative charges they were training centers for Communists.

Education of workers became an increasingly important part of the New Deal regardless of conservative objections. Under FERA auspices, unemployed teachers, male and female, were trained in local universities to conduct workers' adult education programs, designed to examine social and economic problems and develop skills in critical thinking. Initial union suspicion was overcome in 1934 by a National Conference on Workers' Education and from a subsequent Labor Advisory Committee of representatives from the AFL, the CIO, and the Railroad Brotherhoods. As a result, not only did superintendents of schools avail themselves of the service, but unions such as the UTW, the United Automobile Workers, and the United Rubber Workers, sponsored classes and often used the teachers in union education programs. When the experiment ended in 1942 a committee, formed as a result of a White House conference inspired by Eleanor Roosevelt, attempted to promote legislation making these services a permanent duty of the Labor Department. Although financed by unions, the effort was abandoned in 1950, primarily because of the success of General Motors in opposing the whole concept.

Workers' education was only a part of one of the most exciting and innovative New Deal agencies, the WPA. Designed to make work for the unemployed, its administration was of special interest to Eleanor Roosevelt. Along with the head of its Women's Division, Ellen Woodward, and Women's Bureau officials, Roosevelt ensured that WPA staffs at all levels of government designed specialized female programs. Women were trained in traditional areas like sewing and domestic service, also in educational, library, clerical, and musical work, as well as in welding and shipbuilding. In some sections of the country rather than refuse employment to mothers of young children, the WPA established day care centers managed by other WPA female employees.[4]

Although eligibility rules did not differentiate between men and women, the experiment was not an unqualified success for women. Special women's agencies, and the utilization by Hopkins of the novelist Martha Gellhorn and Lorena Hickok, a former A.P. correspondent, to report on poverty and programs, did little to correct the inequalities inherent in the system for the WPA limited its jobs to "economic heads" of families, a qualification many women failed to meet since their husbands were physically able to work. As it was difficult to devise suitable projects for the unskilled, sewing programs frequently provided the most work for women. Blacks encountered special problems because it was hard to obtain sponsorship for their projects, furthermore, most communities desired to relegate them to domestic service. Enrolled women were periodically restricted to a specified percentage of WPA employees, due to public criticism of working women and also in an attempt to check the desire of some women to be breadwinners. Protesting the arbitrary dismissal of fifty women in Colorado, because 27 percent of that state's WPA force was female, the 1936 AFL convention urged an enlarged WPA to provide suitable and useful employment for all needy persons.

A TROUBLED AFL

That resolution was but an indication that the AFL was undergoing a painful, vacillating reassessment of its relationship to female workers. On the one hand, the Federation was unable to estimate the number of women members since internationals refused to supply information on this subject. For two consecutive years it attacked legislative means of obtaining equal pay, yet Green refused financial assistance to WTUL organizers. In 1933 Elisabeth Christman, a League fraternal delegate, antagonized the convention by stating women must be organized in functional unions such as rubber and textile and demanding their representation and participation on responsible union governing bodies. Not until 1944 was another League representative invited to address a national convention.

On the other hand, the AFL endorsed the principle of equal pay, appointed a new woman organizer, Agnes O'Connor, to work in the rubber industry, and commended the work of the Women's Bureau. Revealing the Federation's indecision was Daniel J. Tobin of the Executive Council, who admitted that unions had inadequately supported the League, and promised to do better. Mary Anderson believed this concession was based on WTUL influence in the White House. Bitterly recalling the occasion of the League dinner honoring

Eleanor Roosevelt she wrote: "You would have laughed, if you had been there to hear Billie Green extolling the Women's Trade Union League - 'this noble organization' and 'the noble women'! I suppose it is too much to expect these men will ever put us on a par with them. It will be the next generation, maybe the next, before that will happen."

THE WOMEN'S BUREAU

This cynicism was understandable based on Anderson's experiences in the Women's Bureau. Studies by that agency during the 1930s clearly demonstrated that women were not working for "pin money," yet they also showed that union non-support forced females to rely on protective legislation. More disappointing than the absence of union cooperation was the attitude of the Secretary of Labor, herself a woman. Despite her experiences in reform movements, her social work background and her being a woman limited Frances Perkin's range of activities in the Department of Labor. The historian Arthur Schlesinger states social work had persuaded her that labor never had any ideas of its own, consequently, she was inclined to do things for labor rather than have it develop its own self-consciousness and do for itself.

Union leaders resented the appointment of a nonunionist woman to a cabinet position they believed should go only to a labor man. To disarm the suspicions directed toward a female in a male world, Perkins overcompensated by tending to slight needs of working women. Such an attitude became apparent early in the depression when, as industrial commissioner of New York State, she denounced women who worked for "pin money" as "menace[s] to the society" and urged those who did not need jobs to devote themselves to motherhood and the home. To relieve females from the necessity of working and enable them to fulfill their proper familial role, she urged increased men's wages. As Secretary of Labor, she changed little. Apparently not reading her subordinates' reports, she assumed, contrary to Women's Bureau research, that most women worked "selfishly" just for "pin money." As late as 1953, eight years after leaving office, she pontificated that it was unprofitable for women with children to work, especially as no machine has yet been built that will "tend a baby" or "teach a child not to wiggle in church."

Anderson, who soon came to resent Perkins' lack of identification with women's problems, found that her "entree" to the Secretary was closed and that the Women's Bureau suffered from a "lack of backing." By the time

Eleanor Roosevelt asked Anderson to have the Bureau investigate domestic workers, the situation had become so critical that Anderson, who had already had such a request rejected by Perkins, asked Roosevelt to approach the Secretary. In 1943 when Perkins attempted to pare the Women's Bureau budget, an embittered Anderson used her WTUL friends to apply public and private pressure on Perkins and the administration to restore the cuts. Retreating rapidly the Secretary perceived the stratagem, leading to a further deterioration of relations, as shown by a rather sharp exchange of correspondence between her and Anderson. These clashes, in part prompted Anderson to support as her successor in the Bureau, Freida Miller, a friend of Perkins. Miller, a non-trade unionist did have extensive union ties, but more importantly, Anderson believed "her contacts in the department were such that she might be more effective than I."

WTUL ENDEAVORS

Anderson's frustrations must have been assuaged to some extent from the continued support given the Women's Bureau and its programs by her old ally, the League. Fighting the Equal Rights Constitutional Amendment, the WTUL advocated protective legislation, and in general endorsed most of the liberal measures of that decade, including elimination of the poll tax, enfranchising Washington, D.C. residents, day care centers for the children of working women, low rent housing, and justice and opportunities for blacks. Along with encouraging measures of this type, the League continued to try to organize and to protect women, especially those in exploited and unskilled fields. Devoting great time and energy to domestic workers the WTUL attempted to obtain legislation limiting hours, establishing a minimum wage, and providing Social Security coverage for them. After ten years of lobbying, workmen's compensation was extended to these women in New York. In conjunction with the YWCA, the League conducted an educational campaign to alert the public to abuses suffered by household workers and encouraged voluntary contracts providing for vacations, insurance, bathing facilities and written agreements on wages. With AFL cooperation it even tried the nearly impossible task of organizing domestics, but by 1940 there were only three household workers' locals. Consequently, the WTUL adopted a policy of keeping the "problems of household workers before the public until such time as a real organizational drive can be worked out."

Endeavors to help women workers in hotels and restaurants met with slightly more success even though, in the early 1930s, the Hotel and Restaurant Employees Union was uncooperative. Ignoring a League appeal to organize in Detroit, and refusing a charter to black women tavern workers in Chicago, it thereby precipitated a strike by male union waiters against the employment of unorganized females. Elisabeth Christman of the League, nevertheless, served as an advisory board member on NRA codes on the hotel industry and incorporated some protections therein, and on behalf of the New York Minimum Wage Board the WTUL investigated conditions in hotels and restaurants. In 1936 a WTUL organizer, Eleanor Mishnun, assisted a general strike of hotel workers. Though beaten and the women blacklisted, the League through contacts with insurance companies and mortgage holders, exerted pressure on the hotels forcing them to reemploy the strikers. In that same year it hired a former waitress, Helen Blanchard, as a part-time organizer for cooks, waitresses, chambermaids, and clerks in small hotels. Its persistence finally impelled the establishment of the New York Hotel Trades Council, a joint board of nine locals that worked very effectively with the League.

Most appreciative of the New York League's efforts was the ILGWU. Not only did the two organizations cooperate with each other in the garment industry but as the International Laundry Workers Union was unable to mount a campaign they attempted to organize the steam laundry workers, failing when a four-week general strike was defeated by the owners. Nevertheless a League organizer led the Brooklyn Laundry strike of 1933, favorably settled through the intervention of Mayor Fiorello LaGuardia.

With the exception of the ILGWU the League was frustrated as most unions requested assistance only after a strike had begun. Answering organizational appeals from working women, the League frequently found locals and internationals opposed or indifferent to its efforts, and therefore undertook an educational campaign for union support of working women.

CIO AND WORKING WOMEN

To protect unskilled women the League urged organization along industrial lines. Others, too, encouraged by federal legislation moved in this direction. After the Supreme Court invalidated the NIRA, Congress passed the Wagner Act, establishing a new National Labor Relations Board to guarantee labor's right of collective bargaining through representatives of its own choosing.

Given authority to determine appropriate bargaining units, the board was authorized to supervise elections and prohibit unfair employer practices. Encouraged when the legislation was upheld by the Supreme Court in 1937 and infuriated by AFL conservatism, industrial unionists broke with the Federation and established the Congress of Industrial Organizations. Since two of the most powerful unions founding the CIO, the Amalgamated Clothing Workers Union and the ILGWU, represented industries that were substantial employers of females, there could be little doubt that organization would be undertaken without regard to sex. Furthermore, the United Mine Workers' John L. Lewis, new CIO president, had long been sympathetic with working women, contributing annually to the WTUL, vigorously supporting equal pay in NRA codes, and enthusiastically championing the Women's Bureau. In a *New York Times* interview he committed the new organization to equal pay for "substantially the same work." As a result Mary Anderson and Mary Heaton Vorse both envisioned a better future for working women and the League executive board, although torn between the AFL and CIO, pledged itself to assist any group appealing for help.

One of the first major CIO drives was to recruit massive numbers of textile workers (39 percent of whom - about 428,000 - were female) and to equalize Northern and Southern wage scales. To achieve this, Lewis created the Textile Workers Organizing Committee. Under the direction of Sidney Hillman, whose Amalgamated Clothing Workers contributed $500,000 to a well-financed campaign chest, the committee eventually became a union itself, the Textile Workers Union of America. By 1941 it claimed 230,000 members and the UTW (AFL) declared 42,000, some of whom were recruited to counter the TWOC drive. Despite increased membership the campaign had succeeded only in part, for organizational efforts were checked in the cotton industry and thwarted in the South.

Southern gains, limited as they were, could not have been achieved without Lucy Randolph Mason, a deeply religious daughter of an Episcopal minister. At nineteen-years of age after teaching Sunday school to young, female, tobacco-field hands, she decided on a career improving working conditions. When appointed as CIO publicist to the TWOC campaign, she was general secretary of the National Consumers' League. Experienced in promoting the Union Label League, addressing union meetings, and campaigning for protective legislation, Mason had earlier served as industrial secretary of the Richmond YWCA and helped develop NRA codes for the textile industry.

Soon a familiar figure throughout the South, the white-haired, soft-spoken Mason travelled over 60,000 miles in her blue Plymouth coupe modifying opposition to the CIO campaign. Demanding from churchmen, newspaper editors, and police chiefs the right to organize, picket, and strike without interference, she based her case on NLRB and other federal rulings and exploited her impeccable Southern lineage, gentility, and wide range of Southern friends. Persuading many critics that the CIO drive was neither a Communist nor a Yankee conspiracy, she also relied on personal contacts including Eleanor Roosevelt, to whom she appealed for assistance on at least three occasions. Her gratitude for Roosevelt's support, including a Justice Department intervention in the case of a badly beaten organizer in Georgia, was such that she wrote: "What on earth would I do without you in the White House."

Displaying unusual courage, Mason was never deterred in her activities by threats or by the presence of violence. In 1937 she worked with Ida Sledge in Mississippi, after the latter had been threatened and run out of town and a male organizer beaten. Upon completion of the TWOC drive, Mason continued to head the Southeast public relations campaign for a total of seventeen years and was also a member of the CIO's Political Action Committee from 1941 to 1946.

Another contributing greatly to CIO organizational efforts was Rose Pesotta, who after being elected vice president of the ILGWU, undertook major campaigns in Buffalo, Puerto Rico, and Seattle, where in addition to management she contended with the negative attitudes of males who resented female unionists. At the request of the CIO and with the approval of the ILGWU, she assumed a leading role in the 1936 Goodyear Rubber Workers strike in Akron, imploring women to support their husband's efforts, addressing church and fraternal groups, raising money, and devising projects to maintain the morale of strikers. After victory in Akron, she organized automobile workers in Detroit and participated in sit-down strikes in Flint and Montreal. Pesotta then resumed her efforts for the ILGWU and led drives in Montreal, Cleveland, Boston, and Los Angeles, where as secretary of a general strike committee she was arrested. Resigning in 1944 as ILGWU vice president she returned to work as a sewing machine operator until illness forced her retirement.

Similar courage was exhibited by hundreds of women in CIO organizational drives. In North Chicago they picketed with striking husbands, and were gassed and beaten. At the Memorial Day 1937 Massacre at Chicago's Republic

Steel plant, women were at the head of the mass picket line when obsessed police fired into the demonstrators, seriously wounding one woman. A few weeks later, June 19 was proclaimed Women's Day by the striking steel workers in Youngstown, Ohio. In front of the gates of Republic, tear gas and shots were fired at massed female pickets, some of whom were accompanied by their children. Rushing from a union meeting, men joined the demonstration, and a general melee with the deputies followed, two strikers were killed and forty-two, several of whom were women, were injured. The following day the labor reporter Mary Heaton Vorse was herself wounded by gunshot.

Women contributed even more in building the United Auto Workers. About fifty of them established an auxiliary of wives, daughters, and female employees to support the striking males of the General Motors Michigan plants. During the violent days of 1936-1937, they distributed literature and ran around-the-clock picket lines. Their sex provided no protection from the plants' "bully boys," who assaulted them when provoked. These women also maintained soup kitchens, nursed casualties, ran a day care center for the children of striking mothers, and established a welfare committee and a speakers' bureau. Their commitment was best reflected in a verse of their theme song:

> The women got together and they formed a mighty throng,
> Every worker's wife and mom and sister will belong,
> They will fight beside the men to help the cause along,
> Shouting the Union forever!

Even more significant than the auxiliary was the Women's Emergency Brigade instituted by Genora Johnson, the twenty-three-year-old wife of one of the strikers. On short notice this semimilitary organization would mobilize thousands of women from Pontiac, Flint, Lansing, and Detroit, uniformed in berets and armbands whose colors identified their home city. Dispatched to weak or embattled points these fearless women were armed frequently with clubs and blackjacks. Creating a ruckus, they lured police to Chevrolet Plant 9 at Flint, so that male strikers could seize Plant 4, the key to the motor assembly division. On Woman's Day, about 7,000 marched through the streets of Flint surrounding Fisher Body Plant 1 in "one of the most amazing labor demonstrations ever seen in America."

Usually under colorful, flying banners, the brigade attempted to defend men from company police and scabs, often smashing windows at plants where police had used tear gas against the male sit-downers. Their actions not only kept the morale and determination of the striking men high, but also served as a sort of union consciousness-raising episode for many heretofore unconcerned women.

Encouragement was also given the male strikers by prominent women who appeared in Flint. Rose Pesotta obtained clothing for the pickets; Dorothy Day, Mrs. Gifford Pinchot, and Ellen Wilkinson, a Labour Party member of the British Parliament, met with some, and addressed others. Dorothy Thompson provided sympathetic press coverage.

Proving itself an effective weapon the sit-down strike rapidly spread across the United States. Frequently and successfully used in all types of firms by women, there were even sit-downs in Woolworth's and Grand's Five and Ten Cent Stores in New York where blankets, cots, guitars, and food (including fish on Friday for Roman Catholics) were passed to the striking "girls." Women adopted this technique in department stores, hosiery mills, drug companies, restaurants, cigar manufacturing plants, and hotels. In Detroit the police had to resort to tear gas to disperse them from a manufacturing plant.

One of the most prominent of the new CIO members was not recruited by the sit-down. When Eleanor Roosevelt began her daily column she joined the American Newspaper Guild, much to the chagrin of her conservative critic Westbrook Pegler. A few years later, she used her articles to urge workers to join unions. A favorite of the CIO, she was guest at its conventions in 1943, 1944, and 1945 where her addresses were warmly received, even when she appealed for women to be more active in unions and thereby achieve independence.

Another woman enthusiastically greeted by the CIO was Josephine Roche, who addressed the 1938 convention when she was chairperson of the President's Inter-Departmental Committee on Public Health and Industrial Hygiene. Introduced as "the greatest woman of our time in our country," Roche must have found the convention a reunion with old friends. A 1908 Vassar graduate with a master's degree in social work from Columbia, Roche, early in her life, had been engaged in a variety of social justice activities, including active membership in the WTUL and the National Consumers' League. Inheriting in 1927 the controlling interest in the Rocky Mountain Fuel Company, one of the largest producers of lignite coal in the United States, she quickly became president and general manager. Recognizing the UMW, she raised wages from $6.25

to $7.00 daily, and established a medical and sanitary department for employees and their dependents, jointly managed by the union and the company. She so thoroughly endorsed unionization that John R. Lawson, formerly of the Executive Board of the UMW, was made a second vice president. The company urged other firms to recognize the UMW but they failed to do so, and with the support of Colorado banks fought Rocky Mountain Fuel because of its liberal union practices. Nevertheless, the firm prospered, and Roche became the miners' idol.

Resigning from Rocky Mountain Fuel in 1934 to enter the federal department of the Treasury as assistant secretary in charge of public health, Roche helped organize emergency and long-range programs for the prevention of disease. She also served on the committee on Social Security, secured relief money for state health programs and industrial hygiene, and sometimes represented Henry Morgenthau at cabinet meetings. In order to run (unsuccessfully) in the Democratic primary for governor of Colorado, she resigned in 1937. Beginning a new career in 1946, she was appointed director of the UMW Welfare and Retirement Fund, capably supervising the pension and health benefits program and instituting UMW hospitals in the coal fields.[5]

Conventions may have had female guests, but until World War II, they seldom passed resolutions bearing on the difficulties of working women. Even the *CIO News* rarely published features or special articles on their problems (rather typically, though, it printed pin-up photos - usually of union girls). However, this type of inattention was relatively insignificant, for CIO drives and revitalized AFL efforts resulted in about 800,000 women union members by 1939, a sevenfold increase in six years, contrasted with that of males which had only tripled.

DOROTHY DAY: THE CATHOLIC WORKER MOVEMENT

Dorothy Day's Catholic Worker Movement was one of the most interesting groups to encourage unionization and aid workers, strikers, and the unemployed during the 1930s. Born in 1897, the daughter of a sportswriter father, Day left the University of Illinois after two nonconforming years as a Socialist. Obtaining her first job as a reporter, at the age of eighteen, for the Socialist *New York Call*, her radical leanings, as well as new friends like Elizabeth Gurley Flynn, attracted her into the IWW and, in the early 1920s, into Communism. Participating in a multitude of demonstrations she was arrested for picketing the White House with the Woman's Party on behalf of suffrage and was arrested again in Chicago when the police raided the Wobbly residence where she lived.

Born an Episcopalian, Day became increasingly attracted to Roman Catholicism. Her infant daughter (from a common law marriage) was baptized in that faith and she herself became a Catholic in 1927. For the next relatively quiet five years she supported herself through her writings and studiously explored her new religion.

In 1932 Peter Maurin, a French peasant, poet, and Roman Catholic social philosopher, convinced by her writings that Day would be sympathetic to his proposals, persuaded her to establish with him the Catholic Worker Movement, an "institution of radical personalist action." Grounded in the poverty, love and charity of Christ and the social encyclicals *Rerum Novarum* and *Quadragesimo Anno*, the organization revolved around the needs of workers and the poor, by providing for their dignity and material welfare and by participating with them and with unions in the creation of a new social order. Through discussions and lecture groups, houses of hospitality, and a Catholic workingman's newspaper, Day hoped that "Month by month, in every struggle, in every strike, we shall do our best to join with the worker in his struggle for recognition as a man and not as a chattel."

Selling for "a cent a copy," the newspaper, the *Catholic Worker*, for which Day chose the news, wrote the copy, and composed the editorials reached a circulation of 150,000 by 1936. Dedication to impoverished workers led to a commitment to racial equality, reflected in its masthead depicting a black and a white worker, and in articles defending the Scottsboro boys, attacking lynching, and denouncing racism. Supporting every liberal movement of the 1930s, the *Worker*, although anti-Communist, commiserated with the Communist dedication to social and working-class objectives.

To raise the consciousness of its readers, the *Worker* sympathetically covered just about all the major strikes of the 1930s, beseeching its audience to exercise moral responsibility by supporting workers and by boycotting the products of oppressive managements. As early as 1938, under Day's leadership, the paper began championing migratory workers, a cause for which she would be jailed for eleven days in 1973. Going beyond support of the traditional New Deal legislation and union membership, the paper advocated that employees "share in the ownership, management and profits of industry and business" as a means of ending bitterness and class war.

Somewhat suspicious of the AFL as an elitist, conservative organization, the *Worker* enthusiastically endorsed the new CIO, whose president, John L. Lewis, had captivated Day at their first meeting. Nevertheless, believing that the division was detrimental to American labor the journal urged a reunification of the unions. Pressing for better conditions for working women and covering women's strikes sympathetically, it also implored every Roman Catholic girl to join a union. Yet the newspaper reflected Day's rather traditional views on women. Notwithstanding that she herself was almost "pure action," Day had written: "Men who are revolutionaries . . . do not dally on the side as women do, complicating the issue by an emphasis on the personal." Thus the *Worker* asserted that the only reason females worked was to support a family, and that if men were paid adequate wages women's labors would be unnecessary.

The paper was but one aspect of the Catholic Worker Movement's service to American labor. At hospitality houses established by Day and Maurin for unemployed men and women free board was available. Forty of these houses throughout the nation by 1939 sheltered as many as 150 poor at a time and the first, in the New York slums, quartered the *Worker* staff, who were living in poverty as were the other volunteers. In addition to providing refuge for the unemployed, and relief for strikers, the houses rallied dispirited workers. For a month during the New York Seamen's strike of 1936-1937, the Worker Movement provided rooms for fifty strikers and served as many as one thousand meals a day. It set up kitchens for strikers in the mills of Lawrence and Lowell, Massachusetts the following year, and for the 1940 Bethlehem Steel strikers in Pennsylvania and provided room and board during the 1941 Seattle Machinists strike. Joining with pickets at New York department stores and five and tens, Catholic workers including Day herself, also organized steelworkers in Pennsylvania, biscuit workers in New York, stockyard workers in Chicago, and Day joined the 1937 sit-down strikers in the Automobile and steel industries. At the request of the Typographical Union, Catholic workers distributed literature in Springfield, Massachusetts, when an injunction prevented the strikers from doing so. Years later, in 1949, the *Worker* even assailed Francis Cardinal Spellman for his reactionary stand on striking Catholic cemetery workers.

Participation in labor disputes and organizational drives started to slacken after 1937 as the economy began to recover. Increasingly the movement came to emphasize pacifism, imploring workers not to manufacture war implements and encouraging conscientious objection. These trends persisted into the Cold War, when Day was arrested five times and imprisoned on four occasions for defying civil defense drills. During the Vietnamese war, several members of the Worker movement (contrary to Day's views) destroyed draft cards in order to protest American policy. Not as active in unionization as in the 1930s, the Worker organization continues to care for the poor and to assist the aged, the handicapped, and the unskilled.

NATIONAL DEFENSE

Diverting the efforts of the Worker movement toward pacifism, the approach of World War II encouraged other organizations to capitalize upon new industrial opportunities for women. Unlike the pre-World War I period, the WTUL supported preparedness and Roosevelt's internationalism, thereby avoiding the pacifist stigma that had crippled it two decades earlier. Reveling in women's job opportunities created by the defense industry the League urged unionization, pay and seniority equal with men and a full employment program, so that women would not be dismissed at the war's end. However, the League actually did little more than publicize these issues and hold rallies and meetings, for unions themselves organized women workers (many of whom were in jobs traditionally men's) and labor cooperated with government and industry thereby negating much of the League's mission. Furthermore, WTUL leadership was spread too thin to espouse new causes or to undertake new reforms. Schneiderman served as secretary of the State Department of Labor of New York until 1943 and Elisabeth Christman, the devoted executive secretary, who in the previous decade and a half had done even more than Schneiderman to make the organization viable, took a leave of absence to work as a troubleshooter for the Women's Bureau.

An ideal choice for this task, Christman was a former glove worker who with Agnes Nestor organized Local 1 of the International Glove Workers Union and served as its shop steward. A member of the War Labor Board during World War I, she became the international secretary-treasurer of the Glove Workers Union as well as an NRA advisory committee member. In her new position representing the Women's Bureau, she investigated working conditions of women in manufacturing plants and prevailed upon management and unions to agree to equal pay. A convincing and forceful woman, she was quite successful in persuading unions that the male wage scale would effectively be reduced if women were paid less than men and replaced by veterans at the conclusion of the war. Despite the significance of Christman's work and her achievements, Schneiderman refused to grant an extension to her leave of absence for the League's "very life" would be "in jeopardy" without her.

Even more determined than the League to exploit the wartime labor shortage for the advancement of females was the Women's Bureau which under Anderson's leadership attacked the reluctance of employers and unions to use women in war production jobs. As early as 1940, after consulting with female representatives from the Amalgamated Clothing Workers Union, International Association of Machinists, International Brotherhood of Electrical Workers, Steel Workers Organizing Committee, United Rubber Workers Union, and WTUL, Anderson drafted women's employment criteria for the federal government, state labor commissions, and unions themselves. A few months later she convinced male unions to force the National Defense Advisory Commission and the Office of Education to accept the right of women to be vocationally trained the same as men. Continuing to hammer away at any restrictions on women, the Bureau, nevertheless, insisted on the maintenance of proper norms, such as adequate rest rooms, lighting, and chairs.

To protect standards for working women the Bureau also cooperated with the War Manpower Commission and the War Labor Board. The former urged further recruiting of women, day care centers if necessary, and with the War Labor Board established a policy of equal pay. Because employers sometimes attempted to avoid this principle through arbitrary job classifications the Bureau persuaded many unions to incorporate nondiscriminatory provisions in contracts. To further protect women from prejudicial wage scales Anderson, after her resignation in 1944, chaired the Equal Pay Committee for federal legislation and was secretary of the National Committee to Defeat the Unequal Rights Amendment.

Continuing to advance Anderson's policies was her successor, Freida S. Miller, who taught at Bryn Mawr during World War I and functioned as secretary of the Philadelphia WTUL from 1918 to 1924. After moving to New York, she was for three years a factory inspector, two years a researcher in the Welfare Council of New York City, and for a decade director of the Division of Women in Industry of the New York State Department of Labor. Industrial Commissioner of New York State from 1938 to 1942, she was also special assistant on labor to the American ambassador to England, John Winant.

A vigorous supporter of equal pay and an opponent of the Equal Rights amendment, she distrusted unions less than Anderson believing as early as 1938 that collective bargaining and trade unions were the primary means of improving the status of American women. Beginning to work more closely with labor organizations she instituted a Labor Advisory Committee to the Women's Bureau in 1945. Composed of female unionists such as Dorothy Bellanca of the ACWU and Ruth Young of the United Electrical Workers Union, the women suggested policy positions and recommended areas of investigation for the Bureau, which in turn shared its data with unions. Under Miller, the Bureau also sponsored frequent conferences attended by union representatives. Some of the early gatherings dealt with Postwar Problems of Working Women, Employment Problems, and the Changing Role of Women.

Modified attitudes of American unions eased considerably the Bureau's task of protecting women workers. With over six million women newly employed because of the war the female labor force increased 50 percent, necessitating the organization of women if a viable trade union movement were to be preserved. Consequently membership drives increased the number of female union members from about 800,000 in 1939 to over 3 million in 1945. Not confining themselves merely to gathering members, many unions implemented special programs to protect their female constituents. AFL conventions exhorted the federal government to issue contracts only to employers who paid equal wages. Entreating the War Manpower Commission to maintain the principle of equal pay, they even endorsed federally assisted day care centers for the children of working mothers and cooperated with the WTUL in preserving protective laws and opposing the Equal Rights Amendment because it might invalidate them.

Also attempting to counter the misogyny of many unionists, the *American Federationist* featured women engaged in industrial work on its cover six times during the war years. In 1943 there was a special photo spread of World War I women industrial workers demonstrating that this was not a new experience for females. Stressing the necessity for working women to meet manpower requirements, articles and editorials pressed for unionization, and equal pay, and President Green advocated that "each defense area should plan for adequate day nurseries and nursery schools."

CIO conventions followed a similar course, urging equal pay, unionization, ending all discrimination, and full utilization of women's talents in unions. Its frequent support of day care centers for the children of working mothers was tempered by the caution that single women should be hired before women with children. Attacking the Equal Rights Amendment and referring to it as "bogus," Philip Murray's union chastised organized labor for not exposing vigorously enough the dangers in an amendment sponsored by "a group of rich and elderly upper crust women with nothing better to do," who were puppets for "sinister forces" desiring "to destroy all social legislation."

CIO conventions were more sympathetic to the sensibilities of women than were those of the AFL, repeatedly calling for women to have positions of responsibility and leadership in unions, and advocating state equal pay legislation. Contractual maternity benefits, and full cooperation with the Women's Bureau were among its resolutions. Furthermore, the CIO Political Action Committee sponsored a Conference on Full Employment in January 1944, headed by Dorothy Bellanca of the ACWA, Ruth Young of the UEW, and Jeanette Brown, Executive Secretary of the National Council of Negro Women. The conference pressed for adequate employment for women after the war, equal pay, child care, and total integration of females into unions. With the increase of distaff members, the *CIO News* added a Woman's Page, edited by the secretary-treasurer of the Women's Auxiliaries. Although similar to such pages in the regular press with dress patterns and recipes, the *News* frequently mentioned the need for additional women workers, postwar plans for women, and the status of child care proposals. In 1944 the column was used by the Political Action Committee to encourage the women's vote.

WARTIME ACTIVITIES

With the influx of women into war industries, many internationals abandoned their exclusionary policy and opened up membership to females. West Virginia United Mine Workers were persuaded by Elisabeth Christman not to strike over the employment of women, but instead accept them into the union. Insisting that locals admit women and modify seniority rules if necessary to do so, the Mine, Mill and Smelter Workers' convention of 1942, however, strongly advised adopting policies to ensure female membership would not deprive returning veterans of jobs. With 5,000 women employed in welding and hundreds more scheduled to be hired, over two-thirds of the membership of the Brotherhood of Boiler Makers voted affirmatively on a government request to admit women. By war's end, all AFL and CIO unions had admitted women and only one, the Brotherhood of Bookbinders, still had a separate women's organization.

The increase in female union membership was accompanied by the assumption of more responsible positions. Typical of emerging female leadership in locals was Mrs. Herschel Davis, a drill press operator in an auto plant in Indiana. Joining a United Auto Workers local in 1941 Davis was elected vice president in 1943, and assumed the presidency when the incumbent was drafted. By 1947 she had negotiated four contracts and won wage increases and fringe benefits without a strike. Other women held national positions. In 1941 Kathryn Lewis, John L.'s daughter, was chosen secretary-treasurer of District 50 UMW (all miners in fields other than coal), and Pauline Newman served the ILGWU as educational director of the union health center, where 200 physicians, nurses, and pharmacists staffed a clinic for women tailors. Representing the AFL on the National Women's Advisory Committee of the War Manpower Commission was Jennie Matyas, manager of the Knit Goods Workers in San Francisco. Gladys Dickason's contributions to the Amalgamated Clothing Workers were such that, following the war in 1946, she was elected vice president, the highest union office of any female in the nation. Holder of an economics Ph.D., she was the union's director of research from 1935 to 1954, organized shirt workers in Troy in 1941, was assistant director of the CIO's postwar organizational drive in the South, and was the only woman in *Fortune Magazine's* list of the ten most efficient labor leaders in the country.

Responding to the needs of their female members, unions began to bargain collectively to eliminate wage differentials. AFL organizers in the California canning industry negotiated equal pay contracts as early as 1941, and the CIO Steel Workers Organizing Committee eliminated wage differentials for 6,500 women that ran from five cents to as much as twenty cents an hour. United Automobile Workers in 1941 struck the Kelsey-Hayes Wheel Company machine gun plant in Detroit because women were paid only eighty-five cents an hour compared with one dollar for men. Albeit motivated chiefly by a desire to protect men's wages, the UAW was usually solicitous of its women members, studying and responding to their needs, and in 1945 warning locals that women's seniority rights must have the same protection and backing as men's. As early as 1941 the UAW began advocating the inclusion of sex and age provisions in the nondiscriminatory clause of Executive Orders dealing with fair employment, and a few years later at its fourteenth convention, pledged that pay, hiring, promotions, and seniority rights would be equal. Insisting that locals were not to allow wage differentials based on sex, the UAW empowered its Women's Bureau to supervise this program, conduct an educational campaign, provide consultants on contracts pertaining to women, and to publish a special bulletin for distaff members.

Apparently, women's response to the feminist orientation of the UAW was wanting. Addressing the New York WTUL in 1943, President R.J. Thomas claimed that women accepted the advantages of union membership, but rejected responsibilities by begrudging dues and refusing an active role in union affairs. Supporting the charge were many women unionists, but Thomas was probably more frustrated than they for the UAW and United Electrical Workers had pushed the equal pay ruling through the War Labor Board.

Very sensitive to the needs of the 683,000 women comprising 40 percent of its 1944 membership was the UEW, whose Woman's conference in 1941 endorsed equal pay, higher minimum wages for both sexes, industrial training for women, maternity leave, and equal representation of women in union activities. Establishing child care, recreational and housing programs for its members the UEW requested that stores extend their hours for the shopping convenience of women workers. In all major and most minor contracts it negotiated equal pay agreements, and frequently incorporated maternity leave provisions without loss of wages. Of its national full-time organizers 35 percent were female, furthermore, the union encouraged locals to select women as shop stewards and presidents.

Union growth did not mean a proportional increase in labor turbulence for in keeping with the defense effort wartime strikes were held to a minimum, but when they occurred women members participated and sometimes assumed the leadership as in the 1941 Los Angeles North American Aviation plant. Striking in New York for seven months in 1940-1941 were about 1,700 members of the International Brotherhood of Electrical Workers many of whom were women. They demanded union recognition, minimum wage, and a forty-hour week. Rose Schneiderman, Mrs. Henry Morgenthau, and Eleanor Roosevelt visited with the demonstrators and addressed their rally. Informing the workers that it was Schneiderman who had educated her in unionism, the president's wife exhorted everyone to join a union and expressed her gratitude for efforts of strikers to make life better for all Americans. Probably the largest wartime women's strike was that of the telephone operators in 1944. Beginning in Dayton, Ohio, it was triggered by the company's decision not to raise the basic wage rate but to offer an $14.25 weekly expense bonus to women transferring from small towns to war production centers. The walkout spread throughout Ohio to Detroit and Washington ending with War Labor Board intervention before it could reach other cities.

Despite improving attitudes, working women still suffered injustices, many deliberately overlooked or even encouraged by union locals. According to some observers the rank and file of union members really were opposed to the employment of women believing that, regardless of the wartime emergency, they still belonged in the home instead of working for "pin money." In keeping with these views locals allowed seniority discrimination and frequently circumvented equal pay by negotiating wage differentials under a job classification system or by accepting lesser wages for women when they worked in a shop separate from men. Assailing unions for these injustices and charging locals with using women's wages as a negotiating pawn, the WTUL still pressed unions to regard women as homemakers as well as workers and to undertake special programs for them such as day care, housing, and education. There was even a note of surrender in Rose Pesotta's resignation as ILGWU vice president: "Ten years in office had made it clear to me that a lone woman vice president could not adequately represent the women who now make up 85 percent of the International's membership of 305,000."

Overall, the war had transformed the attitudes of many trade union leaders, who not only came to accept women in the work force but learned that they could be employed in large numbers without reducing the prevailing wage scales, and that seniority based on sex endangered the entire system. Furthermore, many of these leaders had begun to bargain collectively for such "typically" female demands as rest periods and clean washrooms, thereby broadening their whole range of negotiating items. But even more dramatic than the change in attitude of union leaders was the change in women's attitudes toward work. Of the almost six million women who entered the work force, it was frequently reported the overwhelming majority, about 75 percent, hoped to continue their employment after the emergency. Even more startling was the attitude of married women, 23 percent of whom worked and of those, 57 percent planned to continue after the war. Consequently the Women's Bureau, women unionists, and the WTUL agitated for postwar planning that would take into account this phase of the women's revolution.

Chapter 12

THE PERSISTENT REVOLUTION [1]

At the conclusion of World War II, skilled women, replaced by returning veterans in better paying jobs, eased less skilled workers from their positions. However, unlike World War I a large percentage of women continued in the labor force. Although 3.25 million left work between September 1945 and November 1946, nearly 2.75 million were hired, for a net decline of only 600,000. By 1947 the percentage of working females not only exceeded that of 1940, but continued to increase, as did the percentage of married women workers. With the outbreak of the Korean War in 1950, it was easier for men to accept women on the assembly line, for women had come to look on work as more than temporary. Once begun, it was to be interrupted only to establish a home and raise children, and then be resumed several years later. World War II tolerance of women's work as patriotic, was followed by an inflation necessitating female labor for most middle-class families. Both events had combined to make the working female an integral part of American life.

POSTWAR LABOR DISPUTES

Like her prewar sister, the new woman frequently participated in labor struggles, displaying courage and fortitude as she joined with working men in organizational drives and in the rash of postwar strikes. Both the CIO (Textile Workers Union of America) and the AFL (United Textile Workers) launched major campaigns in the South. Like those of the 1930s they were followed by strikes and violence, for management retorted with scabs, sheriff's deputies, state police, and militia. Women pickets, beaten and gassed, continued to demonstrate even in the face of gun battles, assaults, and kidnapping of female organizers. Yet despite such heroism, organizational gains were infinitesimal. By 1952 textile unionism in the South was again on the defensive.

Courage was displayed not only by Southerners, but was also demonstrated by twelve women pickets in a 1951 Philadelphia textile strike. As they pleaded with a truck driver not to cross their picket line, the manufacturer pushed the driver aside. Muttering that he would get through "if he had to kill them all," the manager drove into the women and seriously injured three of them.

Perhaps not as dramatic, but still an inspiring example of human persistence, was the Kohler Manufacturing strike in Wisconsin. This 1954 dispute was in many ways a continuation of a lengthy and bitter walkout begun in 1934 as a result of deplorable working conditions. In July of that tumultuous year four strikers were killed and all during the summer and fall under the dynamic inspiration of Maud McCreery, editor of the Sheboygan *New Deal*, women workers and wives picketed and as a result were clubbed and gassed along with their men. After the company union won an election (probably rigged) in September 1934, the strike was virtually broken. Appealing for a national boycott of Kohler products the workers maintained only a skeleton crew of pickets until 1941, when the strike was officially called off. Postwar difficulties began when the new United Automobile Workers local attempted to obtain recognition and negotiate wage and pension grievances (women employees had objected particularly to the lack of provisions for maternity leave). For several years women workers and men picketed the plant and stumped the country, urging a boycott of Kohler products while a Ladies Auxiliary performed clerical work, raised funds, and ran soup kitchens. Kohler was ordered to rehire 1,700 strikers in 1960, when the National Labor Relations Board found the company guilty of unfair labor practices and of prolonging the strike. The union called off the walkout, but victory was not really achieved until 1965, when the company, after exhausting all legal appeals, finally made a $4.5 million back pay settlement.

Another dispute exemplifying the resoluteness and courage of women workers was in the laundry and dry cleaning industry in Boise, Idaho. Unorganized underpaid victims of lengthy hours and deplorable conditions were on strike for two months before the union sent organizers and relief funds. Using children as strike-breakers, management was able to delay a settlement for two years, nevertheless, women won a forty-hour week, a seventy-five cent hourly wage, and adequate rest rooms.

But an increasingly technological society impaired the effectiveness of the traditional strike. Nowhere was this more apparent than among telephone company employees. Unionism in the American Telephone and Telegraph Company had been virtually crushed during the 1920s by management opposition and the weakness of the International Brotherhood of Electrical Workers. Encouraged by the Wagner Act and the ensuing decline of company unions, delegates from forty-two labor organizations in that massive conglomerate established the National Federation of Telephone Workers in 1939. After achieving a modicum of recognition from the War Labor Board, the Federation supported a general strike in 1947 of 350,000 to obtain industry-wide collective bargaining and a wage increase. In spite of the bitterness and vastness of the walkout, violence was at a minimum; however, many strikers were jailed or fined including three women leaders in New Jersey. Government pressure, adverse public reaction, and acceptable offers from regional branches of the telephone company compelled the NFTW, a month after the strike began, to allow affiliates to settle individually. There really was little alternative, for each member organization, according to the federation's constitution, was "forever autonomous."

To eliminate this weakness the NFTW reorganized into the Communications Workers of America wherein affiliates were grouped into divisions and subjected to central control on strike and contract issues. President of the revised union was the young and liberal Joseph Beirne, one of its founders and former NFTW president. Beginning to emphasize governmental protection as well as collective bargaining the CWA supported political candidates and championed federal legislation on behalf of workers. The new direction was not taken because the CWA was primarily a women's union for Beirne was convinced of the loyalty, energy, and militancy of its members, and believed that any difference between his and men's unions had to be "resolved in favor of the women." However, during an eleven-week walkout against Southern Bell in 1955, large numbers of strikers and pickets, due to automation were unable to prevent the completion of phone calls. Urging then that strikes be deemphasized Beirne advocated the reconstruction of all unions so as to participate more fully in the economic, intellectual, and especially political life of the nation.

Decreased effectiveness of strikers was not the major reason for inconsequential postwar gains toward the goal of working women's equality. Despite the increasing numbers and stability of females in the work force, justification for their employment was still based on necessity, not on their right to work, for the notion that women belonged at home competed with the desire for middle-class living standards that rationalized their employment. Even Alice K. Leopold, President Dwight Eisenhower's director of the Women's Bureau, reenforced traditional shibboleths by informing a press conference that: "After all, the most important function of a woman is to run a home, be a mother, and contribute to the life of her family and community." Furthermore, society was warned of dire consequences if females ignored these duties. Dr. Eli Ginzberg of Columbia University, a consultant to the Child Study Association of America and director of staff studies for the National Manpower Council's study on womanpower, charged that as a result of women's work, families suffered from psychological strain. Daughters were denied any clear image of a woman's role, fathers and husbands "resented" and "suffered" from being forced to modify demands on working wives, and mothers would be susceptible to mental ills later in life. Such views led to renewed demands to curtail the number of working women during the recession of 1958.

With these schizophrenic attitudes prevalent among many educated Americans, it is little wonder that as early as 1945 union leaders had to contest their own membership in order to secure or preserve equal pay and equal job opportunities for women. Lower echelon male unionists were so role conscious that the AFL's Women's Auxiliary president reproved husbands for being reluctant to let wives participate in that organization. Male predelictions also resulted in innumerable cases of pay discrimination for females as only about one-quarter of collective bargaining contracts included equal pay provisions. Locals, even in such traditionally liberal and feminist unions as the ILGWU, constantly flouted national policy by signing discriminatory wage agreements. As late as 1962 one Pennsylvania union circumvented the state equal pay law in its contract thereby forcing thirty-eight female employees of the Continental Can Company to seek relief in the courts.

EQUAL PAY LEGISLATION

Increasingly frustrated by both management and locals, women's organizations and unions rallied behind equal pay legislation first introduced in Congress in 1945. To develop a program designed to eliminate discrimination, a two day conference of female unionists was conducted by the Women's Bureau the following year. It was agreed to encourage union support for equal pay measures and have the Bureau undertake a publicity campaign on their behalf. Annually thereafter the Bureau agitated for this reform, frequently publicizing it through national conferences and even pressuring Eisenhower to include equal pay in his 1956 State of the Union Address. The National Federation of Business and Professional Women's Clubs and the Women's Trade Union League also enthusiastically endorsed the measure.

Concerned with justice for women and the unskilled, the CIO recommended at its 1945 convention, and annually thereafter, that collective bargaining agreements include equal pay clauses. Representatives of that union and its affiliates, including officers of the United Automobile Workers, Amalgamated Clothing Workers, International Union of Electrical, Radio, and Machine Workers, and Communications Workers of America, frequently testified before congressional committees for such legislation. AFL conventions also upheld equal pay but only through collective bargaining agreements. This method, the Federation alleged, was the quickest way to obtain the objective and would preclude unnecessary and impractical governmental interference. However, when the AFL and the CIO merged in 1957, the CIO position on the issue prevailed. In December 1955 the Joint Resolutions Committee recommended that officers of each union study equal pay legislation to determine appropriate action. The following year the Executive Council endorsed it; thereafter, until its passage, each AFL-CIO convention sanctioned such measures.

Political support for equal pay also mushroomed. From 1948 until the enactment of the bill, Democratic and Republican platforms favored it in principle, usually in the form of federal legislation. President Eisenhower, calling the proposal a matter of justice, included it on his list of priority measures and President Kennedy described it as "essential" at the first meeting of his Commission on the Status of Women.

By 1962 many groups had rallied behind the concept. At that year's Senate hearings, administration and labor spokesmen and representatives of the National Federation of Business and Professional Women's Clubs, the American Civil Liberties Union, and the National Consumers' League testified for the measure. Claiming that federal legislation was unwise and detrimental to women, the bill's major opponent, the Chamber of Commerce of the United States, further asserted that if employers had to pay equal wages they would hire males in preference to females. Such testimony only confirmed that women, earning an average wage less than two-thirds that of men, with starting salaries lagging behind as much as $50 to $100 a month, were deliberately exploited. Of 24.5 million women workers, only 3.5 million were protected by collective bargaining agreements, consequently, both President Kennedy and the AFL-CIO hailed passage of a federal law in 1963 as a landmark for human rights.

Because the Equal Pay Act was based on the Fair Labor Standards Act of 1938, it did not protect millions of employees in agriculture, hotel, restaurant, laundry, small establishments, administrative, and management positions. However, amendments in 1972 and 1974 extended coverage to nearly all workers including administrators and most domestic servants. Furthermore, after filing its first suit in 1971, the Department of Labor has won an overwhelming majority of cases against violators, recovering over $75 million in back pay.

Fear that the influx of women workers during World War II would undercut men's wages contributed substantially to equal pay proposals. These same trepidations led to the massive organizational drives that increased female union membership threefold and thereby undermined the rationale of the WTUL. Consequently that organization began to emphasize "public relations" at the expense of unionization. By 1947 neither AFL nor CIO representatives mentioned organizational activities in their address to the League convention. James Carey of the CIO even urged the WTUL to concentrate on encouraging housewives to become active in political, economic, and consumer problems of the nation.

DISBANDING THE WTUL

Perennial financial difficulties precluded the League from effectively implementing any new program, for on more than one occasion it was unable to pay the executive secretary her salary. It also lacked the resources to put into effect a convention resolution creating a national advisory committee of trade union and professional women to develop contacts with unorganized females. Funding from hard-pressed trade unions was chimerical for according to the League's president, union officials failed to realize the importance of having an organization "to interpret trade unions to women, both in and outside the labor movement."

In the spring of 1950, with a sense of pride in past achievements and a note of sorrow for unrealized goals, the WTUL's national office disbanded because most of its functions had been assumed by the labor movement. However, it expressed the hope that action would be taken by unions in those areas left incomplete: protection of migratory workers and household employees, equal pay for women, and the entry of females into positions of responsible union leadership. After the demise of the national League, locals rapidly closed; the last was in New York, whose women's clubhouse ceased activity in 1955.

Although the League believed that most of its functions had been assumed by unions, the attitude of the AFL toward women workers had not undergone any fundamental change. It fought the Equal Rights Constitutional Amendment, because by endangering protective legislation that proposal challenged the position of working women as "mothers - actual or potential." Along with the CIO it censured Alice Leopold, director of the Women's Bureau, for abandoning that agency's opposition to the amendment, nevertheless, it urged women workers not to depend upon legislation for protection but rather upon the unions. President Green claimed that women and unions needed each other and repeatedly urged women to join. However, little was done to encourage their membership other than to exhort affiliates to provide special organizational programs for them and to include equal pay in collective bargaining agreements.

CHANGING UNION ATTITUDES

On the other hand, CIO conventions, continuing to show awareness of the needs of women, endorsed equal promotional and seniority rights, recommended maternity leaves in contracts, legislation for equal property rights, full custodial rights for children, and tax deductions for child care. A Women's Status bill was supported that would commit the nation to an anti-discrimination policy by prohibiting sex bias in federal law and by authorizing a presidential women's commission. (The commitment was more apparent than real, since the measure allowed exceptions on the grounds of biological differences and social function.) Like the AFL, the CIO encouraged female unionists, as well as the wives and daughters of male members, to engage actively in politics. Furthermore, it urged affiliates to draw women into active participation in locals, including positions as union officers.

But Victorian attitudes limited even the CIO's vision. An article in the *CIO News* promoting women for union leadership positions concluded with the banality: "Women are known to be more emotional than men and this very emotionalism can give them the fire and power which will be a great benefit."

Instead of supporting equal pay and seniority rights as a matter of justice, conventions emphasized their relationship to male wages and seniority and justified an increase in Social Security benefits to decrease the necessity of working wives.

As the two major federations inched toward acceptance of women workers, some of their affiliates approached that goal more rapidly. President Beirne of the Communications Workers of America was one of the first union leaders to testify for equal pay, and at the 1951 CWA convention the number of male and female delegates was identical. Another early supporter of non-discriminatory wage legislation was the International Union of Electrical, Radio and Machine Workers, whose president, James Carey, testified before the 1962 congressional hearing. Encouraging contracts with special benefits for females, the IUE also hosted a 1957 working women's conference stressing their right to qualify for all occupations. Its rival, the United Electrical Workers whose constitution called for the unity of all workers regardless of sex, also supported equal pay during the same period, winning, in 1961, over $87,000 in back wages for female employees of the Allen Bradley plant in Milwaukee. At the first conference sponsored by any major union on the problems of women the UEW emphasized that in 1953 women should hold positions of leadership in unions, committed itself to the support of day care centers, and began a campaign to publicize the needs of working women.

Equally concerned with its female members the United Packinghouse Workers of America in 1954 forced American Sugar to return women to the so-called "male jobs" from which they had been displaced at the conclusion of the Korean War, resulting in a twenty cent hourly wage restoration. In addition to sponsoring three National Women's Activities conferences during the 1950s, the UPWA required all locals to develop woman leadership programs and to make a sincere effort to include a proportional number of both sexes in all delegations, committees, and local activities.

New organizational drives, frequently in industries that employed large numbers of females resulted from the merger of the AFL and the CIO. Over $2 million was spent on a successful twenty-one-month strike of chambermaids, waitresses, housemen, and bellmen in luxury Miami hotels. As the Southern textile industry resisted efforts of the merged unions the organizational campaign ultimately centered around the Harriet-Henderson Mills in North Carolina. When the company insisted that it be permitted to veto union arbitrable requests the largest strike in the twenty-four year history of the Textile Workers

Union of America began in 1959. Under the existing contract, there had been an average of only one case of arbitration a year, but management still claimed that the process encroached upon its time and disrupted their authority. Despite large numbers of male and female pickets, the plant reopened with scab labor under the protection of state troopers. Violence abounded in the area. Boyd Payton, TWUA regional director was beaten in his hotel room; his assailants were never found. However, Payton, a Presbyterian elder, was easily convicted of conspiracy to damage the company's property, and sentenced from six to ten years on the testimony of a paid hoodlum, clandestinely employed by the state bureau of investigation. After two and a half years and expenditures of over $15 million, the strike was officially called off by a defeated and demoralized union with only 90 of 1,038 workers rehired, unions were on the defensive throughout the South.

The South's successful fight against unionization helps to explain the numerical imbalance between men and women union members. As most of the new employees in Southern manufacturing plants were nonunion females the increase in the work force was not matched by a proportional increase in female union members.

Even more significant in accounting for sexual disparity in national membership was the phenomenal postwar growth of white collar and service industries, both largely female and traditionally hard to organize. By 1956, for the first time in American history, if not in the history of the industrial world, white collar workers outnumbered blue collar workers. Achieving notable success in unionizing some of these employeees, was the American Federation of Teachers, for postwar belligerency stimulated new membership and promoted substantial gains in that profession. But other efforts to organize this changing work force failed, consequently many labor leaders feared that unless new approaches were found, unions would represent only a dwindling minority of American workers and thereby lose their influence.

Continuing to press for organizational campaigns directed at women the newly merged AFL-CIO held that unions were essential for women's "advancement" and "human dignity," and urged affiliates to include maternity leave provisions in collective bargaining agreements, to seek the cooperation of local communities and governmental agencies in the establishment of child care facilities, and to include full participation of women in union affairs. At the same time, the AFL-CIO looked to the federal government for assistance in protecting the rights of women workers, suggesting increased appropriations for the Women's

Bureau and advocating a study of existing protective legislation. It endorsed the recommendations of Kennedy's Commission on the Status of Women and appealed to the President to issue executive orders preventing sexual discrimination in governmental contracts. Although women constituted one-third of the work force, and the AFL-CIO exhorted locals to utilize female talents, only a disproportionate number achieved leadership positions. Surveying its membership in 1957, the Building Service Employees International Union found that 187 women were local officers or business agents and only fifteen of these were presidents, and most were participants in the smaller locals. The Union viewed this neither as a problem nor as a starting point, but as an achievement. In the same year President George Meany expressed pride that women held 200 full-time administrative positions, hundreds of regional officers, and thousands of local presidencies in the AFL-CIO. Aware that this representation was inadequate he attributed it to the traditional union method of promoting from within, a system that decreased the opportunities for women relatively new to unions.

Nevertheless scores of women did hold highly visible positions in the trade union movement. Among these were Gertrude Lane, a founder of Local 6 of the Hotel and Club Employees Union, with a membership of 27,000, the largest culinary local in the country. Lane served as organizer and was a labor member of the New York State Hotel Minimum Wage Board. One of the most visible officers, Bessie Hillman, was elected vice president of the Amalgamated Clothing Workers Union in 1946 after the death of her husband. This was more than a sympathetic gesture to a grieving widow, for she had helped lead strikes as early as 1910, in the 1930s she organized shirtworkers in Connecticut, Pennsylvania, and New York, and from 1937 to 1944 she was educational director of the Laundry Workers Joint Board. As vice president, Hillman directed her efforts to the educational program, encouraged young women to leadership careers in trade unions, and was appointed to the subcommittee of President Kennedy's Commission on the Status of Women. Caroline Davis, the director of the Women's Bureau of the United Auto Workers, was an example of leadership developing from within the ranks. In 1941 she recruited her fellow employees at an Elkart, Indiana auto plant into the UAW, and then became negotiator, vice president, and president of the local she had founded. In 1948 she was appointed to the bureau by Walter Reuther to formulate women's programs and to help provide contract coverage for equal pay, maternity leave, and seniority.

Several years later, Lillian Roberts of Chicago was the first black woman elected vice president of an international. After twelve years of membership, she was elevated to that office in the Federation of State County and Municipal Employees. Yet she continued to walk picket lines and to rally labor forces in a strike against the New York City Welfare Department.

THE NEW FEMINISM

Union reluctance to struggle for women's benefits and the absence of federal legislation to promote equality increasingly became a matter of concern as women's attitude toward work changed. By the mid-50s married and single women viewed employment as a means of providing personal and social worth and a degree of independence. This was especially true of the more educated who found recognition, achievement, and psychological satisfaction in work and younger women who began employment with the conviction that they would work most of their lives, except for a few child-bearing years. These new attitudes were reflected in a Women's Bureau study showing that labor turnover was based not on sex, but on age, skill level required for the job, and the workers' length of service.

As this "new working woman" emerged and feminism reappeared in the late 1950s and 1960s, critics tended to ignore the advances of the employed female and focused instead on inequalities and injustices. Statistical studies emphasizing pay differentials and the limitations in mobility, opportunities, and advancement, also revealed the decline in the percentage of professionally employed women. Increases in service, white collar, semiskilled, and unskilled jobs, traditionally women's, reduced their average income in relationship to that of men.

Even federal equal pay legislation in 1963 was unable to reverse this trend for the disparity between male and female wages has increased. In 1955 women's earnings were 64 percent that of men, however, by 1961 they had dropped to about 59 percent where they have remained since. Some of this differential is attributable to the concentration of women workers in low paying jobs in low paying industries and a reduction in the percentage of women employed in professional and technical positions. However, both the Manpower Report of the President and the President's Council of Economic Advisors have attributed a significant proportion of the gap to sexual discrimination, as did the EEOC in its 1980 study.

Unions were attacked for slighting and even for discriminating against women. Elizabeth Pidgeon, of the Women's Bureau, as early as 1947 pointed out that unions still did not record membership by sex. Eleanor Flexner's scholarly study on the history of American women, *Century of Struggle*, assailed unions for their disregard of female members and the absence of female leadership. Even Bessie Hillman was uncomfortable over their token numbers at conventions and absence from key positions. Some critics urged women to fight union prejudice through a more vigorous and aggressive membership and many female members made known their resentment at the tendency of males to "talk at" them during union meetings, demanding that locals undertake meaningful women's programs.

Moved by the seriousness of these charges Esther Peterson, director of the Women's Bureau, persuaded President Kennedy in 1961 to establish the President's Commission on the Status of Women to recommend programs to "demolish prejudices and outmoded customs" impeding full realization of women's rights. Verifying the deplorable status of women the commission suggested the extension of equal pay protection, increased minimum wage, executive orders to equalize employment opportunities, paid maternity leaves, and state legislation to extend equal pay and to protect the rights of workers to join unions.

CIVIL RIGHTS ACT OF 1964

The commission's damning report, the precedent of federal equal pay legislation, and the growing political power of women contributed to a major legislative triumph for working females. During the debate over Title VII of the Civil Rights Bill of 1964, prohibiting racial discrimination in employment, Representative Howard Smith (Democrat, Virginia), an opponent of the measure, introduced an amendment to add the word "sex" to the equal employment provisions. Several congresswomen rallied to his support and only one, Edith Green (Democrat, Oregon) objected, claiming that it was not the "time or the place" for such a proposal.

If the amendment were introduced in an effort to defeat the bill, as has been charged, the stratagem failed. No substantive arguments were offered against Smith's addition, and President Lyndon B. Johnson endorsed it at a press conference. The amendment passed 168 to 133, and the amended bill was enacted by a vote of 290 to 130 in the House and 73 to 27 in the Senate.

Under Title VII most unions and employers (except for government and educational institutions) were prohibited from discriminating on the basis of race, color, religion, or sex. This safeguard was to be administered by a five-member Equal Employment Opportunity Commission (EEOC) appointed by the President. Upon receiving complaints, the EEOC was authorized to investigate and seek compliance through the use of "informal methods of conference, conciliations and persuasion." If unable to obtain acquiescence it could *recommend* that the Attorney General's office institute a law suit on behalf of the aggrieved, an option also available to the individual complainant. However, the measure did permit an employer to discriminate when sex was considered a reasonably necessary qualification to a particular business enterprise, a "bona fide occupational qualification" (bfoq).

Enforcement of the legislation was at best cumbersome, at worst reluctant. Title VII has had no visible effect on the widening wage gap between men and women. Women earn 40 percent less than men, and although their number in the labor force has doubled in the last twenty-five years, 70 percent are in traditionally female jobs with occupational segregation greater now than at the end of the nineteenth century. Six years after the enactment of the Civil Rights law, a study conducted by the American Society for Personnel Administration and the Bureau of National Affairs concluded that one-half of all companies disqualified women from certain jobs, usually on grounds of physical strength. Even the authors of the 1973 Economic Report of the President felt compelled to comment on the "striking" low representation of women in positions of responsibility, concluding that there was no drastic change from 1950 to 1970 in occupational segregation by sex and expressed the belief in 1974 that the amount of job segregation by sex was greater than by race.

Embarrassing to labor was the Department of Justice's first suit under Title VII in 1970 charging Libby Owen Ford Glass Company and Local 9 of the United Glass and Ceramic Workers with entering into collective bargaining agreements establishing seniority, promotion, demotion, and layoff procedures detrimental to female employees. Five months later, the case was settled by a consent decree amid accusations by women activists that the Department of Justice had "sold out." Aggrieved female employees, often with the support of NOW (National Organization for Women), undertook their own suits against unions. Among the most significant, was the case in 1969 against Local 15 of the International Chemical Workers Union and the Colgate Palmolive Company. The defendants were charged with cooperating in a system of job classification depriving women of work opportunities and subjecting them to discriminatory layoffs. Compensation for the women and changes in company procedures were required by the appeals court. Although the union was not found liable the court asserted that it "was not entirely blameless in permitting discrimination to exist and could have worked harder to eliminate the residual and continuing effects of the blatant prior discrimination."

Apparently receptive to the protections guaranteed racial minorities by the Civil Rights Act, union reaction toward sex provisions was ambivalent. In a rather lengthy analysis of the measure, the *American Federationist* merely mentioned that it applied to women. For four and a half years after the bill was passed, that journal did not publish any articles on women workers, nor did it devote any special attention to them in its features on organizing. Its first piece on females after passage of the Civil Rights Law dealt with women's auxiliaries and was written in 1969 by a staff member of the Department of Public Relations. Assuming that the normal women's role was homemaking, the author sought to glamorize the task by stressing the old maxim that to educate a man was to educate an individual, but to educate a woman was to educate a whole family. AFL-CIO conventions, fearful that Title VII would invalidate protective legislation, sought to retain these laws through the application of bfoq exemptions. Resolutions were passed endorsing protective legislation for both sexes and urging child care centers and tax deductions for child care. Conventions also pressed for expanded organizational efforts directed toward women and counseled affiliates to encourage female participation in policy-making positions.

Some unions did utilize civil rights provisions to champion the cause of women members, the UTW filed complaints with the EEOC when individual members failed to do so, an action upheld by the Eighth Circuit Court. A suit was initiated by the IUE against the General Electric Company claiming its policy of providing males with sick pay while denying females maternity benefits was in violation of Title VII. (Provision for maternity benefits was later incorporated into EEOC guidelines, however, the Supreme Court in 1976 defied the Commission, overturned six U.S. Courts of Appeals and found for General Electric.) As a result of the unions charge of a sex discriminatory classification system, General Electric in 1974 was ordered to increase wages $700,000 for 1,650 employees. On the other hand, the CWA fought the EEOC case against American Telephone and Telegraph Company. When the Department of Labor forced that firm to pay $15 million to 15,000 women and minority workers for "pervasive and systematic discrimination," the union objected that the agreement infringed upon collective bargaining rights.[2] A flagrant defiance was that of the Teamsters and fifteen building trades unions accused in 1976 by the Civil Rights Commission of discrimination resulting in reduced wages for women and minorities.

Weaknesses of the Civil Rights Act were attacked by many women's groups, including the Citizen's Advisory Council on the Status of Women, an organization appointed in compliance with recommendations of the 1963 President's Commission on Women. Under pressure from these associations changes were gradually made wherein the EEOC revised guidelines on discrimination because of sex. After examining state protective legislation the commission in 1969 ruled such laws irrelevant in a modern technological society and in conflict with Title VII. Guidelines also narrowed the application of sex as a "bona fide occupational qualification" to positions where "it is necessary for the purpose of authenticity or genuineness."

In 1972 the Employment Opportunity Act strengthened the EEOC, authorizing it to initiate action without awaiting complainants, to recommend legal proceedings to the Justice Department, and extending its jurisdiction to practically the entire labor force. New guidelines the same year prohibited employers from denying females jobs because of pregnancy and provided that disabilities relating to pregnancy, miscarriage, and abortion, would be treated as any other illness for purposes of leave time, seniority, reinstatement, and insurance payments. They also disallowed restrictions on the employment of married women and extended to males laws providing benefits for females, such as rest periods.

TRIBULATIONS OF THE EEOC

Despite these improvements, equality for working women still remains a tenuous proposition. EEOC does not have the authority to issue cease and desist orders, and although influential in the courts, guidelines do not have the force of law and have been disregarded by the Supreme Court. Dependent on sympathetic administrators and adequate financing it has not been very successful in protecting women's rights. One of its earliest appointees, Aileen Hernandez, quit in frustration, charging that the agency, headed by an executive director who made sexist jokes, had little if any commitment to preventing sex discrimination. Due to the pressure of women's organizations attitudes improved. Nevertheless, in March 1975 chairperson John H. Powell, censured by his fellow commissioners, resigned amid charges of fiscal carelessness, destruction of records, a mushrooming backlog of cases, and pressuring complainants into accepting reduced settlements.

The General Accounting Office, late in 1976, revealed that because of mismanagement the Commission has had only a "minimal effect" on the problems of job discrimination facing women and minorities. Two years was the average waiting period for an EEOC settlement, the GAO reported, and some petitioners still awaited action after seven years.

Meanwhile Karen DeCrow, former President of the National Organization for Women, has charged that many male employees at the understaffed, underfinanced agency find sex discrimination a humorous subject. This attitude is not really strange as the Department of Labor itself failed to comply with EEOC maternity guidelines. During his 1972 confirmation hearings as Secretary, Peter J. Brennan, in reply to a question about the rising dissatisfaction of workers, retorted: "We'll get'em some go-go girls to watch. That'll satisfy'em."

OFFICE OF FEDERAL CONTRACT COMPLIANCE

Additional hazards of protecting working women through administrative agencies are illustrated by the anti-sexual discrimination program in federal contracts. As a result of women's lobbying, President Johnson signed an executive order in October 1967 prohibiting sex discrimination by federal contractors and subcontractors. After public hearings, the Office of Federal Contract Compliance issued a proposed set of guidelines to implement this policy. However, formal procedures were not promulgated until June 1970, seven months later. Weak and ridden with loopholes, they differed from the suggested ones. James D. Hodgson, President Nixon's Secretary of Labor, admitted that job discrimination against women was "subtle and more pervasive than against any minority group." However, he stated that the Department of Labor would not take immediate steps to combat this injustice. "I have no intention," he declared "of applying literally exactly the same approach for women" as has been applied to minority groups.

After the appointment of Brennan, proposed guidelines that conformed more with those of EEOC were issued in December 1973 but their promulgation was inordinately delayed. In the spring of 1977 Lawrence Lorber was appointed head of the OFCC and charged with straightening out its rules and regulations.

Selecting the easy way out for his understaffed agency, the victim of both courts and business, Lorber proposed new guidelines. His suggestions exempting companies with less than 100 employees or $100,000 in contracts from filing affirmative action programs were defended by his assertion, "To say that I am selling out is a lot of crap. There's nothing to sell out."

Lorber's actions substantiated feminist charges that the agency had demonstrated its insensitivity to women by its reluctance to debate contractors because of sex discrimination and by submitting its findings to the greatly overburdened EEOC. When the "affirmative action" program developed by the office was undermined by Presidents Nixon and Ford, the staff had become demoralized and practically inoperative. During the 1973 Joint Economic Committee Hearings, Congresswoman Martha Griffiths (Democrat, Michigan) asserted that the Civil Rights Act, Equal Pay Legislation, and Executive Orders on Contracts have been enforced only sporadically at best, and Congressman Augustus Hawkins (Democrat, California) in 1975 hearings criticized the OFCC for not implementing effectively the appropriate executive orders.

RECENT DEVELOPMENTS IN THE EEOC AND OFCC

As the administration of President Jimmy Carter was more sympathetic to the needs of working women than its predecessors, directors of agencies tasked with preventing sex discrimination approached their responsibilities with enthusiasm. Furthermore working-class feminism, especially as manifest in the leadership of the AFL-CIO and the Coalition of Labor Union Women, spurred supervisors to efforts that contrasted sharply with the ineffective operations of the first half of the decade.

In 1977 a thirty-nine-year-old black lawyer, Eleanor Holmes Norton, formerly the head of the New York City Commission on Human Rights, was appointed to chair EEOC. After reorganizing that troubled agency, she concentrated on reducing the backlog of cases and pared the time required to process a complaint from two years to two months. Additionally, settlements were made with General Electric for $32 million in back pay and to implement affirmative action policies for minorities and women, and with the Chase Manhattan Bank for $1.8 million. Her success was such that Carter designated the EEOC as the principal agency for equal employment enforcement.

Even the much maligned OFCC after suffering through six chairmen in ten years became energized under its new director, Weldon J. Rougeau, who proclaimed "a brand new day in enforcement of the executive order." At the time of his appointment in 1978, only eighteen contractors had been declared ineligible in the office's thirteen-year history, and ten had been reinstated. In its first major enforcement action, proceedings against Uniroyal Tire were initiated, resulting in a $5.2 million award for 750 women. In just two years fourteen companies, including Firestone Tire and Rubber and Prudential Insurance, were debarred for discriminating against women and minorities in hiring, firing, and promoting, while the Kellogg Company paid close to $600,000 in back pay and for affirmative action programs.

Nevertheless, working women cannot rely on federal agencies for protection against discrimination, because their effectiveness is in direct proportion to administration support: dedicated appointees, adequate budgets, and political leadership. There is little doubt that the cost-conscious, *laissez-faire* administration of Ronald Reagan will not enlarge or improve these agencies, and already his advisory unit has assailed the EEOC for creating "a new racism in America."

FEDERAL COURTS AND WOMEN'S RIGHTS

It is also apparent that it would be risky for working women to seek protection in judicial interpretations of the Fourteenth Amendment and the Civil Rights Act. Administrative shortcomings in that 1964 legislation have not been sufficiently offset by the courts to convince feminists that women are adequately protected under Title VII. Early federal decisions interpreted the law conservatively: for example, it was ruled that the dismissal of an airline stewardess for marriage, when male employees were not required to remain single, was a discrimination on the basis of marriage not sex. As recently as December 1973 a Federal Court upheld Delta Airlines refusal to rehire a woman after childbirth as a "business neccessity," declaring that EEOC guidelines on pregnancy did not have the force of law and that "there appears to be no factual basis upon which these requirements were drawn."

On the other hand, courts have upheld the right of maternity leave and increasingly have invalidated protective laws that discriminate rather than protect, such as restrictions on hours and weight lifting. These cases usually were initiated by working-class women claiming that protective restrictions prevented them from working overtime and decreased their opportunity for promotion. Very few suits have actually arrived before the Supreme Court because employers seldom contest appellate decisions.

Appeals that have reached the highest tribunal have not resulted in an un-equivocal definition of Title VII. Decisions rendered on "bona fide occupational qualification" have been perplexing. A unanimous ruling held that an employer could not refuse to hire a woman as a trainee solely because she had preschool-age children and that the company could not have "one hiring policy for women and another for men." However, in an interpretation described by Justice Thurgood Marshall as a manifestation of "ancient canards about the proper role of women," the justices also ruled that "family obligations, if demonstrably more relevant to job performance for a woman, than for a man, could arguably be a basis" for discrimination in employment. A few years later, although the Court judged "that the bfoq exception was in fact meant to be an extremely narrow exception to the general prohibition of discrimination on the basis of sex," it upheld Alabama's height and weight requirements for "corrective counselors" even though they excluded over 40 percent of female applicants and only one percent of males. In a rationale attacked by Justices Marshall and Brennan as perpetuating "one of the most insidious of the old myths about women — that women, wittingly or not, are seductive sexual objects," the majority upheld these requirements as a legitimate "bfoq" for the "ability to maintain order in a male, maximum-security, unclassified penitentiary . . . could be directly reduced by her womanhood."

Furthermore in the case of *Gedulig v. Aiello* (1974) the Court ignored EEOC guidelines and implied that discrimination because of pregnancy was not discrimination because of sex, and in *General Electric v. Gilbert* (1976) overturned agency directives that the exclusion of pregnancy from a disability program was a violation of Title VII.

Although the Supreme Court has disallowed arbitrary sexual classification as a violation of the Fourteenth Amendment to the Constitution, it has imposed a test of reasonableness in so doing. By a six to three decision it reversed in June 1974, a three judge Federal District Court ruling that California's denial of disability benefits to women, incapacitated by normal pregnancy, was a violation of that amendment. In what Justice William Brennan in his dissent described as a "retreat" and the creation of a "double standard for disability compensation," the majority cited the increased cost to the employer of such a social insurance program. The Justices left room for "gender-based discrimination" even when ruling that a compensation law that provided death benefits automatically for a widow, but for a widower only if he had been dependent on his wife, violated the Amendement by discriminating against the female wage earner and her spouse. Such distinctions were legal if they served "important governmental objectives . . . and used discriminatory means . . . substantially related to those objectives."

President Nixon's appointees also have been reluctant to challenge traditional societal classification. In 1973 the Supreme Court ruled discriminatory military requirements that a female officer, unlike a male, must demonstrate that her spouse is dependent upon her for over one half his support to obtain a quarters allowance and medical benefits. One Justice, however, dissented (William Rehnquist), and three others (Lewis F. Powell, Harry A. Blackmun, and Chief Justice Warren Burger) took exception to the "far reaching implication" of the majority view, that classifications based on sex are inherently suspect and must be subjected to strict judicial scrutiny. These Justices also asserted that the Court was premature in accepting the case and should have practiced judicial restraint until the Equal Rights Amendment to the Constitution had been decided on by the states. Furthermore, with new Court appointments, the stereotyped views of the dissenting minority of Rehnquist, Burger, and frequently Blackmun, may become a majority opinion.

EQUAL RIGHTS AMENDMENT

Confusion surrounding Title VII further incited adherents of the Equal Rights Amendment. Because organized labor seemed to be the most respectable opponent of that measure, charging that it would invalidate protective legislation, amendment supporters reexamined the relationship between unions and women. Friendly critics, noting that sexism had not decreased in twenty years, assailed unions; according to one study they perceived protection for women as a government responsibility and thus felt no specific contractual obligation to female members. To help fight tax inequalities and sex discrimination in employment and education Women's Equity Action League (WEAL) was established in 1968. Two years later its founder, Dr. Elizabeth Boyer, testified before a congressional committee that about one-third of the complaints received dealt with the failure of unions to act on behalf of female members.

Trade unions and feminists increasingly became adversaries on the issue of women's rights as female members often subverted union policy from within, and occasionally intertwined "feminism" and "unions" in such a way that it was impossible to separate the two. Disgruntled California unionists established Union WAGE (Women's Alliance to Gain Equality) in 1972 "to fight discrimination on the job, in unions, and in society." These workingwomen publicize their grievances at rallies, lobby before the state legislature for a variety of measures, and persistently demand greater benefits for women in collective bargaining agreements. Through their newspaper, *Union W.A.G.E.*, they maintain that females should establish committees to fight sexism in unions, the "last bastion of male supremacy," and "to raise the consciousness of male unionists." Like most feminists, they support the Equal Rights Amendment, but with the proviso that it should be interpreted to extend labor standards to both sexes.

In 1973 and 1974 a series of regional conferences was held to "bring together women trade union members to deal with our special concerns as unionists and women." These meetings culminated in a Chicago rally where 3,200 women from 58 unions established the Coalition of Labor Union Women (CLUW) under the presidency of Olga Madar. Indicative of their resolution was Madar's defiant message to George Meany, Leonard Woodcock, and Frank Fitzsimmons that "we didn't come to Chicago to swap recipes." Determined to expand their policy-making role in unions and to increase female membership to 30 million, CLUW also aspires to extend protective laws to both sexes and to obtain additional legislation for child care facilities and maternity benefits. Planning to make unions more responsive to the needs of women and undertake positive action against sex discrimination CLUW has conducted programs to train women in labor leadership and in March 1976 established a special task force to rally female unionists behind the Equal Rights Amendment.

Working-class feminism led to the questioning of protective legislation. As early as 1947, traditional support for such measures began to erode when a WTUL convention divided over the wisdom of legislation that prevented night work for women. Two years later the New York State Department of Labor reported that women who worked the night shift preferred doing so because they were free to care for their children during the day. Further challenging the value of these laws was the National Manpower Commission report that in certain fields and localities such legislation affected women workers adversely. Female workers also registered their dissent. At the 1964 Women's Bureau conference on Women and Unions the only disagreement during workshops was on the desirability of protective legislation, and during its first two years women filed 291 complaints with the EEOC concerning the injustice of these statutes.

Elizabeth Koontz, appointed in 1969 by President Nixon to head the Women's Bureau, steered that agency into the new feminist movement. At the first major women's conference under her direction (American Women at the Crossroads: Directions for the Future) 1,100 delegates from a broad spectrum of the women's movement endorsed the Equal Rights Amendment to the Constitution. As a result of Koontz's pressure the Secretary of Labor reversed that agency's traditional stand and announced to the conference his support of the amendment. This step was enthusiastically hailed by Koontz, who continues to identify the Bureau with the Equal Rights Amendment, warning that "if society is permitted to assume that the goal of every woman is marriage to a man earning enough to support her and educate their children," then what happens to the economic and social development of the country "will be founded on a false assumption."

Supported in major party platforms since 1948, and endorsed by the Women's Bureau and by President Nixon's Task Force on Women's Rights and Responsibilities, nonetheless, the path of the Equal Rights Amendment remained tortuous. Passing the House of Representatives (352 to 15) for the first time in history in 1970, it was not acted on in the Senate, probably because of labor opposition. Kenneth A. Meiklejohn, legislative representative of the AFL-CIO, testified against it at congressional hearings, as did women representatives of the CWA, ACWA, and Hotel and Restaurant Employees and Bartenders International Union. Even the ILGWU submitted a dissenting statement. Most of the rational remonstrations were based on the contention that women's rights could be protected by the Fourteenth Amendment. Thus the Equal Rights Amendment was unnecessary and would endanger that legislation which protected women not covered by union agreements, as well as those in small firms not protected by Title VII or the Equal Pay Act.

Labor however, was no longer in complete accord with itself. Testifying for the proposal was Olga Madar, a vice president of the UAW. This union, with 200,000 women members, had endorsed the amendment at its national convention, and had attacked protective legislation for effectively prohibiting overtime for women. Additional favorable evidence was given through a brief paper submitted by James R. Hoffa, president of the Teamsters Union, and by Carl J. Megel, the legislative director of the American Federation of Teachers.

Georgianna Sellers of the League for American Working Women (LAWW), a national organization consisting primarily of female factory workers, also testified for the proposal. Sellers emphasized sexual discrimination within unions, accusing the Hotel Workers' Myra Wolfgang, an opponent of the Equal Rights Amendment, of being a female "Uncle Tom" who neglected the rights of women in her own union. Sallies against Wolfgang were unfair, for she headed a coalition for women's advancement in the Hotel Workers Union, publicly criticized male labor leaders for their prejudices against women workers, and later participated in the establishment of the CLUW.

Responding to charges that the Amendment was advocated only by middle-class and upper-class women and not by workers, female members of the UAW, IUE, Meat Cutters and Butcher Workmen, and the American Federation of Government Employees announced their endorsement at a press conference, charging that the issue of protective laws was a false one, since they were illegal under Title VII and usually were enforced selectively to help men. In Ohio fifty union women met with the media to challenge the testimony of a male AFL-CIO official on the necessity of protective legislation. Accusing unions of hypocrisy in opposing the Amendment, Betty Freidan, the founder of NOW, charged them with "gross neglect and blindness" in their organizational policy, with willingly tolerating lower wages for women, and conspiring with management to suppress female workers.

Hearings were again held on the Equal Rights Amendment in 1971, but they were neither as long nor as dramatic as those of the year before. The addition of the IUE to the list of union opponents was more than offset when the United Steel Workers of America, the American Newspaper Guild, and the Chemical Workers Union joined the UAW and AFT as amendment advocates. On the key issue of protective legislation, UAW vice president Madar testified: "The truth, more abundantly clear with each passing week, is that 'real' workingwomen in the factories of the land, with or without the support of their unions, have been making a charge at the discriminatory practices authorized or not prevented by the State protective laws . . . Not professional nor businesswomen but women who work for wages have brought most of the suits." In October the House passed the Amendment 354 to 24. President Nixon then urged passage by the upper branch, and despite the warning of Senator Sam Ervin (Democrat, North Carolina) that "women were being crucified upon the cross of dubious equality and specious uniformity," the measure passed 84 to 8 in March 1972.

AFL-CIO AND THE NEW FEMINISM

Judicial rulings that protective legislation usually violated Title VII and the increasing enthusiasm of women workers for the Equal Rights Amendment forced the AFL-CIO to reassess its original opposition. Delegates to the 1973 convention resolved to support the Amendment as "a symbol of commitment to equal opportunities for women and equal status for women." Pointing out that female wages amounted to only 60 percent of male earnings, they urged affiliates to lobby for ratification in their states and also amended the AFL-CIO constitution to prohibit sexual discrimination in its membership.

But union support was not able to overcome the opposition of those who viewed the Amendment as endangering traditional values. In an effort to garner the approval of three more states, Congress in 1978 extended the deadline for ratification until June 30, 1982. Despite this maneuver the situation remains bleak; three states are still needed to complete the process, but the new Reagan administration is not supportive of the Amendment.

As a result it appears that more significant than the AFL-CIO reversal on Equal Rights was the approval by the 1975 convention of the most feminist program in its history. The union pledged to fight discrimination at the bargaining table and to press for child care legislation and maternity leave protection. Delegates further endorsed full participation of women in all union activities and resolved to cooperate with CLUW. These advances were described as mere concessions to feminist members by CLUW's Myra Wolfgang. Declaring them only "half a loaf" she criticized the convention for refusing to endorse CLUW fully and for rejecting a CWA resolution for a separate standing committee on women's issues. However, the 1975 meeting marked the rejection of AFL-CIO misogyny and was a turning point in union policy for females; the convention established a Women's Activities Committee and a Coordinator in an expanded Civil Rights Department. Furthermore the AFL-CIO, International Association of Machinists, and United Auto Workers began to provide financial support to CLUW, and Robert Georgine, president of the Building and Construction Trades Department AFL-CIO, exhorted affiliates to include women in apprenticeship programs. By 1978 George Meany, who had described himself as a "closet feminist," addressed a national Equal Rights rally, endorsed extending the Amendment's ratification deadline, encouraged Congress to amend the Civil Rights Act to require employers to provide regular disability benefits for pregnancy, and, at the request of CLUW's president, shifted the 1979 convention from Florida, a non-ERA state, to Washington, D.C.

Joyce Miller, a forty-nine-year-old University of Chicago graduate and vice president of the Amalgamated Clothing and Textile Workers Union was elected president of the Women's Coalition in 1977. Because of her aggressive leadership and many joint undertakings with the AFL-CIO, tensions between CLUW and the union have eased. In 1979 Miller, whose organization now has 12,000 members, addressed the AFL-CIO Convention, the first president of CLUW to do so. Lane Kirkland, incoming AFL-CIO president, encouraged by an Illinois resolution advocating women on the Executive Board, named a committee of fifteen to explore ways and means to better reflect the contributions and roles of women and minorities in the highest level of the union movement. A few months later the Executive Coucil waived rules requiring that its members be general officers of affiliates and represent entirely different unions, thus making possible the naming of Miller to the Executive Council, the first woman ever to hold that position (Miller's national union president, Mark Findley, was also a member). Her election reflected the growing importance of women in union leadership roles; by 1980 12 percent of the nation's union leaders were female, a 5 percent increase since 1976.

It now seems that male and female unionists have reached a juncture where collaboration in redressing the injustices suffered by working women is possible. This partnership should not exclude middle-class women whose allegiance has been demonstrated in the long history of the WTUL and more recently in campaigns supporting the United Farm Workers and employees at Farah Slacks and J.P. Stevens. The possibility of a liberal-union alliance of this type has been increased by CLUW's recent action welcoming non-union women as associate members. One of the major issues facing such a coalition is the continuing wage gap between male and female workers. A new organizational drive by CLUW and the Industrial Union Department of the AFL-CIO may help, as there is less pay differential between union women and union men. Furthermore, 85 percent of workers covered by collective bargaining agreements are protected by antidiscrimination clauses, while a federal appeals court has ruled that data on hiring, pay, and promotion of women and minorities cannot be withheld from unions. As the future of EEOC seems bleak and since most courts rule against compensatory and punitive damages in Title VII cases, protection of women by unions is essential to prevent employers from finding it an acceptable business practice to continue to discriminate against them.

But the basic wage difficulty stems from the fact that 70 percent of women are employed in fields traditionally female and thus are underpaid in relation to men (the average woman college graduate earns $3,000 a year less than a male high school graduate). The AFL-CIO Human Resources Development program designed to gain jobs for women in non-traditional areas is a step in the right direction, but not enough. If the disparity is to be corrected, it is imperative that unions and reformers rally to the banner of "equal pay for comparable work," described by the EEOC as the "last frontier" of Title VII. Such a policy has been urged and publicized by that agency, while a federal appeals court has made union implementation possible by ruling that the IUE had the right to challenge a pay structure wherein women were paid less than men for jobs of comparable skill and responsibility.

Another major hardship is the lack of adequate day care facilities for working mothers. This problem is typified by a distraught secretary who in 1979 testified before the President's Advisory Committee for Women that $3,255 of her yearly salary of $6,800 went to day care services. If the situation is not alleviated, it will rapidly become worse, for the government has projected by 1990 that 45 percent of children under six will have mothers in the labor force. Although CLUW's goal of federally financed centers seems illusory at this time, it should be pursued in principle, while unions incorporate provisions for child care facilities in contracts and possibly manage centers themselves.

Finally, to meet the specific needs of women, unions should fight sexual harassment on the job by providing remedies in collective bargaining agreements and by cooperating with federal agencies. The EEOC has issued interim guidelines declaring sexual harassment illegal and holding supervisors in business and labor accountable, while the OFCC requires contractors to maintain a working environment free of harassment, intimidation, and coercion. To deal with this problem the AFL-CIO Department for Professional Employees has implemented programs which can provide guidance to affiliates and other interested groups.

With seven out of eight women unorganized these steps can only be the beginning. To recruit large numbers of women it is necessary for unions to undertake an educational campaign directed toward their own members and local officers, dispelling the myth that women work only for "pin money" and are hard to organize as well as troublesome. Studies of the history of working women and of physiology would be one means to surmount these irrational concepts. Changing female work patterns should also be emphasized, stressing their permanence in the work force as newer contraceptive methods and an emphasis on population control further reduce the number who leave work for child bearing.[3]

Nearly 75 percent of employed women are in clerical, service, professional, and technical work where labor consciousness is lacking. To attract these workers, unions should make an effort to contribute to the well-being of all Americans. They must, dramatically and publicly, become more involved in community affairs both at the local and national levels. In combating the problems of the aged, minorities, housing, municipal services, ecology, pollution, charities, and medical care, the experience of unions is unmatched. With increased political activities, unions should be able to obtain legislation to protect domestic and migrant workers. However, in keeping with the recommendations of the late Joseph Beirne of the CWA, collective bargaining and the strike should not be abandoned. Although automation has decreased the possibility of success, strikes still can be a rallying point for other forces to exert pressure on management. New feminism can contribute greatly to such a tactic, as manifested by middle-class housewives who successfully boycotted Farah slacks and picketed supermarkets on behalf of the United Farm Workers.

History may well demonstrate that the Women's Trade Union League program of organizing, educating, and lobbying under the combined leadership of workers, trade unionists, and middle-class citizens is really the most effective means of obtaining equality for the working woman.

NOTES

[1] An interesting survey of American working woman's history from colonial times to the eve of World War I is Barbara M. Wertheimer, *We Were There: The Story of Working Women in America* (New York, 1977); extracts from a wide variety of sources may be found in Rosalyn Baxandall, Linda Gordon, and Susan Reverby, eds., *America's Working Women: A Documentary History 1600 to the Present* (New York, 1976). The best study of the relationship between unions and nineteenth-century working women is John B. Andrews, *History of Women in Trade Unions, 1825 through the Knights of Labor,* vol. X of the *Report on the Conditions of Women and Child Wage-Earners in the United States* (61 Cong., 2 Sess., Sen. Doc. 645, 19v., Washington, D.C., 1910-1913). John R. Commons, *et al., A Documentary History of American Industrial Society* (10v., New York, 1958) contains much source material, including NLU proceedings. Succinct biographies of women workers and reformers can be found in *Notable American Women 1607-1950: A Biographical Dictionary* (eds. Edward R. James, Janet W. James, Paul S. Boyer, 3v., Cambridge, 1971). Contemporary accounts of the adversity of women workers are in Virginia Penny, *Think and Act. A Series of Articles Pertaining to Men and Women, Work and Wages* (Philadelphia, 1869); Helen Campbell, *Prisoners of Poverty, Women Wage Earners, Their Trades and Their Lives* (Boston, 1887); Jennie Collins, *Nature's Aristocracy: Or Battles and Wounds in Time of Peace, A Plea for the Oppressed* (Boston and New York, 1871); Edward and Eleanor Aveling, *The Working Class Movement in America* (2d ed., London, 1891); also see the annual reports of the New York Workingwomen's Protective Union. Many insights into the relationships between suffragists and unionists can be obtained from Israel Kugler, "The Trade Union Career of Susan B. Anthony," *Labor History,* II (Winter, 1961), 90-100; and Sylvis'

position is stated in James C. Sylvis, *The Life, Speeches, Labors and Essays of William H. Sylvis Late President of the Iron-Molders International Union; and also of the National Labor Union* (Philadelphia, 1872).

[2] Sylvis' biographer believes that if the union leader had lived he could have reconciled the differences between the NLU and Anthony. See Jonathan Grossman, *William Sylvis, Pioneer of American Labor. A Study of the Labor Movement during the Civil War* (New York, 1945), 267.

[3] Lewis had also served as temporary chairperson during the formation of the Workingwomen's Labor Union of New York. In 1874 she married Alexander Troup, a printer and one-time (1866-1867) secretary-treasurer of the Typographical Union, with whom she co-published the *New Haven Journal*. For a brief biography of her see Eleanor Flexner, "Augusta Lewis Troup," in *Notable American Women*, vol. III, 478-479.

[4] F.E. Wolfe, *Admission to Trade Unions* (Baltimore, 1912), 80, contends the constitution was amended in 1875 not in 1867 as stated by Bliss, *op. cit.*, 92 and Edith Abbott, *Women in Industry* (New York, 1910), 206.

Chapter 2

[1] The best sources on women and the Knights of Labor are found in the Terence V. Powderly Papers, especially in the correspondence with Leonora M. Barry (Mullen Library, Catholic University of America); also see the Proceedings of the General Assemblies of the Knights of Labor and their newspaper, the *Journal of United Labor*, which includes reports from Barry. Powderly's reminiscences are in *The Path I Trod: The Autobiography of Terence V. Powderly* (eds., Harry J. Carmen *et al.*, New York, 1940), and *Thirty Years of Labor, 1859 to 1899* (Columbus, 1890). Helpful on relations with the WCTU are Frances E. Willard, *Glimpses of Fifty Years: The Autobiography of an American Woman* (Chicago, 1889), and Mary Earhart, *Frances Willard: From Prayers to Politics* (Chicago, 1944).

[2] It was extremely difficult for the Order to obtain statistics on women and working conditions; not until 1913, when the Sixty-First Congress completed its report on the Condition of Women Workers, were adequate data available. Estimates of the number of female Knights vary greatly; apparently membership reached a peak between 1886 and 1888, when there were nearly 200 female locals and a membership that may have reached 50,000. See Andrews, *History of Women in Trade Unions*, 17; Augusta E. Galster, *The Labor Movement in the Shoe Industry with Special Reference to Philadelphia* (New York, 1924), 52; Philip S. Foner, *History of the Labor Movement*

206

in the United States from the Founding of the American Federation of Labor to the Emergence of American Imperialism (New York, 1955), 61.

[3] Terence V. Powderly to Leonora M. Barry, July 25, 1888, Letterbook 43, Powderly Papers.

[4] Stevens had organized a woman's assembly, served as a judge and Master Workman, and was owner and editor of her own newspaper. She continued reform work at Hull House, where she organized for the AFL, and was later appointed assistant factory inspector for Illinois. See *Journal of United Labor*, August 16, 1888, and Ray Ginger, *Atgeld's America: The Lincoln Ideal versus Changing Realities* (New York, 1958), 135. For the best sketch of Stevens' life see Allen F. Davis, "Alzina Parsons Stevens," *Notable American Women*, vol. III, 368-369.

Chapter 3

[1] For a good general survey of the AFL and working women consult W.D.P. Bliss, *History of Women in Trade Unions from the Organization of the American Federation of Labor*, vol. X of the *Report on the Conditions of Women and Child Wage-Earners in the United States*, also see Belva M. Herron, *Labor Organization Among Women* (University of Illinois Studies, vol. I, No. 10, Urbana, 1905) and Alice Henry, *The Trade Union Woman* (New York, 1915) and *Women and the Labor Movement* (New York, 1923). Gompers' antifeminism is clearly revealed in his correspondence (Gompers' Letterbooks, Library of Congress) and obscured in his *Seventy Years of Life and Labor: An Autobiography* (2v., New York, 1925). The Proceedings of the AFL Conventions and the *American Federationist* also provide valuable insights into AFL leadership. Mary Kenney O'Sullivan's dedication to working men and women is dramatically demonstrated in her manuscript autobiography (Arthur and Elizabeth Schlesinger Library on the History of Women in America, Radcliffe College, Elizabeth Morgan's contributions are outlined in Ralph Scharnau, "Elizabeth Morgan, Crusader for Labor Reform," *Labor History*, XIV (Summer, 1973), 340-351; and Eva Valesh's conservatism is manifest in her Reminiscences (Columbia University Oral History Research Office). Very critical of the AFL is Alice Kessler Harris, "Where Are the Organized Women Workers?" *Feminist Studies*, III (1975), 92-110.

[2] The wily Gompers was reluctant to identify closely with the temperance movement. A few years later, when the Federation was lobbying for passage of a bill to exclude convict-made goods from interstate commerce, he asked Mrs. Margaret D. Ellis, Superintendent of the WCTU, not to "kill our bill with kindness . . . We have sufficent difficulty in securing the passage of laws

to protect our fellow-workers from convict labor, without being hampered by the efforts of . . . well disposed persons." See Gompers to Ellis, October 17, 1900, v. 37, p. 738, Gompers Letterbooks.

[3] For Irene Ashby see her articles in the *American Federationist:* "The Fight Against Child Labor in Alabama," VIII (May 1901), 150-157; "Abolish Child Labor," IX (January 1902), 19-20, and "Child Life vs. Dividends," IX (May 1902), 215-223; also Elizabeth H. Davidson, *Child Labor Legislation in the Southern Textile States* (Chapel Hill, N.C., 1939), 25-28, 33-34, 41-45, 80-82.

[4] D. Owen Carrigan, "Martha Moore Avery: Crusader for Social Justice," *Catholic Historical Review*, LIV (April 1968), 22.

Chapter 4

[1] Among the manuscript materials upon which this chapter is based are the Women's Educational and Industrial Union Papers, located in their Boston office; the Papers of the Rutland Corner House, Denison House, Consumers' League of Massachusetts, whose relative fullness supplements the scanty early collection of National Papers in the Library of Congress, and those of Ellen M. Henrotin and Mary K. Simkhovitch, all in the Arthur and Elizabeth Schlesinger Library, Radcliffe College. The YWCA and the Federation of Women's Clubs still await their definitive histories; however, see Elizabeth Wilson, *Fifty Years of Association Work Among Women 1866-1910; A History of the Young Women's Christian Association in the United States of America* (New York, 1916); Mary S. Sims, *The Natural History of a Social Institution - The Young Women's Christian Association* (New York, 1936), and Mary I. Wood, *The History of the General Federation of Women's Clubs for the First Thirty-Two Years of its Existence* (New York, 1912).

William R. Stewart, *The Philanthropic Work of Josephine Shaw Lowell* (New York, 1911), contains many of her speeches and letters. Abbie Graham, *Grace H. Dodge, Merchant of Dreams* (New York, 1926) should be supplemented by Dodge's own *A Bundle of Letters to Busy Girls on Practical Matters* (New York, 1887). The early reports of the Consumers' League in the Supplements to the *Annals of the American Academy of Political and Social Science* are most helpful, as is Maud Nathan's delightful *The Story of an Epoch Making Movement* (New York, 1926). The development and hopes for the union label are treated in Ernest R. Spedder, *The Trade Union Label* (Baltimore, 1910). The evolution of labor statistics is thoroughly analyzed in James Leiby,

Carroll Wright and Labor Reform: The Origin of Labor Statistics (Cambridge, 1960) and Wright's objectives are expressed in his article "The Growth and Purpose of the Bureau of Statistics and Labor," *Journal of Social Science*, XXV (December 1888), 1-14.

Among the most significant surveys and exposés of women's working conditions are Mrs. John Van Vorst and Marie Van Vorst, *The Woman Who Toils: The Experiences of Two Ladies as Factory Girls* (New York, 1903); Maude Younger, "The Diary of an Amateur Waitress, an Industrial Problem from the Worker's Point of View," *McClure's*, XXVII (March and April 1908), 543-552, 665-677; Dorothy Richardson, *The Long Day: The Story of a New York Working Girl as Told by Herself* (New York, 1905); Elizabeth B. Butler, *Women and the Trades: Pittsburgh 1907-1908* (New York, 1909); also see Rheta Childe Dorr, *What Eight Million Women Want* (Boston, 1910) and her autobiography, *A Woman of Fifty* (2nd ed., New York, 1925).

The most thoughtful study of the settlement house movement is Allen F. Davis, *Spearheads for Reform: The Social Settlements and the Progressive Movement, 1890-1914* (New York, 1967). Settlement residents wrote extensively on their work. Among others see Jane Adams, *Twenty Years at Hull House* (New York, 1910); Lillian Wald, *The House on Henry Street* (New York, 1915); Mary Simkhovitch, *Neighborhood, My Story of Greenwich House* (New York, 1938); Philip Davis, *And Crown thy Good* (New York, 1952), and *The City Wilderness: A Settlement Study by the Residents and Associates of the South End House South End Boston* (ed. Robert S. Woods, Boston, 1898).

[2] For testimony indicating that unions had helped improve the welfare of working women, see that of Fanny Ames, Massachusetts Factory Inspector, VII, 60-62, and Clare de Graffenreid of the Department of Labor, VII, 232, in U.S. Industrial Commission, *Reports* (19v., Washington, 1901-1902). Strasser was not as antifeminist as in the 1882 hearings; he testified that previously women lowered wages in the cigar industry but now great numbers enjoyed the same union benefits as men, *ibid.*, vol. VII, 250.

[3] Addams was careful as to the source of donations. In the 1890s she refused a $20,000 gift to the Jane Club because of the donor's reputation as an unjust employer. See Robert H. Bremner, *American Philanthropy* (Chicago, 1960), 113.

Chapter 5

[1] Essential to any account of the WTUL is that organization's papers, located in the Library of Congress and in the Arthur and Elizabeth Schlesinger Library, Radcliffe College; of particular relevance are the reports of the Executive Committee, organizers, and local branches. An excellent account of the founding of the League is Allen F. Davis, "The Women's Trade Union League: Origins and Organization," *Labor History*, V (Winter 1964), 3-17. Gladys Boone, *The Women's Trade Union Leagues in Great Britain and the United States of America* (New York, 1942), although dated, is solidly researched and includes WTUL constitutions in the appendix. Accounts of the League's activities, biographies of its leaders, and first-hand descriptions of organizational drives and strikes can be found in the *Union Labor Advocate*, 1906-1911. Interesting studies of the relationship between feminism and the WTUL are found in *Feminist Studies*; Robin Miller Jacoby, "The Women's Trade Union League and American Feminism," III (1975), 126-140 and Nancy Shrom Dye's articles, "Creating a Feminist Alliance: Sisterhood and Class Conflict in the New York Women's Trade Union League, 1903-1914," II (1975), 24-38; "Feminism or Unionism? The New York Women's Trade Union League and the Labor Movement," III (1975), 126-140.

Memoirs of women who were instrumental in WTUL endeavors provide valuable insights into the League's problems, programs, and relations with organized labor. See the *Memoirs* of Alice Henry (ed. Nettie Palmer, Melbourne, 1944), the Australian-born editor of *Life and Labor*. Much primary source material is in Mary E. Dreier's biography of her sister, the WTUL mainstay and president 1907-1922, *Margaret Dreier Robins, Her Life, Letters, and Work* (New York, 1950). The fascinating life of a cap-maker immigrant from Russian Poland who became WTUL president and a member of the National Recovery Administration is revealed in Rose Schneiderman, *All for One* (with Lucy Goldwaite, New York, 1967). The autobiography of Mary Anderson, *Woman at Work* (as told to Mary M. Winslow, Minneapolis, 1960) is the account of a shoe worker and WTUL organizer who became director of the Women's Bureau from 1919 to 1944. The founder of the International Glove Workers Union, who held office in that organization from 1903 to 1948 and in the WTUL from 1913 to 1948, relates her life in *Woman's Labor Leader, an Autobiography of Agnes Nestor* (ed. Delmar Bordeaux, Rockford, Ill., 1954). There is no published biography of Leonora O'Reilly, who bridged the gap between WTUL allies and workers, and who labored indefatigably for working women; however, her papers at the Arthur and Elizabeth Schlesinger Library, Radcliffe College, are extremely informative, and Frances

H. Howe has written an honors thesis, "Leonora O'Reilly, Socialist and Reformer, 1870-1927" (Radcliffe College, 1952).

[2] Many of the people who participated in establishing the WTUL (Walling, Mary Dreier, McDowell, O'Reilly, Wald, Addams, Barnum) also helped to found the NAACP. See Charles F. Kellog, *NAACP: A History of the National Association for the Advancement of Colored People, 1909-1920* (Baltimore, 1967), 298-299, 300-301, 304.

[3] As late as 1910 25% of working females were between 16 and 20 years of age and another 25% were from 21 to 25. C.E. Persons, "Women's Work and Wages in the United States," *Journal of Economics*, XXIX (February 1915), 216.

[4] From 1903 to 1923 only 38 paid women organizers were employed by the AFL, and many of these worked only for a short time. See Alice Henry, *Women and the Labor Movement* (New York, 1923), 95.

Chapter 6

[1] In addition to earlier references on the AFL and WTUL, a wealth of material is available on labor disputes during this period. Among the better accounts of the Shirtwaist strike are F. E. Sheldon, *Souvenir History of the Lady Waist Makers Union* (New York, 1910); Charles Bernheimer, *The Shirtwaist Strike* (University Settlement Series, New York, 1910); and Melvyn Dubofsky, *When Workers Organize: New York City in the Progressive Era* (Amherst, 1968). A fascinating narrative relating the experiences of a young striker, including incarceration in the workhouse, is Theresa S. Malkiel, *The Diary of a Shirtwaist Striker* (New York, 1910); additional revelation of police brutality is given in McAlister Coleman, "All of Which I Saw," *The Progressive*, XIV (May 1950), 24-27. Leon Stein's *The Triangle Fire* is a classic portrayal (New York, 1962). Published accounts of the confrontation at Muscatine include that of the WTUL member, Gertrude Barnum, "Button, Button, Who's Got the Button?" *Survey*, XXVI (May 1911), 253-255, and the Federal Council Commission of the Churches of Christ, *Report on the Industrial Situation at Muscatine, Iowa by a Special Committee* (New York, 1912). The autobiographies of Nestor and of Anderson are valuable on the Chicago strike, as is Matthew Josephson, *Sidney Hillman, Statesman of American Labor* (New York, 1952). The best account of the women's role in that strike is Chicago WTUL, *Official Report of the Strike Committee* (Chicago, 1911).

The Lawrence strike has attracted many historians. Among the better works are Donald B. Cole, *Immigrant City: Lawrence, Massachusetts, 1845-1921* (Chapel Hill, N.C., 1963), 3-13, 177-194; chapter VIII of Henry F. Bradford, *Socialism and the Workers in Massachusetts, 1886-1912* (Amherst, 1966); and Melvyn Dubofsky, *We Shall be All: A History of the Industrial Workers of the World* (Chicago, 1969), 227-262. A revealing first-hand narrative is Mary K. O'Sullivan "The Labor War at Lawrence," *Survey*, XXVIII (April 1912), 72-74. Important testimony was given to Congress in *The Strike at Lawrence, Mass., Hearings before the Committee on Rules of the House of Representatives on House Resolutions 409 and 433* (62 Cong., 2 Sess., House Doc. 571, Washington, D.C., 1912).

Two of the women "radicals " have published their autobiographies: Mary Heaton Vorse, *Footnote to Folly* (New York, 1935) and Elizabeth Gurley Flynn, *I Speak My Own Piece: Autobiography of the Rebel Girl* (New York, 1955).

[2] Samuel A. Gompers, "The Struggle in the Garment Trade - From Misery and Despair to Betterment and Hope," *American Federationist*, XX (March 1913), 190.

[3] Arthur Bullard (pseudonym Albert Edwards) in his novel *Comrade Yetta* depicts his Socialist heroine as so ill at ease with the reforming nature of the League that she eventually quits, realizing that the WTUL program could not be reconciled with true Socialist reform. His assessment is not dissimilar to William L. O'Neill's contention that the liberal League was destructive of the radical goals of Socialists and that Socialist members weakened their own cause by participation in the WTUL. See O'Neill, *Everyone Was Brave: The Rise and Fall of Feminism in America* (Chicago, 1969), 100-101.

[4] Louis Levine, *The Women's Garment Workers: A History of the International Ladies' Garment Workers' Union* (New York, 1924), 222.

Chapter 7

[1] Much of the source material for this chapter is unpublished; the Gompers Letterbooks (Library of Congress) and WTUL and O'Reilly Papers (Library of Congress, Arthur and Elizabeth Schlesinger Library, Radcliffe College) were used extensively and were of special value in divulging the extent of the AFL distrust of the League; Gompers' articles in the *American Federationist* were also of assistance on this issue. For the WTUL organizers' school, see "Training Women in Union Leadership," *Survey*, XXXVII (December

1916), 312. The hardships of working women are emotionally described by some of the school's students in *I Am a Woman Worker - A Scrapbook of Autobiographies* (ed. Andria T. Hourwich and Gladys L. Palmer, New York, 1935).

For the operators' walkout see Anne Withington, "The Telephone Strike," *Survey*, XLII (April, 1919), 146; Elizabeth F. Baker, *Technology and Woman's Work* (New York, 1964) is helpful, while Jack Barbash, *Unions and Telephones: The Story of the Communications Workers of America* (New York, 1952) a survey sympathetic to the union, is indispensable for a history of the operators. Rose Schneiderman exposes the exploitation of underwear workers in "The White Goods Workers of New York, Their Struggle for Human Conditions," *Life and Labor*, III (May 1913), 132-136, and Benjamin Stolberg is sympathetic to their cause in his revealing *Tailor's Progress: The Story of a Famous Union and the Men Who Made It* (New York, 1944), 65-77.

The women's peace movement still awaits its historian; however, Marie L. Degen, *The History of the Woman's Peace Party* (John Hopkins University Studies in Historical and Political Science, Series LVII, no. 3, Baltimore, 1939), is essential on that subject. See also Leonora O'Reilly's report, "International Congress of Women at the Hague," *Life and Labor*, V (July 1915), 125-128.

[2] Helen Marot's views on the minimum wage are in "The Minimum Wage-Board and the Union," *Unpopular Review*, IV (October-December 1915), 397-411. Her opposition to protective legislation was unusual. Because of the absence of unionization most reformers, if they took any stand, supported such measures. Yet regulations restricting hours, regulating weights, and limiting shifts were justified on the basis of woman's uniqueness, frailty, incapacity to protect herself, and destiny as mother. Not until the 1920s was there forceful, articulate, female opposition to protective legislation, when professional and upper-class women, to the dismay of the Women's Bureau and working-classes, unsuccessfully attacked these laws as inhibiting opportunities for women. The new feminism of the 1960s, technological advances, and the Civil Rights Act of 1964 have rendered such protection obsolete, and today's working women have joined their middle-class sisters in condemning the discriminatory features of such statutes.

[3] Samuel Gompers, "They Don't Suit the Intellectuals," *American Federationist*, XX (February 1913), 132.

[4] For Bellanca's inspiring career see Herbert G. Gutman, "Dorothy Jacobs Bellanca," *Notable American Women*, vol. I, 124-126.

Chapter 8

[1] Mother Jones Papers at the Mullen Library, Catholic University of America, are rather meager and should be supplemented with the Terence V. Powderly and John Mitchell Papers at the same archives; Jones' *Autobiography* (ed. Mary F. Parton, Chicago, 1925) should be used with care, her testimony before the Industrial Relations Commission is quite helpful (64 Cong., 1 Sess., 11v., Washington, D.C., 1916), vol. XI; and Dale Fethering's biography *Mother Jones: The Miner's Angel* (Carbondale, 1974) is penetrating and scholarly but tends to accept her rhetoric at face value. Much of the best material on the strikes in which Jones participated consists of government reports. For Colorado 1903-1904 see U.S. Bureau of Labor, *A Report on Labor Disturbances in the State of Colorado from 1880 to 1904 inclusive with Correspondence Relating Thereto* (58 Cong., 3 Sess., Sen. Doc. 122, Washington, D.C., 1905), and Colorado Bureau of Labor Statistics, *Ninth Biennial Report* (Denver, 1904); for West Virginia, U.S. Congress, Senate, Committee on Education and Labor, *Conditions in the Paint Creek District West Virginia, Hearings before Subcommittee* (63 Cong., 1 Sess., Washington, D.C., 1913); for Colorado 1913-1914, Colorado Bureau of Labor Statistics, *Twelfth and Fourteenth Biennial Reports* (Denver, 1910, 1914), U.S. Congress, House Committee on Mines and Mining, *Report on the Colorado Strike Investigation Made Under House Resolution 387* (63 Cong., 3 Sess., House Doc. 1630, Washington, D.C., 1915), U.S. Congress, House, Sub-committee of the Committee of Mines and Mining, *Conditions in the Coal Mines of Colorado Hearings Before a Subcommittee on Mines and Mining pursuant to House Resolution 387* (63 Cong., 2 Sess., Washington, D.C., 1914), Adjutant General of Colorado, *The Military Occupation of the Coal Strike Zone of Colorado by the Colorado National Guard 1913-1914* (Denver, 1914), George P. West, *Report on the Colorado Strike* (Washington, D.C., U.S. Commission on Industrial Relations, 1915). Other perceptive accounts of these major strikes include Benjamin M. Rastall, *The Labor History of Cripple Creek District: A Study in Industrial Evolution* (Madison, 1908); Harold E. West, "Civil War in the West Virginia Coal Mines," *Survey*, XXX (April 1913), 37-50; George S. McGovern and Leonard F. Guttridge, *The Great Coalfield War* (Boston, 1972).

Elsie Gluck's sympathetic study, *John Mitchell, Miner: Labor's Bargain with the Gilded Age* (New York, 1929), was helpful throughout the chapter; however, I relied more heavily for an assessment of Mitchell on Robert H. Wiebe, "The Anthracite Strike of 1902: A Record of Confusion," *Mississippi Valley Historical Review*, XLVIII (September 1961), 229-251.

[2] Although Mitchell seldom attacked Jones, there is little doubt that he was wounded by her volleys. When he was asked to refute the canard that prior to becoming a labor agitator she was the keeper of a brothel he evasively replied that he was unable to speak on the subject as he did not know her prior to 1894. See Mary Breckton-Mitchell correspondence, March 1904, file 310, Mitchell Papers.

[3] Actually Jones' dedication to Socialism had predated her friendship with Debs, for as early as 1894 she had helped J.A. Wayland establish the Socialist weekly, *Appeal to Reason.*

[4] For Jones and the Steel strike see William Z. Foster, *The Great Steel Strike and Its Lessons* (New York, 1920), 53, 60, 63, and Mary H. Vorse, *Footnote to Folly* (New York, 1935), 287-289.

Chapter 9

[1] There are brief biographies of these Socialist women in *Notable American Women*; both Theodore Draper, *The Roots of American Communism* (New York, 1957) and David A. Shannon, *The Socialist Party of America: A History* (New York, 1955) include the role of women in their accounts. Ella R. Bloor has published her autobiography, *We Are Many* (New York, 1940) and is praised in Elizabeth Gurley Flynn, *Daughters of America: Ella Reeve Bloor and Anita Whitney* (New York, 1942). For Kate Richards O'Hare's views, her *The Sorrows of Cupid* (revised and enlarged, St. Louis, 1912) is indispensable, and Harold Bronco's brief biography, "Kate Richards O'Hare," *World Tomorrow*, IX (February 1926), 55-56 is illuminating. Gilman's *The Living of Charlotte Perkins Gilman: An Autobiography* (New York, 1935) is fascinating and revealing; Carl N. Degler interprets her as a "rationalistic radical" in "Charlotte Perkins Gilman on the Theory and Practice of Feminism," *American Quarterly*, VIII (Spring 1956), 21-39.

For sources on women workers in World War I, in addition to the biographies cited in Chapter 5 see the early reports and studies of the Women's Bureau, *The First Annual Report of the Director of Women in Industry Service* (Washington, D.C., 1919), and the *Monthly Labor Review*; the participants in the Labor Reconstruction Conference were optimistic about the future of women workers because of the war [Samuel M. Lindsay, ed., "War Labor Political Reconstruction," *Proceedings of the Academy of Political Science*, VII, No. 2 (February 1919)], as was Florence Kelley, who was also deeply concerned about protective legislation ["The War and the Women Workers,"

Survey, XXXIX (March 9, 1918), 628-631]. More analytical was Margaret A. Hobbs, "War Time Employment of Women," *American Labor Legislation Review*, VIII (December 1918), 332-338. For the International Federation of Working Women see Boone, *Women's Trade Union Leagues*. The most perceptive account of labor and woman suffrage is found in Aileen S. Kraditor, *The Ideas of the Woman Suffrage Movement 1890-1920* (New York, 1965). Elizabeth C. Stanton *et al.*, *History of Woman Suffrage* (6v., New York, 1881, 1922) frequently touches on the issue and includes convention addresses on the subject.

[2] The League also encouraged revision of the Versailles Treaty, condemned the occupation of the Ruhr, and supported the 1921 Conference on the Limitation of Armaments. Its constitution was amended to commit the WTUL to efforts to outlaw war and to affiliate closely with woman workers of all countries.

Chapter 10

[1] For the 1920s and early 1930s the Papers of Mary Anderson of the Women's Bureau (Arthur and Elizabeth Schlesinger Library, Radcliffe College) are essential; the only major study of women in the period from 1920 to 1970 is William C. Chafe, *The American Woman: Her Changing Social, Economic, and Political Roles* (New York, 1972), which emphasizes the role of working women. J. Stanley Lemons, *The Woman Citizen: Social Feminism in the 1920s* (Urbana, 1973), a first-rate work, is of particular value on the struggle between women's groups over the Equal Rights amendment. For the Bryn Mawr summer school and an optimistic first-hand account of the WTUL educational program see the manuscript autobiography of Hilda Smith, Schlesinger Library. The League's journal, *Life and Labor*, touches on all the strikes of the period involving women; Irving Berstein, *The Lean Years: A History of the American Worker, 1920-1933* (Boston, 1960) is thoroughly researched, as is F. Roy Marshall, *Labor in the South* (Cambridge, 1967). Fred E. Beal's rather bitter memoir, *Proletarian Journey: New England, Gastonia, Moscow* (New York, 1937) is of particular value on Gastonia. Despite the limited subject matter, Louise Prette, ed., *Women Workers Through the Depression: A Study of White Collar Employment made by the American Women's Association* (New York, 1934) remains the best study of the effects of the depression on women workers. There is still need for a biography of Eleanor Roosevelt as a feminist; however, see her reminiscences, *This is My Story* (New York, 1937) and *This*

I Remember (New York, 1949), and Joseph P. Lash's delightful *Eleanor and Franklin* (New York, 1971).

[2] The other member organizations were the National Consumers' League, National Council of Women, General Federation of Women's Clubs, Association of Collegiate Alumnae, WCTU, National Federation of Business and Professional Women's Clubs, National Congress of Mothers and Parent-Teachers Association, National League of Women Voters, American Home Economics Association, and the Council of Jewish Women.

[3] In such an administration and with societal values still rigidly anti-feminist, it is understandable that Women's Bureau recommendations of vocational classes for girls and state women's bureaus were overlooked. In her autobiography Anderson expressed discouragement by noting that the Bureau's most important achievement was gathering data on working conditions, hours, and wages.

[4] Gompers' lack of interest in the WTUL was revealed when he still believed Robins its president four months after Swartz had assumed that office.

[5] There is not a good biography of Fannia Cohn, but her articles in the *American Federationist* and *Labor Age* are revealing, as is her *Workers' Education in War and Peace* (New York, 1943).

[6] Lucy Lang, *Tomorrow is Beautiful* (New York, 1948).

[7] Ann W. Craton, "Working the Women Workers," *Nation*, CXXIV (March 23, 1927), 311-313.

[8] Theresa Wolfson, "Trade Union Activities of Women," *Annals of the American Academy of Political and Social Science*, CXLIII (May 1929), 120-131; Wolfson, *The Woman Worker and the Trade Union* (New York, 1926); Wolfson, "Equal Rights in the Union," *Survey* LVII (February 15, 1927), 629-630.

Chapter 11

[1] Some of the sources listed in Chapter 10, as well as the autobiographies of women cited earlier, were of help also in this chapter. Irving Bernstein, *The Turbulent Years: A History of the American Worker, 1933-1941* (Boston, 1970) is unsurpassed for a history of labor in this period. Sidney Fine, *Sitdown the General Motors Strike of 1936-1937* (Ann Arbor, 1969) is definitive. Grace Hutchens, *Women Who Work* (New York, 1934) is a valuable view from the left; and both Melvyn Dubofsky, ed., *American Labor Since the New Deal* (New York, 1971) and *Labor's Story as Reported by the American Labor Press* (eds. Gordon H. Cole, Leon Stein, and Norman Sobol, New

York, 1961) provide convenient contemporary journalistic accounts. Two of the women who organized for the CIO have published poignant memoirs: Lucy R. Mason, *To Win These Rights: A Personal Story of the CIO in the South* (Westport, Conn., 1952), and Rose Pesotta, *Bread Upon the Waters* (ed. John N. Beffell, New York, 1944). There is not yet a first-rate study on the New Deal and women; however, Donald S. Howard's superb *The WPA and Federal Relief Policy* (New York, 1943) gives full attention to women. The Catholic Worker Movement can be investigated through Dorothy Day's writings, *From Union Square to Rome* (Silver Spring, Md., 1939), *The Long Loneliness* (New York, 1952), *Loaves and Fishes* (New York, 1963), and *House of Hospitality* (New York, 1939). The *Catholic Worker* is essential; many extracts from it can be found in *A Penny a Copy - Readings from the Catholic Worker* (eds. Thomas C. Cornell and James H. Forest, New York, 1968). The best biography of Day is William D. Miller, *A Harsh and Dreadful Love: Dorothy Day and the Catholic Worker Movement* (New York, 1973). The most rewarding approach to working women in the war years is through the *Monthly Labor Review* and *Women's Bureau Bulletins*. One of the best biographies of recent years George Martin, *Madam Secretary: Frances Perkins* (New York, 1976) deemphasizes her difficulties with Anderson.

[2] The stretch-out, a particularly odious abuse in the textile industry, was the gradual introduction of additional machines for the workers' care without an increase in pay. Thomas R. Brooks, *Toil and Trouble* (2nd ed., New York, 1971), 156 writes: "As W.J. Cash notes in his *Mind of the South*, the stretch-out 'violated the whole tradition of the South.' Wrenched out of their easy-going ways, Southerners were put under the sharp-eyed Yankees with their ever-present stop watches. It was too much."

[3] When these no longer served their purpose they were converted into centers for elderly women. Ryder later served as vice president of the Central Trades and Labor Union (AFL) from 1935 to 1943 and as a member of the AFL organizing staff in the St. Louis area. See *AFL-CIO Convention Proceedings, 1961*, vol I. 525.

[4] Howard, *The WPA*, 280, gives the percentage and number of women employed by the WPA:

Date	Number	% All WPA Workers
1935 December	330,700	12.1
1936 June	387,800	17.2
1937 June	323,000	18.2
1938 June	372,100	13.3
1939 June	352,800	14.6
1940 June	243,300	15.4
1941 June	254,800	19.2

[5] There is no biography of Josephine Roche; however, see Newspaper Clippings, Biography File, Josephine Roche, Arthur and Elizabeth Schlesinger Library, Radcliffe College; "Battler for Miners." *Business Week*, April 8, 1967, 100-101; John M. Blum, *From the Morgenthau Diaries, Years of Crisis, 1928-1938* (Boston, 1959), 83-84.

Chapter 12

[1] The papers of Truman's director of the Women's Bureau, Frieda Miller, are quite helpful; those of Eisenhower's director, Alice K. Leopold, are disappointing and consist primarily of published materials. Both collections are at the Arthur and Elizabeth Schlesinger Library, Radcliffe College. In addition to Women's Bureau publications other government documents are essential to the topics covered in this chapter. Among the most valuable are Reports of the EEOC and Citizen's Advisory Council on the Status of Women: President's Commission on the Status of Women, *American Women* (Washington, D.C., 1963); U.S. Congress, House, Subcommittee on Equal Opportunities of the Committee on Education and Labor, *Oversight Hearings on Federal Enforcement of Equal Employment Opportunity Laws* (94 Cong., 1 Sess., Washington, D.C., 1975); U.S. Congress, House, Special Subcommittee on Education of the Committee of Education and Labor, *Hearings on Section 805 of House Resolution 16098, Discrimination Against Women* (91 Cong., 2 Sess., Washington, D.C., 1970); U.S. Congress, House, Subcommittee No. 4. of the Committee on the Judiciary, *Hearings, Equal Rights for Men and Women* (92 Cong., 1 Sess., Washington, D.C. 1971); U.S. Congress, Hearing Before the Joint Economic Committee, *Economic Problems of Women* (93 Cong., 1 Sess., Washington, D.C., 1973); U.S. Congress, Senate, *Equal Rights 1970, Hearings before the Committee on the Judiciary* (91 Cong., 2 Sess., Washington, D.C.,1970); U.S. Congress Senate, *The Equal Rights Amendment, Hearings before the Subcommittee on Constitutional Amendments* (91 Cong., 2 Sess., Washington, D.C., 1970). Walter Uphoff, *Kohler on Strike, 30 Years of Conflict* (Boston, 1966) is an objective in-depth narrative of that conflict. An excellent summary of the Harriet-Henderson strike is Douglas Cater's, "Labor's Long Trail in Henderson, N.C.," *The Reporter*, XXV (September 14, 1961), 36-40. For the organization of the CWA see Jack Barbash, *Unions and Telephones: The Story of the Communications Workers of America* (New York, 1952); Joseph A. Beirne, late CWA president, outlined fresh approaches for labor in *New Horizons for American Labor* (Washington, D.C., 1963) and *Challenge to Labor: New Roles for American Trade Unions*

(Englewood Cliffs, N.J., 1969). The 1951 convention traced the history of AFL policy on equal pay, see AFL *Convention Proceedings, 1951*, 210-213. A good survey of recent federal legislation is found in Judith Hole and Ellen Levine, *Rebirth of Feminism* (New York, 1971), a work critical of the Nixon administration; a former president of NOW, Karen DeCrow, in *Sexist Justice* (New York, 1974) analyzes the enforcement of judicial rulings pertaining to equal pay legislation and the Civil Rights Act of 1964, and accuses the Nixon administration of having undermined these measures; also see the *Women's Rights Law Reporter*. An analysis of legislative needs and the means of enforcing present laws is Task Force on Working Women, *Exploitation from 9 to 5: Report on Twentieth Century Fund Task Force* (New York, 1975). A scholarly and objective summary of women's labor force activity is Juanita Kreps, *Sex in the Marketplace: American Women at Work* (Baltimore, 1971); also see the special issue of the *Monthly Labor Review*, XCVII (May 1974) entitled "Women in the Workplace." For the establishment of CLUW see Claudia Dreifus, "Trade Union Women's Conference," *Nation*, CCXVIII (March 30, 1974). For recent developments, see Mimi Kelber, "AFL-CIO — For Men Only," *Nation*, CCIX (November 17, 1979), 490-492. In addition to the Supreme Court cases cited in the text see: *Phillips v. Martin Marietta* Corp. 400 U.S. 542 (1970), *Frontiero v. Richardson*, 411 U.S. 677 (1972), *Dothard v. Rawlinson* 433 U.S. 321 (1976), *Winger v. Druggists Mutual* 466 U.S. (April 22, 1908), as the complete volume has not yet been printed it must be consulted in the "slip version."

[2] On May 30, 1974 AT&T consented to additional back pay and future pay adjustments of $30 million for discrimination in violation of the 1972 amendments extending the Equal Pay Act of 1963 to management employees. See *New York Times*, May 31, 1974.

[3] In 1979 43% of wives, husband present, with preschool children were in the labor force, U.S. Department of Labor, *Childcare Centers Sponsored by Employers and Labor Unions in the United States* (Washington, D.C., 1980), 1.

Appendix 1

Women in the Work Force

Year	No. Women Employed	No. Women in Unions	% Female in Work Force	%Female Union Members
1890	3,704,000		17	
1900	4,999,000		18	
1910	7,789,000	76,750	21	3.5
1920	8,229,000	397,000	20	8.0
1930	10,396,000	260,000	22	7.7
1940	13,783,000	800,000	25	9.4
1944*	19,170,000	3,000,000	35	21.8
1950	17,882,000		29	
1954**	19,718,000	2,950,000	29	16.6
1960	23,200,000	3,304,000	33	18.3
1970	31,560,000	4,282,000	37	20.7
1980	45,480,000	6,700,000	42	30.0

* 1944 selected as peak of wartime employment for women.

** 1954 selected as post-Korean-war slump and first year Bureau of Labor Statistics began collecting data on women labor union members.

Sources: The data on women's employment through 1960 are from U.S. Department of Labor, Women's Bureau, *Handbook on Women Workers,* 1969 (Bulletin 294, Washington, D.C., 1969), for 1970 from *Statistical Abstract,* and 1980 from *Employment and Earnings,* XXVIII (January, 1981), 162.

The data on women in unions from 1910 to 1944 are from Glady's Dickson, "Women in Labor Unions," *Annals of the American Academy of Political and Social Science,* CCLI (May, 1947), 70-78; for 1960 and 1970 from U.S. Bureau of Labor Statistics, *Directory of National and International Labor Unions in the United States* (Bulletin 1665, Washington, D.C., 1979); and for 1980 from CLUW estimates as in *AFL-CIO News,* November 22, 1980.

Appendix 2

Women as the Percentage of all Persons Employed in Select Occupations

Occupation	1950	1960	1970	1980
Professional and Technical Workers	39.0	38.4	39.9	44.3
Managers and Administrators (except farm)	13.7	14.8	16.6	26.1
Clerical and Kindred	61.9	67.9	73.6	80.0
Craftsmen	3.1	3.1	5.0	6.0
Operatives	27.4	28.7	31.5	40.0
Laborers (except farm)	3.6	5.1	8.4	11.5
Farm Workers	8.8	9.6	9.5	17.9
Service Workers	58.1	61.9	60.0	62.0
Sales Workers	34.2	36.2	38.6	45.2

Sources: *Economic Report of the President, 1973* (Washington, D.C.), 155-159; *Employment and Earnings*, XXVIII (January, 1981), 178.

Appendix 3

Presidents of National Women's Trade Union League

Name	Years	Affiliation
Mary Morton Kehew	1903	Social Reformer
Ellen M. Henrotin	1904-1907	Social Reformer
Margaret D. Robins	1907-1922	Social Reformer
Maud O'Farrell Swartz	1922-1926	Typographical Union
Rose Schneiderman	1926-1950	Cap Makers Union

INDEX

Civil Liberties Union

Civil Rights Act (1964), 194; bona fide occupational qualification (bfoq), 190, 191; Title VII, 189, 190, 197, 199, 201-203; Title VII and federal courts, 195-197; Title VII and unions, 190-192; also see Equal Employment Opportunity Commission and bona fide occupational qualification.

Civil Rights Commission, 192

Civil Works Administration, 158

Civilian Conservation Corps, 158

Clayton Antitrust Act, 79, 80

Clerks International Protective Union, 48

Clothing Workers Union, see Amalgamated Clothing Workers Union

Coalition of Labor Union Women, 194, 201-203

Cohn, Fannia, 140-141, 145, 153

Cole, Elsie, 62

Colgate Palmolive Company, 190

Collar Laundry Workers Union of Troy New York, 10

College Settlements Association, 40

Collier's, 105

Collins, Jennie, 8, 28

Communications Workers of America, 180, 182, 185, 191, 199, 201, 204

Communist Party, 78, 119, 120, 121; and textile workers strike, 148-149

compositors, 8-9

Conboy, Sarah, 70, 77

Congress of Industrial Organizations, 159, 164, 167, 170, 178, 182; Political Action Committee, 165, 174; women workers, 1930s, 164-168; World War II, 173-174; post World War II, 184-185; Women's Trade Union League, 183

Congressional Record, 110, 135

Consumers' League, 32-36, 40, 59, 63, 65, 80, 125, 164, 167, 182, 215 (f.n. 2); of Massachusetts, 34; of New Jersey, 40

Continental Can Company, 181

contract compliance, see governmental contracts and discrimination

Coolidge, Calvin, 117, 137

cotton textile industry, NRA code, 155

Council of Jewish Women, 217 (f.n. 2)

Council of National Defense, 128, 129

Craton, Ann, 143, 144

Crawford, James, 116

Creel, George, 113

Daly, Charles P., 3

Darrow, Clarence, 20, 93

Daughters of St. Crispin, 6, 7-8

Daughters of the American Revolution, 135, 136

Davis, Caroline, 187

Davis, Mrs. Herschel, 175

Davis, James, 137

Davis, Jeff, 144

Davis, Philip, 45, 48

Davis, Polly (Mrs. Philip), 45

day care facilities, 159, 162, 172, 173, 174, 176, 186, 191, 201, 203

231

ABOUT THE AUTHOR

JAMES J. KENNEALLY

James J. Kenneally, Professor of History, Stonehill College, North Easton, Massachusetts, received his education at Boston College and Tufts University. A frequent contributor to scholarly journals, he has also indexed and catalogued the papers of the late Speaker of the United States Congress, Joseph W. Martin Jr. In addition to membership in several professional organizations, Kenneally is a colonel in the Air Force Reserve, a member of the National Association for the Advancement of Colored People, the Boston Labor Guild, and of St. Joan's Alliance (a Catholic feminist organization). He formerly served on the Peace and Justice Commission of the Archdiocese of Boston.